D1330289

Piano
FOR
DUMMIES®
A Wiley Brand

3rd Edition

Cardiff Libraries
www.cardiff.gov.uk/libraries

Llyfrgelloedd Caerdydd
www.caerdydd.gov.uk/llyfrgelloedd

CARDIFF
ERDYDD

Revised by Adam Perlmutter

FOR
DUMMIES®

CA

ACC. No: 02959281

Piano For Dummies,® 3rd Edition

Published by: **John Wiley & Sons, Inc.,** 111 River Street, Hoboken, NJ 07030-5774, www.wiley.com

Copyright © 2014 by John Wiley & Sons, Inc., Hoboken, New Jersey

Published simultaneously in Canada

No part of this publication may be reproduced, stored in a retrieval system or transmitted in any form or by any means, electronic, mechanical, photocopying, recording, scanning or otherwise, except as permitted under Sections 107 or 108 of the 1976 United States Copyright Act, without the prior written permission of the Publisher. Requests to the Publisher for permission should be addressed to the Permissions Department, John Wiley & Sons, Inc., 111 River Street, Hoboken, NJ 07030, (201) 748-6011, fax (201) 748-6008, or online at http://www.wiley.com/go/permissions.

Trademarks: Wiley, For Dummies, the Dummies Man logo, Dummies.com, Making Everything Easier, and related trade dress are trademarks or registered trademarks of John Wiley & Sons, Inc., and may not be used without written permission. All other trademarks are the property of their respective owners. John Wiley & Sons, Inc., is not associated with any product or vendor mentioned in this book.

LIMIT OF LIABILITY/DISCLAIMER OF WARRANTY: WHILE THE PUBLISHER AND AUTHOR HAVE USED THEIR BEST EFFORTS IN PREPARING THIS BOOK, THEY MAKE NO REPRESENTATIONS OR WARRANTIES WITH RESPECT TO THE ACCURACY OR COMPLETENESS OF THE CONTENTS OF THIS BOOK AND SPECIFICALLY DISCLAIM ANY IMPLIED WARRANTIES OF MERCHANTABILITY OR FITNESS FOR A PARTICULAR PURPOSE. NO WARRANTY MAY BE CREATED OR EXTENDED BY SALES REPRESENTATIVES OR WRITTEN SALES MATERIALS. THE ADVISE AND STRATEGIES CONTAINED HEREIN MAY NOT BE SUITABLE FOR YOUR SITUATION. YOU SHOULD CONSULT WITH A PROFESSIONAL WHERE APPROPRIATE. NEITHER THE PUBLISHER NOR THE AUTHOR SHALL BE LIABLE FOR DAMAGES ARISING HEREFROM.

For general information on our other products and services, please contact our Customer Care Department within the U.S. at 877-762-2974, outside the U.S. at 317-572-3993, or fax 317-572-4002. For technical support, please visit www.wiley.com/techsupport.

Wiley publishes in a variety of print and electronic formats and by print-on-demand. Some material included with standard print versions of this book may not be included in e-books or in print-on-demand. If this book refers to media such as a CD or DVD that is not included in the version you purchased, you may download this material at http://booksupport.wiley.com. For more information about Wiley products, visit www.wiley.com. All music engravings and illustrations © John Wiley and Sons, Inc.

Library of Congress Control Number: 2014936393

ISBN: 978-1-118-90005-5 (pbk); ISBN 978-1-118-90006-2 (ebk); ISBN 978-1-118-90007-9 (ebk);

Manufactured in the United States of America

10 9 8 7 6 5 4 3 2 1

Contents at a Glance

Table of Contents

Introduction

. . . .

*W*elcome to *Piano For Dummies,* 3rd Edition. Don't be nervous about wanting to play the piano; it's just a big, lazy piece of oversized furniture with a bunch of black and white keys on it. By selecting this book, you're taking the appropriate action to keep your piano from becoming a giant dust collector.

If you've never seen or put your hands on a piano or keyboard, no problem. This book starts at the very beginning and walks you through everything you need to know to tame that beast and make it sing sweet music. You'll also have fun along the way.

About This Book

Because you're in possession of a piano or keyboard or you have access to one, you may need this book to figure out how to play it. Or you may want to study how to read music. Maybe you already know how to play and you just want to improve your playing skills or develop your style. Could be you're interested in knowing more about pianos and their performers. Or you may need some help buying a keyboard or finding a teacher. For any of these reasons, this is the book for you.

You can use *Piano For Dummies,* 3rd Edition, as a teaching aid or just as a reference book. Even if you already know how to play music, you may run across some new tricks or techniques in these pages. If you read every page of this book and set about to play the examples and listen to the audio tracks and watch the video clips at www.dummies.com/go/piano, you'll be able to read piano music; know the names of notes, scales, and chords; understand a lot about different musical styles; and in general get a solid handle on some fundamental piano skills.

If you have a few specific questions about playing piano or want to go directly to something you've been dying to know, you'll find the part titles, chapter titles, and section headings practical and helpful. They make it easy to maneuver through the book and find what you're looking for.

Note: Truth be told, reading music and coordinating your hands and fingers to play musically on the piano are skills not learned in a day. It takes a bit of time and dedication. Although you may have seen or heard about methods to play the piano without reading music, this book isn't one of them. *Piano*

For Dummies, 3rd Edition, follows the tried-and-true method of teaching the basics of reading notes and rhythms from the get-go. And this book aims to do all that in a simple and fun way.

Within this book, you may note that some web addresses break across two lines of text. If you're reading this book in print and want to visit one of these web pages, simply key in the web address exactly as it's noted in the text, pretending as though the line break doesn't exist. If you're reading this as an e-book, you've got it easy — just click the web address to be taken directly to the web page.

Foolish Assumptions

In writing this book, I made a few assumptions about you, the reader:

- ✔ You like to listen to music and especially like the sound of a piano.
- ✔ When you hear someone play the piano, it sparks something in you. You say to yourself something along the lines of, "I wish I could play the piano."
- ✔ You haven't had any piano lessons before, or you had some lessons at some point in your life but you basically see yourself as a beginner. Either way, you'd like it all laid out and explained in a simple and easy-to-understand way.
- ✔ If you have a piano or keyboard, you aren't playing it as much as you want to and need some help getting to the music-making.
- ✔ If you don't have a piano or keyboard, you're considering the purchase of a keyboard and welcome some help with the whole process. Most likely, your keyboard will have at least 25 black and white keys, may or may not plug into the wall, and will cost you as much as you're willing to part with.
- ✔ You like to discover things for yourself.

If any of these assumptions is true for you, you're reading the right book.

Icons Used in This Book

As you go through the chapters of this book, you'll find the following friendly icons designed to draw your attention to different bits of information, from helpful guidance to pleasant diversions.

Be sure to pay attention to anything that has this icon attached. As you may guess, it's something important that you shouldn't forget.

When you see this icon, you know some handy-dandy information follows that can save you time, money, energy, and more.

This icon lets you know that there's an audio track and, in many cases, a video clip that demonstrates the concept, playing technique, or song discussed in the text. Check out these online resources at www.dummies.com/go/piano to deepen your understanding and speed your progress.

Pay attention to text featuring this icon. You can thank me later for showing you how to avoid mistakes and problems.

This icon points out bonus material you can find online.

This icon suggests different music that you can play on your keyboard.

Beyond the Book

In addition to the material in the print or e-book you're reading right now, this product also comes with some online goodies. Check out the eCheat Sheet at www.dummies.com/cheatsheet/piano for common musical symbols, piano fingerings, and the names of the piano keys.

You can also find several other tidbits of information online about rhythm, mode, and arpeggios. Go to www.dummies.com/extras/piano to read them.

You can view and listen to various techniques and songs that I discuss throughout the book. Go to www.dummies.com/go/piano to download the audio tracks and video clips. You can also discover a list of ten additional tips for making the most of your practice sessions at this same site. When prompted, enter the username of pianofordummies and the password of wiley.

Where to Go from Here

If you don't know much about the piano as an instrument, start with Part I and get to know the different types of pianos. Pianos are a wonder of the world.

If you're thinking about buying a piano or keyboard, turn to Chapters 3 and 4. They'll leave you feeling so much more prepared for the tasks of shopping and buying.

Check out the guide to reading music at the beginning of Chapter 6 and test yourself by trying to identify the elements of music notation on a page of piano music. (Don't worry, there's a key that tells you where to look for a reminder or an explanation of each element.)

Go through Chapters 7 and 8, which cover rhythms. Reading and responding to rhythm smoothly are huge components of reading music. If you can get your rhythm down, it will make all the other elements come together much more easily.

If you already know how to read music, try Parts III and IV for some scales, melodies, chords, and more that fit your taste and technique. Skip around and play fun songs while you expand your knowledge. If you have trouble playing something, backtrack to where you can brush up on a particular technique.

To get an idea of the music you play as you work through this book, check out the audio tracks and video clips on the accompanying website (`www.dummies.com/go/piano`) and enter the username (pianofordummies) and password (wiley). Use the audio track table at the back of the book to direct you to the written music.

Part I

Getting Started with Piano

Visit www.dummies.com/cheatsheet/piano for great free Dummies content online.

In this part . . .

- Find out what makes playing the piano so satisfying and what elements come together to make beautiful piano music (you're probably aware of some without even knowing it). Also check out some tips that will make your piano-playing journey a smooth one.

- Take a tour inside the piano and meet the extended family of keyboard instruments. Get the lowdown on the two major players in the keyboard arena — acoustic and electric pianos — along with an introduction to the organ and the harpsichord.

- Gather advice for finding and purchasing a piano or keyboard, getting one that's not only right for you now and but will also allow you room to grow as a musician.

- Keep your instrument — be it a traditional piano or a digital instrument — clean, in tune, and in perfect working order.

- Get to know the keyboard, what makes it tick, where to put your hands and feet, and what all those keys are for.

Chapter 1

Preparing to Play a Piano

"*I* love to run my fingers o'er the keys, the ivories."

These lyrics from the 1915 Irving Berlin song, "I Love a Piano," were no doubt true for many people when they were written nearly 100 years ago. The piano was in its heyday, and your average Joe and Jane felt owning and playing the piano in their home was almost as important as putting a roof over it. But neither the song nor the sentiment has lost its charm; the lyrics certainly ring true for a whole bunch of people. The piano remains a very popular instrument, with the number of piano lovers growing and its popularity spreading throughout the world. Even as the piano is treasured for its quality as an instrument, it also adapts itself to the changing times through technological advances.

This chapter helps you understand what makes the piano unique and what's involved in learning to play the piano. You may find out that you know a lot more about music than you thought you did, even if you're a beginner.

Knowing Why the Piano Is So Special

Playing the piano involves the following fundamentally musical tasks:

✔ Playing different pitches and melodies

✔ Controlling the attack and release of a note

✔ Playing different dynamics (relative loudness and softness)

But playing the piano is different from playing other instruments in some important respects, and the piano has several attributes that make it an ideal tool for learning and understanding music.

Advantages to playing the piano

The piano occupies a central position in the world of music. It's the gold standard of musical instruments, utilized by composers and arrangers and featured routinely in nearly all musical styles, in chamber groups, rock bands, and jazz trios (everything except marching bands). The following characteristics make the piano a wonderful instrument:

- **You can play many different notes at the same time.** The fancy word for this characteristic is *polyphonic*.

- **It's a completely solo instrument.** You can play a complete song or other musical work without requiring additional accompaniment or other help from your musical friends. That makes the piano satisfying and self-sufficient.

- **It's the perfect choice for accompaniment.** You can accompany a singer, a choir, a dance class, a silent movie, your own opera, or your own soap opera, not to mention any other instrument.

- **You can play almost anything on the piano.** The piano has an unmatched repertoire of music. You name it, there's piano music for it.

Advantages to studying music at the piano

The piano is an ideal instrument for studying all about music, starting with the design of the keyboard. As you sit in front of your keyboard, the notes are laid out before your very eyes in a clear, organized, and orderly way. Understanding and playing musical pitches is quite easy because the keyboard presents a clear visual image for your brain to process the way musical notes go up (higher in pitch), down (lower in pitch), or stay the same.

Each key produces a single, distinct pitch, and you can't beat that for simplicity. Not much skill is required to make a nice, musical sound. Compared with some other instruments I shall refrain from naming (well, okay: oboe and tuba, to name just two), playing any key on the keyboard, no matter how high or low the pitch, is as easy as playing any other key.

Another advantage of the piano is that you can play chords and layer sounds. The keyboard makes it easy to play harmonies and immediately hear how a combination of notes sounds. This really seals the deal.

A skill and an art

After all is said and done, the reason playing piano is so special may be that it's an activity that invites your full participation and rewards you just as completely. It has its mental side and its physical side. It requires both creativity and discipline, and engaging your mind and body is deeply satisfying.

As you learn to read music and play the notes on the piano, you create information loops from your brain throughout your body. The first loop is from your eyes to your brain, as you take in the notes on the page and process the information. In the second loop, your brain sends signals to your hands and fingers, telling them how and where to move. Your fingers start to develop a sense of what it feels like to move around the keyboard and use different kinds of touch to produce different results from the piano. A third loop is made as your ears hear the sound from the piano and send information back to your brain for it to process: Did I play the right notes and rhythms? Did I play a note too loudly or softly? Does what I play sound musical, overall? All this information helps you to modify the signals you send throughout your body to improve the results.

This full-sensory experience is paired with an interpretive element, as your inner artist is at work. The notes and directions on the page can only go so far in describing how the music should sound, which is why two pianists playing the same piece may create noticeably different performances. Even two performances by the same pianist will come out differently. Playing the piano lets you be the decider when you make music: how fast, how slow, how much more, how much less, how many encores to give your audience.

The combination of executing skills and interpreting the music is something that happens each time you play. Even when you simply play what's written, your personal interpretation comes through. With the piano, you're a musician from day one.

Understanding Why People Take Piano Lessons (And Why They Often Quit)

Many people start taking piano lessons as kids, when they don't have much say in the matter. But adults come to the piano for many reasons, including wanting to take it up again because it didn't stick the first time around, when they were kids. Following are some reasons you may want to learn or relearn to play piano:

- **You want to re-create your favorite songs and compositions.** When you play a piece of music on the piano, you bring that music to life. Written music is like a blueprint — a set of directions that tell you what notes to play and when and how to play them. It takes a performer to complete the process that starts in the composer's mind but is unfulfilled until the music reaches the listener's ear.

- **You like a challenge.** There's no doubt that getting to the intermediate and advanced levels of piano takes time, patience, and practice. Some people relish this challenge. Whatever your ambition, learning to play piano is a never-ending challenge given the wealth of material at all levels. Some people set goals for themselves — to be able to play a certain piece or to play piano for others at a party or family gathering. There are plenty of rewards to be had along the way, and sticking with it pays off when you start playing your favorite songs or when you get the chance to play music with others. There's nothing like being able to say, "I'm with the band."

- **You want to be able to play music in almost any style.** Playing a pop song or a classical sonata on piano doesn't require a different set of notes; when you know how to read and play piano music, you can play classical, jazz, rock, country, folk, cabaret, Broadway show tunes, and more. If you can play piano, you can speak the universal language of music.

- **You think it will make you better at math.** It's true that math plays a big part in music, from the nature of sound itself to the formula for the notes in a scale to the symmetrical structure of a 32-bar song form. Piano teachers know from experience that playing piano requires focus and concentration. They also know that piano students improve in these areas as their playing improves and they gain experience. But some experts (for example, your eighth-grade algebra teacher) strongly refute the notion that playing the piano improves math skills.

Unfortunately, failure to quickly reach any of these goals leads some piano students to throw in the towel. Be realistic with your timetable and your expectations as you begin playing the piano. With that in mind, here are some top reasons people give up; don't let yourself fall victim to them, too:

- ✔ **Frustration:** Mastering the piano takes patience. Coordinating hands and fingers, reading music, and committing to practice, practice, practice are the refrain of musicians everywhere, but making it all fun is the goal of this book.

- ✔ **No time:** Getting yourself to a basic beginner level of piano doesn't require hours and hours of keyboard work every day. Short but regular practice sessions in which you can focus and learn comfortably do wonders for improvement.

- ✔ **Self-criticism:** No doubt you're your own worst critic, and nobody likes playing wrong notes. Short-circuit your inner critic by celebrating small achievements (they're achievements nonetheless), and show off to your friends and family along the way so they can support you.

For tips on making the most of your practice sessions, see Chapter 18.

Getting to Know Your Instrument

The first step in learning to play the piano is familiarizing yourself with your instrument. The piano is a complex and fascinating contraption, and the modern piano reflects hundreds of years of developments and improvements in design and sound. In Chapter 2, you find out all about the piano's structure: the names of its parts and how it, through you, produces sound. I also cover the major modern development of digital pianos, which produce sound electronically, and the ways they differ from their acoustic counterparts.

A prospective buyer has plenty of options when approaching the keyboard market today. The two styles of acoustic piano, grand and upright, come in a variety of sizes and prices, and both produce sound in a similar way. Their hammer action design allows you to control the volume and tone quality through the speed and nuance of your touch as you press down a key and send a felt-covered wooden hammer to strike a string, or set of strings, inside the piano. The resonance of the string vibrating is amplified by the wooden soundboard, which is parallel to the strings.

The wide range of digital keyboards available today offers some attractive alternatives to acoustic pianos, even if they fall short of capturing the sound and feel of the real thing. As I explain in Chapter 2, these keyboards use sampled sounds — of pianos, electric pianos, harpsichords, and organs, as well as other instruments and sound effects — that are stored as digital information. You play these sounds by pressing a key and hearing the sound amplified electronically. Digital keyboards put a greatly expanded library of sound at your fingertips. Other advantages include greater portability and "silent" practicing with headphones.

The hybrid piano, covered in Chapter 3, combines acoustic and digital technology and is another enticing option available today. Though expensive, these pianos are well on their way to fulfilling their promise to combine the best of both worlds.

Check out Chapters 2 through 4 to find out more about all the keyboard instruments, compare styles and designs, prepare yourself to go keyboard shopping, and find out how to care for your keyboard at home.

If some folks predicted that the piano would grow obsolete with the development of electronic instruments in the last 50 years, they have been proved wrong. (And hopefully they're happy things turned out for the better.) The piano is popular in both its old-fashioned acoustic version and all the newer versions that feature digital sound; automatic playing features; and recording, editing, and web-integration technology. In other words, pianos are the best of both worlds these days, and no one needs to compromise. The piano has adapted and changed with the times, yet it's still treasured for the fundamental things that haven't changed. It's still an ideal solo instrument to have at home, it's ready to be played whenever the mood strikes you, and its intuitive design satisfies both your fingers and your ears.

Comprehending the Language of Music

Playing the piano means reading music. The best thing to keep in mind is that, in a way, you already know the language. You've heard it, sung it, danced to it, and gone to beddy-bye to it your whole life. If you haven't read music before, think of it as assigning new names and concepts to things you already know and making connections from the new language to the language you already comprehend aurally.

Coordinating mind and body

At the heart of playing the piano is movement. The subtle movements required to play piano may not be as big as those required of ballet or swimming, but they're numerous. As a result, playing piano involves lots of coordination, which is where practice comes into the picture.

Playing while you read involves counting, reading, and responding. You achieve a smooth choreography as you coordinate your mind and body and continually isolate and integrate your hands and fingers and the melody and the harmony. You may start by playing a melody in your right hand, adding a left-hand part when your right hand is secure, and adding facility as you go. Keep in mind that it's normal and necessary to progress by taking one step back and two steps forward.

Reading music means reading pitches, rhythms, and other notational symbols invented to communicate music from composer to performer. Notes (see Chapter 6) and rhythms (see Chapters 7 and 8) simply tell you what pitch to play and how long or short to play it. The grand staff, which joins together a treble clef staff and a bass clef staff (see Chapter 6), matches the keys on the keyboard to the notes on the page and tells you which hand you use to play them. Musical rests (see Chapter 7) tell you when *not* to play (and how long not to play). Time signatures (see Chapter 7) and key signatures (see Chapter 13) help organize music into rhythmic patterns and tonal areas, respectively, that apply throughout a song. Expressive directions (see Chapter 15) make up the remaining elements of music notation you can look forward to discovering: how soft or how loud to play the notes, with what kind of touch you should press the key, the general tempo and feel of the music, and so on.

When you know how to read music, you can play most any song or other musical composition written at the beginner level, no matter the style of music.

Developing an ear for horizontal and vertical music

Among the challenges and rewards of learning piano are understanding and combining the melodic and harmonic elements of music. In a way, a music score is a kind of sound map in which proceeding from left to right represents the horizontal flow of music through time, and any one freeze-frame of the score shows the vertical combination of notes sounding together at that moment, from low to high. A piano player, like the conductor of an orchestra, controls these vertical and horizontal elements and the total content in the music, and expresses the complete musical picture, not just a single component.

You get to know these individual components throughout this book and combine them naturally as you go. Part III focuses on melodies and scales (the horizontal parts), and Part IV focuses on harmony (the vertical part).

Getting to know musical forms and styles

Even the simplest melody, say a lullaby or a folk song, carries with it a musical form and a musical style. To describe its qualities is to define the form and style. For example, "Frere Jacques," a song you play in Chapter 9, gets its form from the way each of its four phrases is repeated, doubling the length of the song. The simplicity of the melody and the repetition define the song's style as a nursery rhyme, perfect for teaching a child.

As you play the other songs in this book, you come to understand that form and style describe how the musical material is used. For example, when you play "Worried Man Blues" in Chapter 13, you see that its opening phrase is repeated with different notes but the same rhythms in its second phrase. The third phrase is the same as the opening phrase, but it leads into a new phrase, the fourth and last one. These four phrases make up the melody to the song and have a form that can be expressed as ABAC, with each letter representing one phrase.

Rhythm plays a powerful role in defining musical style. Both the Mozart sonata and the country riff in Chapter 17 use musical ornaments (covered in Chapter 15), but the songs use them in completely different ways. The most noticeable difference is in the way the ornaments affect the rhythm. Popular music grew increasingly rhythmic in the 20th century and continues to grow and develop rhythmically more than harmonically or melodically. Jazz developed its own rhythmic language that was completely different than anything else that came before it.

Starting to Play the Best Way

You'll pick up quite a lot of new skills as you read and play *Piano For Dummies*, 3rd Edition, but I hope to emphasize a very important point about *how* you learn to play piano. You get the best results when you're comfortable and enjoying yourself, so keep the following tips in mind:

- ✔ **Be comfortable.** Comfort starts with freedom of movement. Make sure you're physically and mentally at ease when you practice, and watch out for signs of fatigue and tension. Take a break when you need it.

- ✔ **Play what interests you.** Find the songs and sections that use material you find interesting and useful for meeting your piano goals.

- ✔ **Appreciate the small steps.** Remind yourself that your rewards will come at all levels but may not come every day.

- ✔ **A beginner can play good music.** Plenty of good music has been published for piano players of all levels, including beginners. If you want to play a song or style that's not in this book, the resources in Chapter 19 can help you find an easy version that you can enjoy while you continue to learn and practice.

Being Aware of What You Already Know about Playing the Piano

Even if you've never touched a piano before, you may be surprised at how many things you can do right away. You also may already know a few pertinent musical facts — and if you don't, you can master them right now.

- ✔ **You can play a pentatonic scale.** Go to your piano or keyboard and play a sequence of black keys, up, down, or both. You've just played a five-note scale with a fancy name: *pentatonic*. The next time your friends ask what you've been up to, tell them you've been practicing some pentatonic scales.

- ✔ **You know the note names used in music.** The seven note names used in music follow the letters of the alphabet from A through G. When you play the white keys, you play notes like C, F, A, and D. And as you find out in Chapter 2, you add either "sharp" or "flat" to those letters to name the black keys.

✔ **You can name the two clefs used in reading piano music.** You read music for piano using the treble clef and the bass clef. Most of the time, your right hand plays notes in the treble clef, and your left hand plays notes in the bass clef.

✔ **You know the total number of keys on a standard piano.** They don't call 'em the old 88s for nothin'. You can count all the keys to see for yourself. Or check out the black and white keys: There's a pattern of 12 consecutive black and white keys from the right end of the keyboard to the left. Look for seven of these groups and the first four keys that begin another group before you run out of keys to count: 7 times 12 = 84, plus four extra equals 88.

✔ **You can identify different musical styles.** Listen to Audio Track 1 at www. dummies.com/go/piano. You hear short examples of four different piano pieces. Match each excerpt with one of the music styles in the following list. Even if you don't know the pieces, you have enough listening experience to hear that blues are different from a baroque piece by Bach. (You can find out the names of these pieces in Chapter 2.)

Composer	*Style*
Scott Joplin	Ragtime
J.S. Bach	Baroque
Erik Satie	Slow, post-Impressionist waltz
W.C. Handy	Blues

Chapter 2

Meeting the Keyboard Family

In This Chapter

▶ Discovering what happens when you press a key

▶ Comparing acoustic and digital keyboards

To be perfectly clear, when I say "keyboard," I mean the type that produces musical sounds — not a keyboard with the letters QWERTY on it that's connected to a computer, typewriter, or NASA space launch. So, did you purchase the right book for your keyboard? Good.

Be it a piano, organ, or digital keyboard, your keyboard is a wonderful and miraculous instrument. You've chosen your instrument wisely.

Keyboards come in all shapes and sizes. They can have many keys or just a few; they can be huge pieces of furniture or small boxes. Whatever the size, shape, or makeup, the instrument is probably a keyboard if any of the following happens:

✔ Musical sound is produced when you press a key or button.

✔ Blowing, bowing, strumming, or plucking it doesn't do much good.

✔ Anyone in the room says, "Hey, dude, nice keyboard!"

If you haven't yet purchased a keyboard, read this chapter to get a feel for your options, decide what kind of keyboard interests you, and then turn to Chapter 3 for tips on buying your instrument.

Looking at the Acoustic Ones

Acoustic means "not electric." So, acoustic keyboards are great for starving musicians because even when you can't pay the electric bill, you can keep playing.

The basic difference between each type of acoustic keyboard is the type of mechanism used to produce a musical sound. The following sections cover the hammer action that's unique to the acoustic piano, the way strings are plucked on a harpsichord, and the pipes that send out sound on an organ. *Piano For Dummies,* 3rd Edition, doesn't teach you how to play the harpsichord or the organ, but it's still fun to know how they make sound.

Pianos

Hands down (pun intended), pianos are the most popular acoustic keyboards, with a 300-year track record, an incomparable tone, and a sound-producing mechanism that has been refined to respond to every subtle variation in your touch. They come in two appropriately named designs:

✔ **Grand piano:** You may need a living room the size of a grand ballroom to house the 9-foot concert grand. If you don't live in a castle, you may want to consider other sizes, from a baby grand (measuring in at about 5 feet) to other sizes up to 7 feet. You can see a grand piano in Figure 2-1.

Figure 2-1:
Owning one
is so grand.

Photo by ©Jgroup/iStockphoto.com

✔ **Upright piano:** These relatively small instruments, also called *verticals,* sit upright against a wall and can vary in height from the spinet up to full-size uprights. You can see an upright piano in Figure 2-2.

Figure 2-2:
Upright, not
uptight.

Photo by ©Klikk/iStockphoto.com

You can hear the marvelous sounds of a piano on Audio Track 1 at www. dummies.com/go/piano. First, you hear an excerpt from Erik Satie's "Three Gymnopédies," followed by a sampling of Scott Joplin's "Maple Leaf Rag," then a bit of Bach's "Gavotte" from his *French Suite No. 4,* and finally some of W.C. Handy's "Yellow Dog Blues."

Thousands more pieces have been written for piano. For a small sampling of various piano styles, I recommend the following recordings:

✔ *A to Z of Pianists* (Naxos)

✔ *Now Playing: Movie Themes — Solo Piano,* Dave Grusin (GRP Records)

✔ *Alfred Brendel Plays Schubert* (Philips)

✔ *Piano Starts Here,* Art Tatum (Sony)

The keyboard: Master of all instruments

Many people regard keyboards as music's most versatile instruments — a big, broad (and slightly biased) statement that can be backed up with some basic facts:

✔ They're capable of a great range of volume, from very soft to very loud.

✔ They can sound more than one note at a time.

✔ They're *toned*, or *pitched*, instruments, which means they're capable of producing different musical notes (as compared to unpitched drums and cymbals).

✔ They have the widest *pitch range* of any instrument, from very low to very high.

✔ They can be played as solo or accompaniment instruments.

✔ They're capable of playing by themselves — just think of the player pianos of a century ago and the computer-controlled models of today.

Sure, your neighbor can (unfortunately) play his clarinet very loud to very soft, but he can only play one note at a time. Your friend with the violin can play two or three notes at once, but she can only play half the notes a keyboard can play. And, yes, the rock concert on Friday night *did* feature a drum solo, but was it very hummable?

Lids

The grand piano has an enormous lid that you can prop open with a stick that comes with the piano. By propping open the lid, you can see the metal strings and other mechanical components . . . and maybe even those car keys that you misplaced last month. Because the sound of a piano starts with the strings inside the instrument, you get a louder and more resonant sound when you leave the lid open, allowing the sound to project off the wooden soundboard.

 The upright piano also has a lid — and may even have a stick to prop it open — but only piano tuners actually use the stick to help them keep the lid open while they tune the strings. Opening the lid doesn't dramatically increase the slightly muffled sound of an upright, but you can try pulling the piano away from the wall to get a bigger sound.

String layout

In the grand piano, the strings are horizontal; in the upright, the strings are vertical and set diagonally — with the treble strings crossing the bass strings — to fit in the smaller upright case.

The difference in the string layout affects the resulting sound of the two pianos. The strings in an upright are perpendicular to the ground, so the sound travels close to the ground. In contrast, the strings in a grand piano are parallel to the ground, which means the sound travels upward from the ground and fills the room.

Keys, hammers, and strings

Most acoustic pianos today have a row of 88 black and white keys. If you have 87, 89, or 32, you may have been cheated! Each of the 88 keys is connected to a small, felt-covered *hammer* (see Figure 2-3). When you press a key, its hammer strikes a string, or set of strings, tuned to the appropriate musical note. The string begins to vibrate extremely rapidly. Your ear picks up these vibrations, and you hear music. The entire vibration process occurs in a split second.

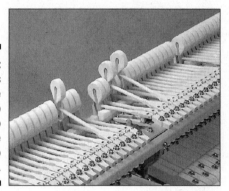

Figure 2-3: Hammers vibrate piano strings to produce music to your ears.

Photo by Kawai America

Try it out: Play a key and watch the hammer hit the string, or have someone else play the keys while you peek inside the case or cabinet of your piano.

To stop the strings from vibrating, another mechanism called a *damper* sits over the strings inside the keyboard. Dampers are made of cloth or felt that mutes the strings by preventing any vibration. When you press a key, in addition to triggering the mechanism that vibrates the string, a piano key also lifts the damper. When you release the key (provided you're not holding down a pedal), the damper returns to mute the string. (To find out about the different pedals on pianos and what they do, turn to Chapter 5.)

Go to www.dummies.com/go/piano and watch Video Clip 1 to see what happens inside the piano when it's played.

Harpsichords

The number of households in the United States with a harpsichord is roughly the same as the number of households with a mural of Beethoven on the front door. Harpsichords are so rare today that it's hard to believe they were once all the rage in Europe.

If you happen to find a harpsichord — perhaps at a university or bingo parlor — you'll notice that it looks a lot like a piano (see Figure 2-4). But check out the ornate lid on the harpsichord.

Figure 2-4:
The ornate harpsichord.

Photo by ©Maxim Anisimov/iStockphoto.com

Some harpsichords have the color of the keys reversed — as do some old pianos. Surely there was a good reason for this switch to more white keys than black ones — perhaps a surplus of ivory.

The harpsichord may bear a striking resemblance to the piano in many ways, but strike a key on the harpsichord, and you'll notice the difference between it and a piano immediately.

The harpsichord achieves its different sound because of the way the strings are played inside the instrument. Instead of a hammer, the keys on a harpsichord connect to small *hooks,* which sit very close to the strings. Pressing a key causes the corresponding hook (also called a *quill* or *plectrum*) to pluck the string tuned to the correct musical tone.

Ol' Bart needed more volume

Contrary to popular belief, the inventor of the piano wasn't named Steinway, nor was it Alec, Billy, Stephen, or any other Baldwin brother. No, the piano was invented by an 18th-century Italian harpsichord-maker named Bartolommeo Cristofori (1655–1731).

It seems that one day in 1709, after a long day polishing his umpteenth harpsichord, Mr. Cristofori thought to himself, "Hmm, instead of each key causing a string to be plucked, what if each key caused a string to be struck?" Rather poetic, don't you think? (I'm paraphrasing, of course, because I wasn't there and don't know Italian.)

Not one to sit still for long, ol' Bart quickly set out to expand his business with the new hammered harpsichord. The marketing pitch? Unlike a harpsichord, which played the same volume no matter how darn hard you hit the keys, the new

instrument could play all volume levels. Thus, the new invention was christened *pianoforte*, which is Italian for "soft loud." Why the name dropped *forte* over the years is probably about as exciting and informative as why you shorten Robert to Bob. Suffice it to say that 18th-century Italians were pretty trendy. With text-messaging, maybe we'll end up calling it a *pf*.

The piano was not an instant success. Wine and cheese parties at the time were all abuzz with heated debates over the "dullness of tone" and "lack of an escapement" in the new piano. (Oh, my kingdom for a time machine!) But after many improvements and many years, such prominent composers as Haydn, Mozart, and Beethoven were abandoning all logic and writing for the crazy instrument.

Many harpsichords have more than one keyboard, which is also called a *manual.* This arrangement is an easy, quick solution to the instrument's one big problem: No matter how hard you hit the keys, the volume stays the same. By adding a second keyboard and a few other mechanisms, the performer can play a second set of strings, or sometimes couple the string "choirs" of each manual, to vary the tonal quality and volume.

Head to www.dummies.com/go/piano and listen to Audio Track 2, an excerpt of Bach's "The Well-Tempered Clavier," which lets you hear the different sound of the harpsichord. I also recommend you listen to harpsichord music as it was meant to be heard. Look for the following recordings:

- ✔ Domenico Scarlatti, *Sonatas,* Trevor Pinnock (Archiv Produktion)
- ✔ Antonio Vivaldi, *The Four Seasons,* Nigel Kennedy and the English Chamber Orchestra (EMI)

  This piece doesn't feature harpsichord as much as violin, but you can still hear the harpsichord plunking away in the background.

- ✔ Johann Sebastian Bach, *Bach: Complete Harpsichord Concertos,* English Concert & Trevor Pinnock (Archiv Produktion)

Pipe organs

As I explain earlier in this chapter, *acoustic* means "not electric." It doesn't mean "having strings." Therefore, a pipe organ is also an acoustic keyboard. It does not, however, have any strings. Instead, it has . . . *pipes.*

You won't find a pipe organ in many of your neighbors' homes. Well, maybe you will if your neighbor lives in a church. You can find pipe organs at churches, synagogues, universities, and some concert halls.

Pipe organs are the world's largest and most complex acoustic instruments. They're great monsters with many, many different-sized pipes. Each pipe has a unique sound, and several pipes played in combination can produce other, non-organ sounds — a trumpet, a flute, or a violin, for example.

Sound is created by blowing air through the various-size pipes. The longer the pipe, the lower the sound. Unless your organist enlists the help of about a hundred hot-aired music enthusiasts, a giant air bag called *bellows* sits under the organ loft — hidden from public view and kids carrying sharp objects. The bellows pushes air through the pipes.

Most pipe organs have two or more rows of keyboards, or manuals. Any single key on a keyboard can trigger 1 to 100 pipes. Which pipes a key triggers is controlled by little knobs called *stops* located on a panel near the keys.

If you have the chance, put your hands on a pipe organ and — as they say in show business — pull out all the stops. *Any* note you play will sound wonderful and terrifying all at once. (But not as terrifying as the organist shouting, "Who did that? Show yourself!")

Familiarizing yourself with some classical lingo

A *concerto* is a composition written for orchestra and one or more featured instruments. So, in a concerto you hear the whole orchestra playing frantically, followed by a solo by a pianist, harpsichordist, or maybe even a kazoo player.

A *sonata* is a composition written in a specific form for a solo instrument. You can find sonatas for piano, harpsichord, violin — you name it.

Other terms like *fugue, passacaglia, mazurka, bagatelle,* and many others appear in the titles of keyboard works. *Classical Music For Dummies,* by David Pogue and Scott Speck (Wiley), can help you to better understand these and other classical music terms.

Go to www.dummies.com/go/piano and listen to Audio Track 3 to hear the ominous sounds of a pipe organ playing an excerpt from Bach's terrifyingly magnificent *Toccata and Fugue in D minor.* If you like the sounds of a pipe organ, find and listen to other classics written specifically for this complex and impressive instrument, including the following:

- ✔ Johann Sebastian Bach's *Toccata and Fugue in D minor* performed by E. Power Biggs on the album *Bach: The Four Great Toccatas and Fugues* (Sony Classical Great Performances)
- ✔ Camille Saint-Saëns, *Symphony No. 3 (Organ),* Peter Hurford with Charles Dutroit and the Montreal Symphony (Decca)
- ✔ Andrew Lloyd Webber, *Phantom of the Opera — Broadway Cast Album* (Decca Broadway)

Identifying the Electric Ones

For considerably less money than you shell out for an acoustic keyboard, you can own a digital keyboard capable of sounding reasonably like just about any other instrument on the planet (including an acoustic keyboard), as I discuss in these sections.

The nuts and bolts of electronic sound

Without taking a screwdriver or welding torch to the body of your digital keyboard, you can probably surmise that there are no vibrating strings inside it like the strings you find in an acoustic keyboard (see "Looking at the Acoustic Ones" earlier in this chapter for more information). Instead, most keyboards of the electronic variety produce sound by one of the following ways:

- ✔ Generating sound waves (the old-fashioned way)
- ✔ Producing sampled sounds (the newfangled way)

These sounds are then amplified, sending vibrations to your eardrum and thus causing you to hear the sound.

Synthesizers

Like bakers, dancers, and burglars, synthesizers derive their name from the work they perform — they *synthesize* sound. First they use an oscillator to generate sound waves electronically. Then, in the *synthesis* part, they alter the shape, frequency, and volume of the sound waves and combine them to create different sounds. Synthesizers can create goofy hums and buzzes as well as imitate virtually any instrument imaginable. A programmable synthesizer, commonly known in hip music-industry lingo as a *synth,* lets the programmer (that's you) shape and modify the sound waves with buttons, knobs, switches, and sliders. You can make your synthesizer sound like the entire Vienna Philharmonic is in your living room!

Audio Track 4 at `www.dummies.com/go/piano` features various bleeps, bloops, and blunders from various synthesizers. One of them even sounds like an orchestra.

To hear some really neat synthesizer sounds, check out these recordings:

- ✐ *Switched-On Bach,* Wendy Carlos (East Side Digital)
- ✐ *Computer World,* Kraftwerk (Elektra)
- ✐ *Oxygene,* Jean-Michel Jarre (Dreyfus)
- ✐ *Witness: Original Motion Picture Soundtrack,* Maurice Jarre (Varése Sarabande)
- ✐ *Synthesizer Mastercuts, Vol. 1,* Magnetic Scope (Peppertoire)

Digital keyboards

Digital keyboards work with sampled sounds. *Sampled sounds* are made by digitally recording discrete audio samples of an instrument (or any other sound) and storing them in the brain of the keyboard. When you choose a sound on the keyboard's display panel and press a key on a digital keyboard, you access the sampled sound and through amplification play the digital information out into the audible realm.

As you can imagine, the quality of digital sound depends on the quality of the sample, and this is one of the features that distinguishes the many digital keyboards. Depending on the model and price, digital keyboards come with a variety of features to simulate the experience of playing a real piano or organ. They also help you to augment the experience with lots of other fun options, like recording and editing your own playing, accessing other instrument sounds at the touch of a button, and connecting to other keyboards or your computer.

Advantages of digital keyboards include the following:

- ✐ **Maintenance:** They never need tuning and are easily cleaned and stored.
- ✐ **Portability:** They come in a variety of sizes and, depending on the model, are a lot easier to move around than an acoustic piano.

✔ **Fun and exploration:** Many allow you to play different keyboard samples (grand piano, honky-tonk, harpsichord, organ, and electric piano) and dozens of other instrument samples (strings, flutes, and other wind and brass instruments).

✔ **Affordability:** The price range of digital keyboards is far below the range of acoustic pianos.

✔ **Privacy:** You can plug headphones into the keyboard in order to practice and play to your heart's desire without disturbing anyone.

Many digital keyboards feature a bonus *auto-accompaniment* feature. With the push of a single button, you can have a nonstop-always-on-the-beat drum and bass line accompanying you. (Bossa nova, anyone?)

Perhaps the biggest downside of a digital keyboard is the sound and touch compared to an acoustic piano. Some digital keyboards don't respond to your touch no matter how fast or slowly you press a key, similar to the action on an organ. Other digital keyboards feature a touch-sensitive keyboard — some with weighted keys and some without weighted keys. Touch-sensitive keyboards produce louder or softer sounds depending on the speed of your touch. I recommend a keyboard with weighted keys because they're closest in feel to an acoustic piano. They may not match the real thing, but technological advances have led to some very decent alternatives. (See Chapter 3 for more comparisons of acoustic and digital pianos.)

Given their capability to put realistic samples of other instruments at your fingertips, digital keyboards are the next generation of the synthesizer. Most people aren't concerned with programming synthesizers; they're happy with the sounds that come with their keyboards and just want to play music, thus the digital piano and organ revolution continues.

A Mager contribution

Not too long after Thomas Edison discovered how to light up Times Square, others began putting electricity in musical instruments. In 1924, Jörg Mager made some attempts at synthesizing sounds. His creations were capable of imitating an infinite number of sounds by slightly altering the sound through a series of knobs and buttons. The world has been oscillating ever since. Although modern synthesizers are far more complex (and, thankfully, more user-friendly) than Mager's early feats, the principle remains the same.

Chapter 3

Finding the Perfect Keyboard

Grandma's old upright piano may satisfy your urges to play the keyboard for a while. However, at some point you may experience the undeniable urge to purchase or rent a piano or keyboard of your own. Probably right around the time that Grandma gets tired of hearing you play "Yankee Doodle" for the hundredth time.

When the urge to acquire a piano strikes, don't pull out that checkbook immediately. If you're prepared to invest the money, spend the time to research, shop around, and choose exactly the kind of keyboard you want.

This chapter helps you decide whether to go acoustic or digital, and then guides you through the features and details to consider in making your purchase. I provide some important tips on buying or renting the keyboard that's right for you, because like a good pair of shoes or a nice felt fedora, the one you choose should fit you just right. I close out the chapter with an introduction to MIDI, digital interface technology that lets you take your keyboard to the next level sound-wise as well as notate and record your masterpieces.

To Hum or Not to Hum: Electric or Acoustic (Or Both)?

The first thing you need to decide when selecting a keyboard is whether you want an acoustic one or not. (See Chapter 2 for an explanation of acoustic and digital keyboards.)

Don't just flip a coin. Choose your type of keyboard carefully, much like you would choose between a lemon or piña colada air freshener in your car. Heck, you're going to be driving it for a while; it should smell right. Make a list of pros and cons to help you decide which type of keyboard is best for you.

In the following sections, I help you get started with lists of some pros and cons for both acoustic and digital keyboards. I also have a section on hybrid pianos, which combine acoustic and digital possibilities. Let these lists get you started, but then personalize them, adding your own perceptions, factors, and concerns. It's *your* keyboard, after all. Base your buying or renting decision on the pros and cons that *you* come up with and that are the most important to you.

Buying an acoustic

Psalteries, virginals, clavichords, and harmoniums are acoustic keyboards. Honestly, you don't need a list of pros and cons for these very rare instruments. If you find one and can't live without it, go ahead and purchase it.

Knowing the right time to buy

Before stepping inside a store, answer the following questions as truthfully as possible:

1. How much can you spend?
   a) Nothing
   b) Less than $1,000
   c) $1,000 to $5,000
   d) More than $10,000

2. Where do you live?
   a) At home with your parents
   b) College dorm or small apartment
   c) House
   d) Castle

3. How much space do you have?
   a) None
   b) Space for one small piccolo player, standing up
   c) Space for an extra couch
   d) Space for the Chicago Bulls to camp out

4. How long have you been playing piano?
   a) One day
   b) Less than a year
   c) One to five years
   d) More than five years

If you answered mostly a's and b's, consider saving your money for a while and keep playing Grandma's upright. Or ask your local music stores about the possibility of renting a piano. If you answered mostly c's and d's, grab your checkbook or credit card and start the hunt for your dream instrument.

Pianos, harpsichords, and pipe organs are also acoustic keyboards. The pros and cons in this section focus on acoustic pianos because they're the most commonly purchased acoustic keyboards.

Pros

The following characteristics are real selling points for an acoustic piano:

- ✔ **Sound quality:** No matter how good a digital keyboard is, it doesn't match the sound and feel of a grand piano — or even a standard upright piano.

- ✔ **Value:** Good-quality acoustic pianos appreciate in value over the years if kept in good condition. You can think of your purchase as an investment.

- ✔ **Aesthetics:** There's nothing like sitting at and playing an acoustic piano. It feels real, it looks great, and you can imagine that you're sitting on a concert stage in front of thousands.

Cons

I would be remiss not to point out the following, which are valid concerns when you consider buying or renting an acoustic piano:

- ✔ **Cost:** Plain and simple, new and even used acoustic pianos are generally more expensive than new digital keyboards (see the next section).

- ✔ **Size and space:** Before the piano movers show up at your door with a special delivery, you need to get practical and think about whether you have room to house the piano and play it. You should also measure the doorway while you're at it to make sure that you can even get the piano where you want it.

- ✔ **Maintenance:** Annual or semiannual tuning at a cost of around $75 to $150 per tuning isn't cheap, but it's essential. (Chapter 4 tells you more about maintaining your acoustic keyboard.)

Buying a digital

You can rent some digital keyboards, but not all. Some of the fancier models are mostly for sale only, although you may find a used one in good condition. On the other hand, plenty of stores offer a rental option on larger digital pianos or digital organs. Many online stores will ship a keyboard to you and provide knowledgeable staff available by phone.

Looking for used keyboards online can yield lots of options, but you really need to be able to see and play a keyboard before you buy. (See the section "Shopping online" later in this chapter for online buying tips.)

This section features pretty well-balanced lists of reasons why buying a digital keyboard can be a good or a bad choice.

Pros

Digital keyboards have the following positive points going for them:

- **Cost:** Unless you're talking about the very high-end models, most digital keyboards are affordable and much less expensive than acoustic keyboards.

- **Size:** No matter where you live, you can probably find a spot for your digital keyboard. Plus, you can move it yourself should the need arise, such as if the acoustics are better in one room than another or if you want to take it on the road for family singalongs.

- **Versatility:** Most digital keyboards come loaded with different sounds, so you can be a one-person band or play a pipe organ without buying the enormous acoustic version.

- **Maintenance:** Digital keyboards require no tuning and no tweaking — you just plug and play. You need to dust your keyboard monthly, but that doesn't cost you anything but a little time. (Check out more of my tips for maintaining your electric keyboard in Chapter 4.)

- **Headphones:** If you have grouchy neighbors, young children, or other housemates who demand quiet, the option of headphones is an important one. You can turn off the sound to the outside world and still hear yourself practicing on your digital keyboard long into naptimes or the wee night hours.

Cons

Yes, even digital keyboards have a few negative characteristics, including the following, which you should consider before making a purchase:

- **Complexity:** Some digital keyboards, such as *workstations,* come with a baffling number of sampled sounds, sequencing tools, and effects. Figuring out how to utilize these features requires a steep learning curve. (There's more on workstations and other digital keyboard types later in this chapter.) Additionally, knobs and levers can break, circuitry can go haywire, and any number of other things can go wrong over the years. Because of the sophisticated gadgetry in most digital keyboards, they tend to run amok more often than your average acoustic keyboard.

✔ **Power:** You must have electricity, or at least a whole bunch of D-size batteries, in order to play your digital keyboard.

✔ **Sound quality:** Some digital sounds are out-of-this-world fantastic, but others are very unconvincing when you're trying to mimic an acoustic instrument.

✔ **Keyboard action:** Many digital keyboards aren't *touch-sensitive,* meaning that whether you play the key hard or soft, you hear the same volume. Only the volume knob can control the volume on some models. The models that have "weighted action" try to give you the feel of an acoustic piano; some succeed where others fail.

✔ **Obsolescence:** Like most electronic devices and computers, today's keyboards probably won't be tomorrow's desire. Eventually you'll want to upgrade to the latest and greatest model, and very few digital keyboards retain their value.

✔ **Addiction:** If you buy one, pretty soon you'll want another, and another, and another. Or you'll want more sound samples, a better amp, a better speaker, a new stand, or a new case. The common mantra among keyboard players in the digital world is, "I need more gear!"

Buying a hybrid

They combine the best of both worlds! They offer unmatched versatility! They cost a million dollars! Well, not that much, but hybrid acoustic/digital keyboards are expensive.

If the idea of a hybrid interests you, there are two ways to go: Buy an acoustic/digital hybrid piano, or have your acoustic piano retrofitted with a digital player system.

Among the growing list of things these hybrid pianos and player piano systems can do are

✔ Record, playback, and mute (muting stops the hammers from hitting the strings — but you can hear yourself by plugging in headphones).

✔ Connect with other MIDI instruments and MIDI files (see the section "The MIDI Places You Can Go" later in this chapter for more on MIDI).

✔ Access sound libraries and karaoke libraries, play along with pre-recorded tracks, and play along with MIDI feeds available over the Internet through a USB or wireless connection. These options open the door to a wide range of instructional and entertainment possibilities.

Yamaha Disklavier leads the field of digital and acoustic technology with its hybrid pianos. PianoDisc, QRS, and Bösendorfer also make player piano systems that can be installed on your acoustic piano.

Be careful if you're thinking about retrofitting your piano with a player piano system. This can involve some significant physical alteration of your piano, and you won't be able to go back after it's done! Consult with a piano technician before signing on the dotted line. Ask how your piano would be affected by an installation, including the sound, the feel, and the value of the instrument.

Picking the Perfect Acoustic Piano

If your pro and con list reveals that an acoustic piano suits your needs best, use this section to help you select the right model piano for you. I even list a few of my own personal favorites; these pianos are all good for the beginning player.

Taking location into account

Most older pianos were produced with a particular climate in mind. The wood used to make them was weathered for the finished product's climate. Japan, for example, has a wetter climate than many locations in the United States. Therefore, the wood in many pianos manufactured for use in Japan has been dried out more than the wood used to make pianos for use in the United States. If you live in the U.S. and you buy a piano made for use in Japan, you may face some serious problems with the wood parts of your piano drying out.

Why does dryness matter? Perhaps the most important element of a piano is its *soundboard* — the very thick and very heavy piece of wood under the strings. If the soundboard ever cracks or breaks . . . well, how do you feel about playing guitar?

For example, if you purchase an older piano that was made for use in Japan, chances are that prior to manufacture, the wood was dried out too much to survive a hot, dry summer in Mississippi. Maybe not this year or next, but one of these days: crack! There goes the soundboard, and there goes your investment.

If it's a brand-spanking-new piano you want, this issue of locale doesn't matter much. New pianos are made with a nod to a more global marketplace. But it doesn't hurt to discuss this issue with your sales representatives, anyway, just to show them that you've really taken the time to get to know the issues surrounding a piano purchase.

Many manufacturer websites allow you to trace the serial number of your piano, so you can check the vintage and country of birth for a piano you're looking at. (See the section "Looking at some specific piano brands" later in this chapter for manufacturer website and contact information.)

Getting all the pedals you deserve

Some underhanded dealers claim that they can save you money by offering you a piano with no middle pedal. (To find out what piano pedals do, see Chapter 5.) Baloney! You may never use the middle pedal, but just in case Lang Lang comes over for lunch, you need to have one.

Getting a middle pedal isn't like adding a sunroof to a new car. Three piano pedals shouldn't be optional or part of a special package that costs more; three pedals are part of the overall purchase. If you want three pedals, ask to see piano models with three pedals.

I must point out that many upright pianos don't have a middle pedal. So, if the piano you want is an upright with only two pedals, it's probably perfectly fine. Just ask about the third pedal to be on the safe side.

If you're buying an older piano, lack of a third pedal sometimes indicates that the piano was made outside of the U.S. Refer to the preceding section to find out why this may not be a good thing.

Finding good buys (and avoiding scams)

If you shop around and find a piano for a ridiculously low price — far lower than the same model anywhere else in town — it's either used, broken, or a Memorial Day sale to really remember.

If you decide to shop for a used acoustic piano, be patient and take a look at a variety of instruments. There are many very good pianos out there, and sometimes people need to sell them because they don't play them anymore, they're moving, or they need to make room for a new 70-inch HDTV setup. And if you've found your dream piano at a garage sale, the low, low price is not necessarily an indication of anything wrong. It's a *garage sale!* You may just find a perfectly good piano with many glorious years left in it for a fraction of the cost of a new one.

Be smart about any deal that seems too good to be true. If most stores offer a certain model for $20,000 and suddenly you're staring at the same model at PianoMax for $5,000, something's wrong. The soundboard may be cracked. It may be missing strings. Who knows? To ensure that you're getting a good deal on a quality instrument, hire a professional to look the piano over before you purchase it. A reputable piano technician can usually spot any faults and is well worth the expense. (See Chapter 4 for more information on finding piano technicians.)

There's nothing wrong with a used piano if it has been kept in good condition. Hire a technician to check it out first, testing that the soundboard is in good condition and the tuning sounds pretty good. Any scratches on the outside? Any sun-faded spots? Well, what do you expect for half price? Cosmetic dings don't affect the sound quality, so the value of your piano's outer beauty is up to you to decide. It's the inner beauty that counts.

Demo models are also good buys. Stores frequently loan pianos to local universities or concert halls for use by students, competitions, and guest artists. Even if it has been used only one time, the piano can no longer be sold as new. Of course, pianos don't have odometers, so you have to take the dealer's word for just how used a piano really is, but most dealers will be honest about this point.

If you've heard one, you haven't heard them all

So you have your heart set on a particular brand of grand piano. Think it's as easy as that? Think again. Not only do different brands sound completely different, but the sound of two pianos made by the *same company* can sound and feel different, too. This is why you must, must, must go to the store and put your hands and ears on every piano you consider. Play every darn key, and play at all volumes.

You think I'm exaggerating? I've played many pianos that sounded beautiful except for one key. If all you ever play is "Camptown Races" in the key of G, you may never notice that silent low D-flat key. But it's more likely that you'll notice the bad key a few days after you get the piano home.

Play and listen to those keys again and again. Trust your instincts. Don't be rushed. Only you know what you like to hear. Some people don't like the sound of a Steinway; some don't like a Baldwin. You're entitled to your own taste.

Give yourself the upper hand in your final negotiation at the piano store by selecting two or three pianos that you like and repeating "Oh, Susannah" over and over on each of them. Sure, you're comparing the sound of each instrument, but you're also driving the sales team insane, hopefully to the point of a discount just to get you to leave the store!

Looking at some specific piano brands

The following are some preferred brands of pianos from around the world. Contact these companies directly and ask where to find their pianos in your area. Trust me, they like hearing from customers.

- ✔ **Baldwin Piano & Organ Company:** Makes Baldwin, Wurlitzer, Chickering, and Concertmaster pianos. Website www.gibson.com/en-us/divisions/baldwin.

- ✔ **Kawai America Corporation:** Offers every Kawai under the sun. Website www.kawaius.com.

- ✔ **L. Bösendorfer Klavier:** Carries all Bösendorfer models. Website www.boesendorfer.com.

- ✔ **Mason & Hamlin World Headquarters:** Makes grands and uprights. Website www.masonhamlin.com.

- ✔ **Pearl River Piano Group America Ltd.:** Makes Pearl River and Ritmüller pianos. Website www.pearlriverusa.com.

- ✔ **PianoDisc World Headquarters:** Carries hardware and software for its player piano systems. Website www.pianodisc.com.

- ✔ **Samick Music Corporation:** Offers the brands Wm. Knabe & Co., Kohler & Campbell, Pramberger, Samik, and Sohmer & Co. Website www.smcmusic.com.

- ✔ **Schimmel Piano Company:** Makes Schimmel pianos in Germany. Website www.schimmel-piano.de.

- ✔ **Steinway & Sons:** Has been making Steinway pianos since 1853; also offers Boston and Essex pianos. Website www.steinway.com.

- ✔ **Story & Clark:** Now makes hybrid pianos, with an optical sensor, USB ports, and MIDI ports standard on all models. Website www. qrsmusic.com.

- ✔ **Yamaha Corporation of America:** Makes all types of Yamaha pianos. Website www.yamaha.com.

Ask the manufacturer which artists play which of its pianos. Any company will be proud to give you a list of famous performers who endorse its products — in fact, you may find the information posted on the company website. Maybe you have your heart set on playing the same piano that Billy Joel plays, for example.

Selecting a Digital Keyboard That Lasts

After much deliberation, and for whatever reasons, you decide to buy a digital keyboard over an acoustic one. Think your job is done? Not so fast, pal. Now you must decide what *type* of digital keyboard you want. Start by breaking them down into the following five categories (you can read more about the basics of digital keyboards in Chapter 2):

- ✔ Digital pianos and organs

- ✔ Arrangers

- ✔ Stage pianos

- ✔ Workstations

- ✔ Synthesizers

Don't assume that you've necessarily gone the cheaper route by selecting a digital keyboard as your instrument of choice. These instruments can be quite expensive, sometimes costing more than an acoustic piano. But they're also very versatile. Instead of being limited to the sound of a piano, you can have literally hundreds or even thousands of different sounds at your fingertips.

The number of sounds you can use depends on the type of keyboard you select. Just like computers, digital keyboards have memory, storage space, and performance limitations. Some you can add memory and sounds to, but some are what they are and no more.

Sorting out all the different keyboard types and styles can leave your mind numb. Here are a few things you can count on across all five categories of digital keyboards:

✔ All digital keyboards today use sampled sounds, which vary in quality.

✔ You can choose from a variety of keyboard actions, or touch sensitivity — everything from nonresponsive action to weighted-action keyboards designed to mimic the touch and feel of an acoustic piano.

✔ The three common keyboard sizes are standard 61-key, 76-key, and 88-key.

✔ Digital keyboards have varying degrees of portability.

✔ Nearly all models come with a music rack, a plug-in sustain pedal, and MIDI (see the later section "The MIDI Places You Can Go" for an explanation of MIDI) and/or USB connection capability.

Although the lines between digital keyboard categories are increasingly blurred, you can still find clear differences when it comes to sequencing capabilities, built-in speakers, sound effects, metronomes, auto-accompaniment features, recording features, extra pedals, and other plug-in devices. The following sections get more in-depth about the differences of these digital keyboards.

Digital pianos and organs

The two types of digital pianos or organs for home use are

✔ Portable models
✔ Upright and grand models

Not surprisingly, the portables are more portable than the uprights and grands, which are designed after their acoustic sisters and are meant to occupy a relatively permanent spot in your home, not unlike an upright or grand piano. Both of these types come with built-in speakers, although the speakers are smaller on the portable models. Both types of digital pianos and organs usually, but not always, offer a few sound options like acoustic piano, electric piano, organ, and maybe vibes. They come with a music rack, a stand (if it's not already a part of the keyboard), and a plug-in pedal.

If you're looking exclusively for a digital organ, some very attractive models come with dual-manuals and multiple organ effects like draw bars and rotary sound. As with other digital keyboards, you can choose from 61-, 73-, and 88-key models. You can find some recommendations later in this chapter, in the section "Recommendations for digital pianos and organs."

Arrangers

If you're looking to have lots of fun with different sounds and accompaniment features and you're not concerned with finding the best acoustic piano samples, an arranger is the digital keyboard for you. This type is loaded with "one-man band" features, like gads of sounds (500 or more); automatic drum, bass, and chord accompaniment; and recording and playback. Lower-end models are quite inexpensive and very portable.

Stage pianos

These keyboards, made for onstage performing, offer more professional keyboard sounds. If you're going to be the keyboard player in a band, or even a solo act, and will be gigging around town, the stage piano may be the choice for you. It doesn't have built-in speakers, so you need to have an external amplifier and speaker to hear yourself play, but you can plug in headphones. Also, a stage piano doesn't have as many functions as an arranger. Stage pianos come with a music rack and sustain pedal, but you need to purchase a keyboard stand and other accessories separately.

Workstations

Essentially a computer built into a keyboard, a workstation has everything: top-of-the-line sound samples, sequencing, recording and editing, and computer integration. Workstations come in 61-, 73-, and 88-key models. These babies can be quite expensive, but if you've got big musical dreams, you may want to try one out.

Synthesizers

You can still buy a good ol' synthesizer and manipulate waveforms, filters, and work with both analog and digital sounds. Today's synthesizers come with more sounds to work with than older models, letting you go to town with some good preset sounds.

Avoiding obsolescence

As with computers, keyboards are updated and become outdated as quickly as they reach the stores. But unlike some unfriendly and money-hungry computer and software developers, keyboard manufacturers are constantly trying to make products that won't become obsolete by creating keyboards that can be upgraded or added to as technology advances.

Ask the manufacturer or a salesperson the following questions to minimize the possibility that your keyboard gets shoved aside when the next big thing comes along:

✔ **Can I add memory?** Adding memory to keyboards is quite common these days. More memory means the ability to accommodate new sounds, software, and hardware at a later date. Also ask what the memory limitations are. If you don't understand the terminology, ask the salesperson to explain it to you in simple terms.

✔ **Is the unit upgradeable?** Workstations offer operating system and software upgrades, making it easy to keep up with the latest improvements. You want to be able to simply upgrade your model, not throw it out.

✔ **Can I purchase extra sound cards or libraries?** Many workstations have vast libraries of sounds. Whether they're developed by the original manufacturer or other sound developers, you can add extra sound cards and libraries to make old keyboards sound new again.

✔ **Is the company still making this model or series?** If not, the keyboard is already headed toward the land of obsolescence. But if it meets all the other criteria on this list and you can get it for a good price, just add memory, upgrades, and sounds over the years.

Don't be embarrassed to ask the preceding questions. If the salesperson looks at you funny or doesn't give you clear answers, call the manufacturer directly (using the information listed in the section "Browsing some specific keyboard brands") to get straight answers.

Knowing the digital features you want

Make a list of the digital keyboard features that are important to you before you even start shopping. This list can be different for each user. For example, if you don't tour with a band, you have no need for a feature allowing "quick live performance flexibility." If you play concerts, however, this may be an important feature.

As technology expands, more and more keyboards feature all kinds of nice little bells and whistles. This list runs through digital keyboard features and tells you which keyboards to turn to for them:

- **Realistic piano sound:** Look at the home digital pianos with the best piano samples.

- **Realistic piano action:** Look at the home digital pianos with the best touch-sensitive keyboards and the best weighted-key action.

- **Built-in speakers:** Home digital pianos, for sure.

- **To perform onstage:** Look at stage pianos, and keep in mind that you also need amplification.

- **Portability:** Look at stage pianos and arrangers.

- **Multi-note polyphony:** Look at home digital pianos, stage pianos, and workstations. The bigger the number, the more notes you can play at once, so try for at least 32-note polyphony. Sure, you don't have 32 fingers, but if you use MIDI (which I explain in the later section "The MIDI Places You Can Go"), 32-note polyphony comes in handy. Some models even have 128-note polyphony, which is excellent.

- **Multi-timbral:** Look at arrangers and workstations for this ability to play more than one sound at the same time. For example, you can play sounds from a piano, a violin, a banjo, and a bagpipe together on "Danny Boy."

- **MIDI capability:** You're okay with any digital keyboard. You can read more about MIDI later in this chapter in the section "The MIDI Places You Can Go."

- **Pitch bend and modulation:** Look at arrangers, synthesizers, and work-stations. These fun little effects make your sounds say "wah wah" and "woob woob."

- **Sound editing:** Look at workstations if you want to change the sounds, making the piano brighter, the horns brassier, and the goose calls goosier, for example.

- **Internal recording, editing, and sequencing:** Want to record what you play without using external recorders or a computer? You need a sequencer, which most digital keyboards have, but only workstations have the most advanced editing and sequencing features.

- **Automatic rhythm, harmony, and bass accompaniment:** Look at arrangers.

- **Strange sound effects:** Look at synthesizers if you want to program your own sounds. Be aware that some synthesizers are *monophonic,* meaning they can play only one note at a time.

✔ **Other mumbo-jumbo:** Flash ROM, DSP plug-ins, BIAS Peak, sub-oscillators, vocoders, modeling filters, arpeggiators — all this is very cool, but what does it have to do with you playing music? Not much. It simply indicates that your model is on the cutting edge of current keyboard features.

Whichever way you go, ask yourself this important question before you buy: Do you like the keyboard as an instrument? Take your time and make sure it sounds good to your ears. If the in-store keyboard is hooked up to an external amplifier and speaker, ask the salesperson if you can listen to the keyboard through an amp and speaker similar to what you'll be using. All the options and models can make you feel like a real novice, but your ears know what they like. Also consider whether the keyboard looks good, and whether you'll enjoy having it set up in a spot in your home where you'll feel comfortable and free to practice and play. And does the keyboard do what you want it to do, whether that's sound like an organ, a string section, or an alien band from a distant galaxy?

Browsing some specific keyboard brands

When you have a good idea of which type of digital keyboard fits your needs, you're ready for some recommendations. In this section, I recommend several top brands and models to help you narrow the search for your keyboard. They're divided into two groups: If your primary requirement is a good piano or organ sound, the first group is for you; if you want a digital keyboard with lots of features and sounds, check out the second group.

Recommendations for digital pianos and organs

Here's my list of recommended brands and models for digital pianos and organs. If you're having trouble finding any of these brands in stores in your area, contact the companies directly; they'll be more than happy to help sell you a keyboard.

✔ **Kawai America Corporation:** Recommended models are CN34 Digital Piano and ES7 Portable Digital Piano. Website www.kawaius.com.

✔ **Korg USA, Inc.:** Recommended models are C-320 Concert Piano and LP380 Lifestyle Piano. Website www.korg.com.

✔ **Nord Keyboards:** Recommended models are Nord C2D Combo Organ and Nord Electro 4. Website www.nordkeyboards.com.

✔ **Roland Corporation U.S.:** Recommended models are RG-1 Digital Mini-Grand Piano, KR-103 Digital Intelligent Piano, and AT-75 Atelier Organ. Website www.rolandus.com.

✔ **Yamaha Corporation of America:** Recommended models are AvantGrand, P140 Contemporary Digital Piano, and P-85 Contemporary Digital Piano. Website www.yamaha.com.

Recommendations for arrangers, workstations, and synthesizers

The following list points you toward some quality manufacturers of arrangers, workstations, and synthesizers. This isn't an exhaustive list of models by any means. Each company makes models with different features and price points (although none are really inexpensive).

✔ **Alesis Studio Electronics:** Recommended model is A6 Andromeda synthesizer. Website www.alesis.com.

✔ **Casio Incorporated:** Recommended models are CTK-6200 Portable Keyboard and WK-6600 Workstation. Website www.casio.com.

✔ **E-Mu Systems Incorporated:** Recommended model is LONGboard 61 USB/MIDI instrument. Website www.emu.com.

✔ **Generalmusic Corporation:** Recommended models are GK360 arranger and Genesys Pro workstation. Website www.generalmusic.us.

✔ **Korg USA, Inc.:** Recommended models are Korg Krome 88-key synthesizer workstation, MicroKORG XL Music Synthesizer, and PA50 Professional Arranger. Website www.korg.com.

✔ **Kurzweil Music Systems:** Recommended models are PC3K8 88-key production station and PC3LE8 88-key performance controller. Website www.kurzweilmusicsystems.com.

✔ **Moog Music Incorporated:** Recommended models are Minimoog Voyager OS Synthesizer and Little Phatty Analog Synthesizer. Website www.moogmusic.com.

✔ **Roland Corporation U.S.:** Recommended models are Fantom G-Series workstations, EXR-5 Interactive Arranger, and SH-201 Synthesizer. Website www.rolandus.com.

✔ **Yamaha Corporation of America:** Recommended models are Motif XF workstation, MOX8 music production synthesizer, and MO6 workstation. Website www.yamaha.com.

Other electric keyboards

Nothing's wrong with a no-frills keyboard from your local toy or electronics store. Many of these instruments have several different sounds and a built-in rhythm section and are very affordable. You probably can't do all kinds of funky little tricks or engineer a hit CD on it, but it will allow you to do the thing that made you buy this book: play the piano.

Make sure that any basic keyboard comes with a power adaptor, or else you may have to buy one (or buy lots of batteries).

Before You Drive It Off the Lot: Sealing the Deal at the Store

If you've ever bought a car, you know that looking at and test driving different models is almost as much fun as taking one home. Buying a keyboard should be a similar experience.

If you've never bought a car (or even driven one), don't worry. This section tells you everything you need to know about being a savvy keyboard shopper.

Taking it for a spin

No matter what kind of music store you walk into, the pianos and keyboards are there for you to try out. Go ahead — touch it, play it. Push the buttons and turn the volume up and down. If it's a piano, have a seat and play a while. It's just you and the keyboard . . . and perhaps a dozen other customers and salespeople standing around listening.

If the salesperson or manager of the store asks you not to touch or play the merchandise, ask him to remind you where the door is and the quickest route to a store that *would* like to make a sale today. Either he'll show you the door or you'll be given a much more comfortable chair and encouraged to resume playing. Either way, you win.

Keep in mind that many digital keyboards on display are routed through processors, effects, and other digital enhancements to make them sound better. Don't be fooled by this extra gear. Kindly ask the salesperson to turn off all effects so that you can hear the keyboard as-is. Otherwise, you may be disappointed with the way it sounds after you get it home — unless, of course, you also buy all the effects and processors.

Notice the following about each piano or keyboard you try:

- ✔ Is the overall sound full or wimpy, bright or dull?

- ✔ Do long notes actually last as long as you play them?

- ✔ On an acoustic piano, do the top five keys sound good, not metallic? Do the lower five keys sound good, not thick and sloppy?

✔ Do you get a quick response when you play the keys? Is the keyboard too sensitive, or not sensitive enough?

✔ Do your fingers have enough room on the keys?

If you like the sound and feel of one particular piano or keyboard, take a good look at it. Do you like the size, color, and overall look? Can you be happy with it taking up half of your living room for the next 25 years? Can you make out any noticeable dents or scratches that would signal you that this is a used piano? Used pianos can be great buys, but not if they're selling at new prices. (I discuss used pianos in the earlier section "Finding good buys (and avoiding scams).")

Loving and leaving it

You found the perfect keyboard for you, and you're in love. This is the one. Now leave the store quickly with a tip of your hat and a polite "I'll think about it" to the hovering sales manager.

You're in trouble if you sit down and negotiate the first time you walk into the store. You're too emotionally attached to think clearly. You think I'm kidding, but this is love — true love. Your keyboard is your baby.

Before negotiating a price, leave the store and spend the next few hours or days searching for that identical piano at a lower price. When you're 100 percent sure that you can't find it cheaper and still can't live without it, head back to the store and start negotiating.

Refusing to pay the sticker price

Many people think that the art of negotiating a price is reserved for car buying and movie star contracts. On the contrary, the wonderful world of instruments and accessories is open for price haggling. The sticker price is merely a starting point. If the price of that baby grand piano you want is $15,000, you could find yourself taking it home (in a very big truck) for as low as $10,000.

Generally, you can hope to get anywhere from 10 to 15 percent off the sticker price. The closer you pay to the dealer's asking price, the more likely the salesperson is to throw in freebies like delivery to your home — which can sometimes cost as much as $300 — or a free year of tuning, piano cleaner, or fuzzy dice. A deal can work the other way, too: If you're buying accessories like a keyboard stand, amplifier, some software, and some cables, the salesperson will be more receptive to making a deal.

Don't be impolite about making a deal, though. Start negotiating a price with the salesperson *only* after you're pretty darn sure you're going to buy that particular instrument. If you're not going to buy it, don't waste the salesperson's time by trying to reduce the price just so you know how much he's willing to move.

Comparing prices is one thing, but using price quotes from two or three different stores is manipulative and unfair, and you probably won't win. Suppose Piano Superstore quotes you $5,000 on a piano. You go to We Are Pianos and say, "Can you beat that?" That store's rep says $4,000. You return to Piano Superstore and say, "I can get the same thing at We Are Pianos for $4,000. Can you beat that?" Guess what the salesperson tells you? "Then go buy it from We Are Pianos."

Go in the store with an absolute maximum dollar amount in your head. When you're sure about a particular model, sit down with the salesperson and ask what the best he can do is on that model piano. If you get an answer equal to or less than the maximum figure in your head, shake hands and write the check. If the price is nowhere close to what you're comfortable paying, stand up and say, "Well, thank you very much. You have my number if you change your mind." Remember, there are more piano stores and more piano models in this world.

A piano store is a store like any other, complete with sales at key times during the year. For example, Memorial Day is always a big piano-buying time. Shop around, and then keep an eye out for sales and promotions.

Shopping online

Surfing the Internet can be great for comparing keyboards and getting a handle on digital lingo. Virtual showroom tours, product demonstrations, and used and new price quotes abound. You can certainly find some available models that your local dealer doesn't carry and preview some models and features that manufacturers are planning to introduce.

As you start to focus on a few keyboards that interest you, read the FAQ and product specifications on the manufacturers' websites (refer to the contact listings earlier in this chapter). Look at what models are being sold as used, and why. Study up on the features that interest you so that when you go to a dealer, you'll be treated as an informed customer and not a know-nothing who can be suckered into a bad deal.

You can buy online, and in some cases pay less doing so, but it's important to keep in mind the limitations. Only a dealer can give you product support, answer your questions, and offer you a store warranty so that you can bring your instrument back for repairs or problems.

The MIDI Places You Can Go

Your new digital or hybrid keyboard is wonderful, exactly what you wanted. But now you want to experiment with all the cool things you've heard about. This section explains several other types of musical devices, including MIDI and other recording systems, that can hook up to your new keyboard and help you go even further in your pursuit of a musical career — or just your desire to get the most out of your keyboard.

After you start investing in recording software and equipment, two things happen: You spend far less time practicing music and far more time studying up on new technology, and your bank account shrinks. For now, it's nice to know these recording options exist, but consider playing music for a while before diving into a new career as a recording engineer.

Always use a surge protector for any and all electronic music equipment you use. You can pick one up at an electronics, office supply, or home supply store. Plug the protector into the wall, and then plug all your equipment into the protector. If lightning strikes, the power goes out, or you accidentally flip the breaker switch while dancing a tango, your expensive music equipment could be fried without a surge protector. And now's not the time to get cheap. The most expensive surge protectors are less than $50, and some have guarantees to repay you thousands of dollars if they should ever fail to protect your equipment.

A MIDI primer

Yes, even musicians use four-letter words, but not just the ones shouted when you play the wrong notes in Beethoven's *Moonlight Sonata.* The four capital letters MIDI stand for *Musical Instrument Digital Interface.* It's not nearly as boring as it sounds. In fact, MIDI (pronounced *mid*-ee) can change your musical life.

In a nutshell, MIDI allows you to connect and communicate with other keyboards, your computer, or other digital equipment from your digital or hybrid keyboard. Suppose you have three keyboards. You select the first one to be the *controller* and set it to sound like a piano. You connect the other two keyboards to the controller and set each of them to different sounds, perhaps a flute and a tuba. As you play the controller, the other two keyboards are sent MIDI *messages* (binary codes) telling them which notes to play, how long, how loud, and so on. But it sounds like three players are playing three separate instruments, instead of just you on a piano.

But that's not all MIDI can do. By connecting a MIDI cable to your computer, you can record, edit, and notate your music using software programs on your computer. You can buy MIDI-recorded CDs and hear the songs played with the sounds of your own keyboard. Hybrid pianos and player piano systems also use MIDI to communicate with other digital equipment. MIDI software and recordings have become quite popular teaching aids because you can follow along note for note as your keyboard plays the songs.

Keyboard to computer

Sooner or later, you'll probably want to record your virtuosic playing for the world to hear. Well, at least for your friends and family to hear. Digital keyboards offer you a host of options that help you record your music. You can record directly on your keyboard, or you can record by connecting your keyboard to your computer using MIDI cables. If you use MIDI, you can record exactly what you play without any fancy recording equipment. The MIDI messages you send from your keyboard as you play can be recorded in a computer or *sequencer.* Later, all you do is push "play" on the sequencer and hear note for note, volume for volume, exactly what you played.

There are many types of recording and sequencing software programs for your computer that give you recording and editing options that may not be available on your keyboard.

Digital recording and sequencing programs allow you to record on several different tracks. So, you can record yourself playing the melody of a song with a piano sound on Track 1, followed by the drum part on Track 2, and then the guitar part on Track 3 and the bass part on Track 4. But you never use any instrument other than your keyboard and the sounds that came with it. Play back the recording, or sequence, and it plays all four tracks at once, which sounds like a quartet. Want more? Just add some violins on Track 5. Perhaps the sound of rain on Track 6. Pretty soon you've got the entire London Philharmonic playing on Tracks 7 through 17.

Software programs allow you to edit, transpose, speed up, or slow down what you've recorded. You can also alter the volume levels on each track and add sound effects, like reverb, to enhance what you've played. But wait! There's more! You can purchase or even download MIDI files that you can load into your recording software so you can play along with files and add new tracks on top.

Recording the old-fashioned way

If MIDI isn't your bag, baby, you can still record your performance using other recording equipment. Several options are available, each unique in what it can offer the aspiring recording artist. First you must decide between *analog* and *digital recording*.

Technical explanations aside, analog is the old-fashioned way of using magnetic tape to record audio; digital is the new and improved means of converting audio into a binary code to be stored on a CD, memory card, or hard drive. Both work fine, but digital is often easier to work with, especially when editing your performance. Digital recorders are very affordable and easy to use; you can just hit the record button, start playing, and have your improvised piano fantasies saved for posterity.

Keyboard to keyboard

You can connect your MIDI keyboard with another MIDI keyboard, or build a chain of three or more. Set each keyboard with a different sound patch and play all the keyboards at once from your main, *controller* keyboard. See what it sounds like to combine piano and string sounds, brass and electric guitar, you name it.

MIDI and music notation

Music notation programs are a great tool to help you learn and improve your music reading and writing skills. When you hook up your MIDI keyboard to a computer and open up notation software, you can write music, read music, and play back whatever you're working on. Plenty of educational programs are available to help you with the basics of music notation; some are interactive and make learning fun. And don't forget that you can use notation programs to write out your latest opus so you can share your music with other musicians.

Chapter 4

Taking Good Care of Your Keyboard

In This Chapter

▶ Finding the right home for your keyboard

▶ Cleaning your keyboard

▶ Realizing when you can't fix it yourself

▶ Taking the pain out of moving day

As with any baby, it's important to be the best parent you can be to your keyboard. Consider this chapter to be your "Bringing Up Baby" manual. From finding the right home in your house to keeping your keyboard clean and professionally maintained, you'll be glad you took the time to take the best possible care of your keyboard.

Providing a Good Place to Live

Whether you bought an acoustic or digital keyboard, the first thing to do when you get your new baby home is to find a spot for it to live. This spot doesn't have to be a permanent resting place, but some spots are better than others in terms of keeping your keyboard looking good and sounding even better for the duration of its life. Your ideal spot has all the following characteristics:

✔ **No direct sunlight:** Even through a window, overexposure to sunlight can damage your keyboard over time. Direct sunlight can cause the wood to warp or dry out, affecting both the sound and overall appearance. You may not mind the look of a faded keyboard, but it will be hard to sell down the road.

✔ **Controlled climate:** Don't expose your keyboard to violent temperature swings. For example, don't leave it on a porch that gets really hot in the summer and dreadfully cold in the winter. To avoid fluctuating temperatures, place your keyboard near an interior wall rather than an exterior wall. Wood responds to changes in humidity, so consider setting up a humidifier or dehumidifier if you and your acoustic piano live in a dry or wet climate. (Your piano tuner will be glad to advise you on humidifiers and dehumidifiers for this purpose.)

✔ **Good ventilation:** For acoustic pianos, good ventilation reduces the buildup of excess moisture, which can affect the wood. For digital keyboards, ventilation keeps the inner workings cooled when the power is on. But you shouldn't put your keyboard right under an air-conditioning unit or right over a heating duct. Just make sure that the area has good airflow through it.

✔ **Safety:** No matter how expensive (or inexpensive) it is, don't set your keyboard in a precarious position where it can get bumped, fall, or have something fall on it.

✔ **Elbow room:** When you feel cramped or uncomfortable, you're more likely to avoid practicing. Lack of practice leads to poor playing, so give yourself ample space for stretching out when you play.

✔ **Convenience:** Don't confine your keyboard to an area that's hard to reach. When inspiration hits, you want the keys close at hand, in a place that allows you to focus on your music. And speaking of convenience, make sure your room has plenty of electrical outlets. Using miles and miles of extension cords is expensive, irritating, and just plain ugly.

✔ **Lighting:** Until you're in a dark, smoke-filled bar or in front of hundreds of adoring fans, you should always play with good lighting. Not only is it easier to see the black and white keys with good light, but reading music is next to impossible in the dark. You can set a lamp on or near your keyboard, but avoid the clip-on kind, which can damage the keyboard's finish.

Also keep in mind how the location of your piano or keyboard may impact your relationship with your neighbors. For example, don't put your keyboard in the room right over your downstairs neighbor's bedroom. All those practice sessions late at night will soon be history.

Making It Shine: Cleaning Your Keyboard

A clean instrument sounds better and looks better longer than one that's neglected — both advantages that can affect its value if you ever need to sell it. You don't have to go overboard when it comes to cleaning your acoustic piano or digital keyboard, but you should keep it free of dust and dirt as much as possible.

Don't be afraid to lay down the law when it comes to keeping your instrument clean, insisting that no one (not even you) eats or drinks around your keyboard. A spilled drink in the back seat of your car is one thing; a spilled drink on your keyboard can be fatal (for the keyboard, that is). And do you really want to clean out old cracker crumbs from between the keys once a month?

In addition to keeping food and drink away from your keyboard, don't allow dust to build up on your instrument. Dust buildup in electric keyboards may eventually short out the circuitry or cause the keys or buttons to stick. Either of these results is bad news. Cover your digital keyboard when you aren't using it, either with a purchased dust cover or a homemade one. Dust buildup in acoustic pianos isn't as critical, but I still recommend that you keep it in check (and constant sneezing because of a dusty piano can be a drawback while playing).

The two most important cleaning tools to have near your instrument are a feather duster and a small, medium-bristle paintbrush. At least once a month, use the feather duster for an overall dusting, followed by a detailing with the paintbrush, where you get in all the grooves and between the keys. Simply press down each key and clean both sides before moving to the next one. If you're in a hurry, just run the brush in between the keys and give it a better, more thorough cleaning later. Digital keyboards have lots of little buttons, digital displays, knobs, sliders, and other gadgets; turn the power off and clean these with a dry, soft, lint-free rag every couple of months.

Be careful what cleaning solvents you use on your keyboard's finish. The wood finish on many grand pianos, for example, can be ruined by normal furniture polish. Ivory keys should be cleaned with a dry cloth or a cleaner made especially for them. (Products made for cleaning piano cases and keys are available online.) For most keyboards (acoustic or electric), I recommend a cloth that's slightly damp with plain soap and water (see the sidebar "Secret revealed: Special piano cleaner"). Don't be embarrassed to ask the dealer what cleaning products are advised and exactly how to use them.

Secret revealed: Special piano cleaner

Your dealer may suggest you buy a special cleaner packaged in a very handy and attractive bottle. Having just written a very large check, you jump at the chance to protect your investment, never mind the added cost.

You get home and decipher the scientific ingredient names on the label only to discover that you just purchased some expensive soap and water. Save your money and make your own by using the following:

➤ An empty spray bottle

➤ A marker

➤ Liquid hand soap

➤ Water

Rinse out the spray bottle until it's free of residue from any previous products. Use your marker to write "Piano Cleaner" on the outside. Add four or five squirts of soap to the bottle, and then fill it up with clean water. Shake well before spraying your rag and then wiping down your instrument. Then, if you'd like, rinse off any residual soap with clean water.

When using a liquid solution on the finish, whether soap and water or window cleaner (sometimes recommended, but ask first!), use an old T-shirt or lint-free rag instead of a paper towel. Fabric cloths don't leave those little white fuzz balls as you clean. Don't spray liquid cleaners directly on your instrument. Spray first onto your rag or cloth, and then wipe the instrument. Continue again and again until the instrument is clean, but make sure you wipe up any excess moisture.

Calling In a Pro for General Checkups and Serious Repairs

Playing the keyboard is one thing. Knowing how to repair and maintain one is another. You should leave such matters to a qualified professional. You have enough to worry about with playing, reading music, and touring around the world.

This section gives you tips on hiring piano tuners, piano technicians, keyboard technical support people, and others who can help you maintain and prolong your instrument's life.

Tuning acoustic keyboards

Okay, so your friend can tune his own guitar, as can your other friends with their violins, clarinets, and kazoos. But keep in mind how much larger your piano is, how many parts are inside, and how much more you probably paid for it. Swallow your pride, pick up the phone, and call a piano technician when it's time to tune your piano.

Piano technicians are skilled professionals with years of education and experience. And this kind of doctor still makes house calls. It may look like the technician's just playing keys and tightening screws, but you won't even know where to begin if you try to do it yourself.

Don't think that you'll suddenly hear your piano go out of tune one day. Loss of intonation is a gradual process that takes place over a long period of time. Your tuning will be much overdue if you get to the point where you actually say to yourself, "Wow! My piano's out of tune." Schedule a tuning at least once a year — preferably twice a year. Generally, the visit will take two to three hours and cost you between $75 and $150, which is well worth the cost! After you establish a relationship with a technician, he'll probably contact you each year, so you don't even have to remember to schedule an appointment for a tuning.

Too many years of tuning neglect results in a piano that's permanently out of tune. Ever heard an old honky-tonk saloon piano? Sure, the sound is sort of fun, but not when it's coming from your $30,000 9-foot grand piano. Frequent tuning ensures that the pitch of your piano doesn't drop (a condition that's reparable but sometimes problematic) and that any problems with the tuning pins, which are tightened and loosened during tuning, or the pinblock, which holds the pins, can be fixed as they arise.

You can get recommendations for a good piano technician from friends, teachers, music stores, and music schools. Then check the recommendations against the member directory of the Piano Technicians Guild at www.ptg.org, which includes individuals who have earned the distinction of Registered Piano Technician (RPT). Don't just select at random from the phone book; a bad technician can ruin a piano.

In addition to tuning, I highly recommend asking the technician to have a look under the hood and make sure everything else is functioning properly. Ask the technician these questions:

- ✔ Do the pedals work?
- ✔ Are the legs secure?

> ✔ Are there any problems with the action?
>
> ✔ Is the soundboard cracked?

Keeping digital keyboards happy

You don't need to tune your digital keyboard. However, it does need some occasional attention. If you keep your keyboard clean and dust-free, chances are it will work and sound just fine for quite some time.

Over time, through constant pushing and pulling, the little buttons, digital displays, knobs, sliders, and other gizmos on a digital keyboard experience normal wear and tear. If a button appears to be stuck, *don't* try to fix it yourself with one of your own tools. Call a professional — perhaps the dealer who sold you the instrument originally or the manufacturer for a dealer reference. For a minimal fee, the dealer can assess the damage (if any) and fix it for you. If your warranty is still good (usually only for one year), repairs may cost you absolutely nothing.

Never, ever, under any circumstances should you unscrew or open the top of your keyboard. Sure, it looks really cool inside with all the computer chips and circuit boards. Sure, you think you know what you're doing and want to save a buck by fixing a problem yourself. But opening up your keyboard voids your warranty automatically and more than likely damages your keyboard irreparably.

Technical support lines

Each and every time you buy a new keyboard, fill out and send in the registration card that comes with it — or fill out the registration online, if that's an option. Don't be afraid that you'll be put on some mailing list; you're simply telling the manufacturer, "Just letting you know that I bought your really cool product. Here's my name and here's where I live." That's all.

Then, day or night, any time you have a problem with your instrument, you can call the manufacturer's technical support line and speak with a knowledgeable professional (maybe even someone who designed your keyboard) about the specific problem you're having and how to rectify it. The call to technical support is usually free — if you've filled out that little card and mailed it in.

To find the technical support line for your instrument, call the manufacturer directly or browse the lists of manufacturers and their contact information in Chapter 3.

Dealing with serious keyboard problems

Unfortunately, some keyboard problems can arise that require some serious time, effort, and money to fix. If you experience any of the following problems, you should get estimates from at least two separate technicians before deciding whether or not to salvage your instrument:

- **The soundboard on your acoustic piano cracks or breaks.** The soundboard is the large, polished board under the strings. The soundboard can break during a move performed by unqualified movers. It can also break due to constant changes in humidity that cause the wood to swell and contract. You probably won't notice a broken soundboard on your own, so have your piano technician check out the soundboard for you during each tune-up.

- **You hear only a thump when you press an acoustic piano key.** Either the hammer, damper, or both are not functioning properly. You may have to replace the mechanism for that one key or replace the entire set of keys and hammers. Hope for the first option. Of course, the culprit could also just be a broken string, which can be fixed for under $20.

- **Your digital keyboard won't power on.** First, make sure you paid last month's electric bill. Unless you have a battery-operated keyboard with old batteries, your keyboard should always power on when plugged in correctly. If not, it may be dead.

- **Your LCD display shows nothing legible.** If the words and program names on the front panel display of your digital keyboard are suddenly a bunch of meaningless letters, the brains of your board may be fried.

- **You spill liquid all over your digital keyboard.** You probably just shorted out the entire board. Few, if any, of your buttons and keys are going to work. This is why you should never have a drink on or near your keyboard. If you spill anything on a digital keyboard, the first thing to do is to shut the power off. To minimize the damage, let it dry out completely before turning the power on again.

- **You spill liquid on your acoustic piano.** Quickly get a towel and start sopping it up. The wood, strings, hammers, and even keys may be damaged, but at least there isn't anything electrical to bug out.

A few mishaps that seem terrible actually aren't that bad, including pedals falling off, strings breaking, headphone jacks snapping off inside the unit, and even keys sticking. True, these are big headaches, but they aren't serious problems. Just leave the problem alone and call a professional for help.

Taking the Worry Out of Moving Your Acoustic Piano

Take these three pieces of advice when it comes to moving your piano:

- ✔ Don't ever try to move the piano by yourself or with friends.

- ✔ Confirm that you're using qualified piano movers.

- ✔ Don't watch the move. You should definitely be present to watch the movers and make sure they take extreme care when moving your precious baby. But you're guaranteed to grimace when you see them flip that piano over on its side. Save yourself the emotional distress and just turn away.

Moving a grand piano involves its own specialized piece of equipment called a *piano board.* This long, flat board has lots of padding and several handles. The movers lay the piano on its side on this board and strap it all to a dolly. The piano board holds your baby securely and cushions any jarring bumps. If your movers show up without a piano board, I strongly advise you to bid them farewell and call new movers. To move upright pianos, movers typically place the piano (upright!) on a flat dolly.

Your local piano dealer can recommend several good moving companies who specialize in piano moving. The good ones actually receive endorsements from piano manufacturers.

If you own or rent an acoustic piano, moving from one residence to another is automatically more expensive. You must hire a qualified piano mover to transfer your baby to its new home. Don't be cheap about hiring a mover. Inexperienced movers can ruin your piano.

Chapter 5

Eighty-Eight Keys, Three Pedals, Ten Fingers, and Two Feet

*Y*ou're staring at all these keys, trying to make sense of the whole thing, and you're wondering why you didn't just buy a pair of cymbals and call it a day. I've been there. It seems quite intimidating, but to paraphrase the Jackson Five: It's as easy as A-B-C, 1-2-3.

In this chapter, I help you get acquainted with all the finer features of your keyboard, including the keys and the pedals. I also advise you on equipment, such as chairs, benches, and racks, that aids you in achieving proper piano-playing posture, and I explain just what that perfect piano posture looks like.

Finding the Keys, Easy Peasy

The first thing you notice on your keyboard is the not-so-colorful use of black and white keys aligned from left to right. The black ones are raised and appear to be set farther back than the white ones, as you can see in Figure 5-1.

If the black and white keys are reversed, you're either playing a very old keyboard or the manufacturer messed up and you got an enormous discount. Congratulations!

Each key on the keyboard represents a specific musical note. These notes use a very complex naming system — the first seven letters of the alphabet, A-B-C-D-E-F-G. The names of the keys correspond to the names of musical notes. (Chapter 6 explains note names.) For now, just remember that a G key plays a G note, an A key plays an A note, and so on.

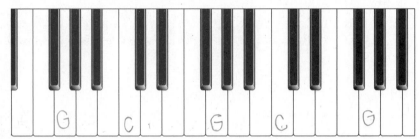

Figure 5-1:
Your basic
set of black
and whites.

You're thinking: "I'm looking at 88 keys, but I only have seven alphabet letters to name all those keys! How do I name the other 81 keys?" For all 88 keys, the basic set of seven letter names repeats over and over, in *octave groupings,* which are groups of eight.

When you name the sequence of seven white keys from A to G, the next (eighth) note is A as the series begins again. You can count seven octaves from the lowest A to the highest A on an 88-key piano.

In the following sections, I show you how to use the E-Z Key Finder technique to locate the different notes on the keyboard. It's an unforgettable way to find any key on the board.

The white keys

To make things really easy, the seven note names (A-B-C-D-E-F-G) are all on the white keys. The black keys have names of their own, which I cover in the next section, but for now you can use the black keys as landmarks to find the correct white keys . . . even in the dark! I present the first instrument ever equipped with a sort of musical Braille system: The raised black keys help you locate any white key quickly and precisely.

The black keys always appear in consecutive groups of two and three. You'll never see two sets of two black keys or two sets of three black keys in a row. This distinction of twos and threes is important and makes the job of finding white keys even easier.

Use your imagination and think of any set of two black keys as a pair of chopsticks. Think of any set of three black keys as the tines on a fork. (Take a glance at Figure 5-2.) "Chopsticks" starts with the letter C, and "fork" starts with the letter F. This handy memory-device forms the basis of my E-Z Key Finder technique for finding the white keys on the keyboard. The main points are as follows:

- ✔ To the left of the chopsticks (two black keys) is the note C.
- ✔ To the left of the fork (three black keys) is the note F.

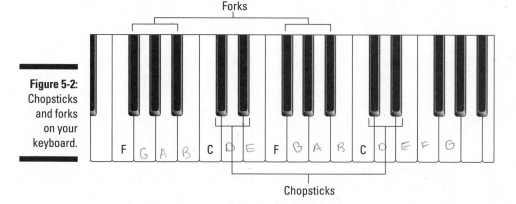

Figure 5-2:
Chopsticks
and forks
on your
keyboard.

Allow that to sink in while you look at your keyboard, and you won't forget it. But what about the other white keys, you ask? You know the alphabet fairly well, don't you? Look at the alphabet letters again: A-B-C-D-E-F-G.

Notice what letters surround C and what letters surround F. The same advanced logic applies to the white keys surrounding C and F. Moving up from C you have the notes D, E, F, G. When you get to G, think "Go" as in "go back to the beginning of the alphabet." The alphabet pattern repeats over and over again on the keyboard, as many times as you see chopsticks and forks.

To practice finding notes, play every C and F on the keyboard, from bottom to top. Then locate every D and G. Test yourself by playing all the other white keys while reciting the names of the keys. With the aid of the E-Z Key Finder, you'll never forget a key's name.

Now that you know the names of the white keys, you can play:

- ✔ The first nine notes of "Over the River and Through the Woods": D, D, D, D, B, C, D, D, D
- ✔ The first six notes of "It's Raining, It's Pouring": B, D, B, E, D, B
- ✔ The first seven notes of "The First Noel": E, D, C, D, E, F, G
- ✔ The first 11 notes to the theme from Ravel's *Boléro:* C, B, C, D, C, B, A, C, C, A, C

The black keys

Play A, then B, then the black key in between A and B. You'll notice that it sounds like a different musical note. You're correct: Black keys represent separate musical notes from white keys. However, because no alphabet letter comes between the letters A and B, the black key between these two can't be given a logical alphabetical name.

The black keys are assigned the same name as the closest white key but with one of the following suffixes added on:

- ✔ **Sharp** is used for a black key to the *right* of (or *higher* than) a white key.
- ✔ **Flat** is used for a black key to the *left* of (or *lower* than) a white key.

Here's another culinary metaphor to help you remember these suffixes. At your imaginary musical place setting, a white key represents a plate. Now imagine that

- ✔ A knife is *sharp* and lies on the *right* side of the plate.
- ✔ A napkin is *flat* and lies on the *left* side of the plate.

Put it to the test: Find the D plate (key). To the right is a sharp knife, D-sharp. To the left is a flat napkin, D-flat. Easy enough? Just remember chopsticks and forks, knives and napkins, and you'll never forget the names of the keys . . . but you may feel a little hungry.

Because each of the black keys lies between two white keys, each black key has two names, depending on the white key you approach it from. For example, the black key to the right of C is C-sharp, but it's also D-flat. The split personality of each black key (note) seems odd at first, but after you get the hang of seeing each key from two different perspectives, it isn't that awkward. The fancy name for one key with two different names is *enharmonic*.

You probably already noticed that no black keys reside between B and C or E and F. Before you demand a full refund from your local keyboard dealer, you should know that this is no mistake. Theoretically, C is also B-sharp and, similarly, E is also F-flat. But this is way too much needless music theory. Suffice it to say that there are no notes between B and C or E and F. You'll survive without knowing why.

Develop a clear mental image of the octave groupings on the keyboard, and then check your mental image against Figure 5-3. These groupings will help you navigate the 88s.

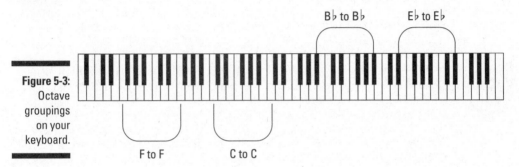

Figure 5-3: Octave groupings on your keyboard.

Now that you know the names of the white and black keys, you can play

✔ The theme from the movie *Jaws*: D-sharp, E, D-sharp, E, D-sharp, E (keep repeating until someone screams)

✔ The first four notes of Beethoven's *Fifth Symphony*: G, G, G, E-flat

✔ The tune of "Shave and a Haircut, Five Cents": G, D, D, E, D, F-sharp, G

Head to www.dummies.com/go/piano to watch Video Clip 2 for more on identifying and mastering both the white and black keys.

Discovering What Your Parents Never Told You about Posture

Good posture, including how you sit and how you hold your hands, keeps you comfortable at your keyboard for hours on end. Practicing good posture while you play also helps you avoid cramped hands, a tired back, and even more serious medical problems like carpal tunnel syndrome. After you're a famous concert pianist, you can look back fondly on this chapter and remember how it helped prepare you for a career with the keyboard.

To sit or not to sit: That's the real question

Depending on the type of keyboard — and sometimes the type of stage — that you're playing on, you can either sit or stand while you play.

As a general rule, most pianists sit at the piano, but many rock keyboardists stand behind their boards. Maybe they want the audience to have a better view of them playing. Or maybe they're just tired of sitting from all those days on tour buses.

As a beginner, you should begin your musical endeavors in a seated position. No matter what kind of keyboard you play, sitting brings you closer to the keys and makes you more comfortable as you practice.

Whether sitting or standing, you should be comfortable at all times. Your feet should rest firmly on the floor. Your hands should have a nice relaxed arch to them. The keys should be at an appropriate height so that your hands and forearms are parallel to the ground, as shown in Figure 5-4.

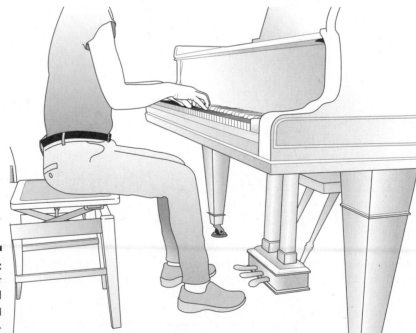

Figure 5-4:
Proper
posture and
positioning
at the piano.

Make sure your back is straight and that you aren't slumping, slouching, or hunching over. Not sitting up straight leads to backaches — the kind that discourage you from practicing.

Sitting down: Chairs versus benches

Both chairs and benches are acceptable options, and both are readily available at most piano stores and concert halls. Of course, both options have their pros and cons, and it's up to you to sort out what's the best fit for your playing.

Chairs

When I say *chair,* I'm not talking about a recliner with flip-out footrest and side pockets for the TV remote. I'm talking about standard-issue piano chairs, which are usually plain, black chairs. Many have a padded seat, and some offer a useful mechanism to raise or lower the height of the seat just a bit, as shown in Figure 5-5.

Figure 5-5:
An adjust-
able piano
chair.

The back on a chair provides some added support, but it also may cause you to slump more just because you can. As Mom and Dad always told you, slumping isn't attractive or good for your back. Also, the extra wood on chair backs often tends to creak, which isn't a pleasant sound during a performance of Debussy's *Clair de Lune*.

But paradoxically, the back on a chair is also its main advantage. The extra support is good for young, sometimes fidgety students because they feel more secure on a chair than on a backless bench. Heck, you can even strap on a booster seat for the young child prodigy. Plus, like it or not, everyone slumps occasionally. As you practice diligently into the wee hours of the night, nobody has to know if you slump against the back of the chair a little bit. At least you're practicing!

Perhaps the biggest drawback of a chair is the inability to accommodate a duet partner. Many pianists enjoy playing duets with friends. You sit side-by-side and play the keyboard in two parts: one person playing the lower notes, and the other playing the upper notes. Sure, you can just pull up another chair, but where's the romance in that?

Benches

The standard piano bench, which you see in Figure 5-6a, measures approximately 2 feet high by 3 feet wide. The width allows ample room for shifting yourself to reach higher or lower notes while you play, and it also accommodates a duet partner.

Height is an important function of whatever you choose to sit on while playing. However, many piano benches aren't adjustable, forcing you to lean up into the keyboard or to sit atop a stack of phone books. The nicer benches come with knobs on the side that let you adjust the bench height for a more personal fit (shown in Figure 5-6b). The better benches also offer padding, which you begin to appreciate after a few hours of hard practice.

Unlike a chair, a bench provides no back support, leaving you to keep a straight spine throughout the performance. On the plus side, a backless bench forces good posture during your playing. However, no back support also means no protection from falling backwards when you become too excited during the climax of a Bartók concerto or your jamming rock solo.

Some piano benches have hinged seats, allowing you to open the seat and store sheet music, books, or even a mid-concert snack. Just don't forget what you leave in there, especially those wallets and car keys!

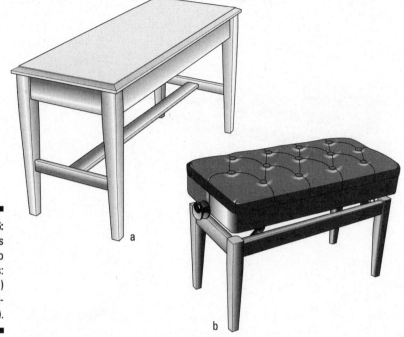

Figure 5-6:
Two types
of piano
benches:
standard (a)
and adjust-
able (b).

a

b

Using stands and racks

Keyboard stands (see Figure 5-7) come in all shapes and sizes. Some are multi-tiered for adding more and more keyboards as your career or bank account grows. Keyboard stands also come in different colors. (If you don't like the colors, you can always buy a can of spray paint.)

Nearly every stand is adjustable because the manufacturer is never exactly sure just how tall its client base is. You can adjust the height of the keyboard so that you can sit or stand, depending on your mood. Just make sure that the keys are at the proper height (refer to Figure 5-4). The adjustability also allows you to spread multiple keyboards farther apart on the stand to allow easy access to the various buttons and knobs on each.

In addition to a stand, you may also need an *effects rack,* which is a wooden or metal box with holed brackets along the edge into which you can screw various components, samplers, effects processors, mixers, or even drawers. Racks can be stationary or on rollers, according to your personal needs and desires.

As always, make sure you have adequate lighting for your keyboard, music rack, and program/patch display.

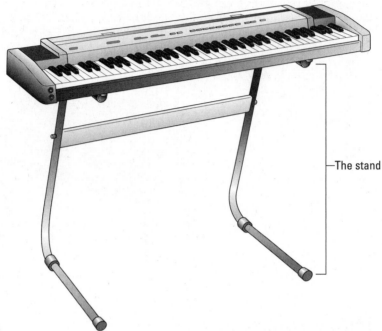

—The stand

Figure 5-7:
Take a stand
for your
electric
keyboard.

Paying Attention to Hand Positioning

I can't stress enough how important comfortable hand position and comfortable posture are while playing the piano or keyboard. Poor hand position can cause your performance to suffer for two reasons:

- ✔ **Lack of dexterity:** If your hands are in tight, awkward positions, you can't access the keys quickly and efficiently. Your performance will sound clumsy and be full of wrong notes.

- ✔ **Potential for cramping:** If your hands cramp often, you won't practice often. If you don't practice often, you won't be a very good player.

These sections examine all you need to know about using your hands and fingers when playing the piano.

Arch those hands and fingers

When you place your hands on the keys, you must keep your hands arched and your fingers slightly curled at all times. It feels weird at first, but you can't improve your playing technique until you get used to holding your hands this way. Arching your hands and fingers pays off with the following benefits:

- Your hands don't get tired as quickly.
- Your hands are less likely to cramp.
- You can quickly and easily access any key, black or white.

To get an idea of the hand shape you're after, find two tennis balls (or similarly sized balls) and hold one in each hand, as shown in Figure 5-8. This is how your hand should look when you play the piano . . . minus the ball, of course.

Go to www.dummies.com/go/piano and watch Video Clip 3 to make sure you have a handle on arching both your hands and fingers.

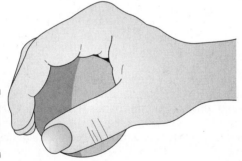

Figure 5-8:
The shape
to emulate.

Trim those nails

It's as simple as this: Keep your fingernails short or at least at a reasonable length. Your audience wants to hear beautiful piano music, not be distracted by the clickety-clack of your nails on the keys.

Fingering

Fingering refers to using the best finger to play each note of a song, and correct fingering is always a very important part of piano playing. Some pieces, even the easy ones, have fingerings marked in the sheet music to help you plan which fingers to use to execute a particular musical passage most efficiently and comfortably.

The fingerings you see in music correspond to the left- and right-hand fingering you see in Figure 5-9. Number your fingers 1 through 5, beginning with the thumb as number 1 and moving toward the little finger, or pinkie.

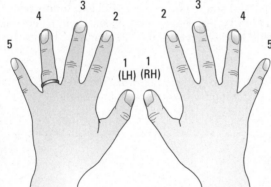

Figure 5-9:
Numbers
and digits.

While you get used to thinking of your fingers in terms of numbers, you may find it helpful to write these numbers on your hands before you sit down to practice. Use washable marker or pen. Otherwise, you'll have to explain those numbered fingers to your date on Friday night, your boss on Monday morning, or your homeroom teacher.

Giving your hands and fingers a rest

Poor posture can lead to the beginning of serious and painful problems in your piano career. The sports claim "no pain, no gain" has no validity when applied to piano playing. Muscle tension and poor posture can cause pain. If you hurt, you won't play. If you don't play, you won't be very good.

Feeling cramped

Even if your posture is absolutely perfect, your hands will inevitably begin to cramp at some point. Cramps are your body's way of saying, "Hey, let's go do something else for a while." By all means, listen to your body.

Generally, you'll experience hand cramps long before you experience any other kind of body cramp during practice. Your back and neck may become sore from poor posture, but your hands will begin to cramp simply from too much use.

If your hands hurt, take a long break and do something that creates a completely opposite hand action. For example, throwing a ball to your dog is an opposite hand action; typing is not. If your whole body hurts, get a massage (including a hand massage) or take a luxurious cruise in the South Pacific. You deserve it.

Avoiding carpal tunnel syndrome

Much has been said about a career-oriented injury called *carpal tunnel syndrome* (CTS). Without getting into its technical definition, which would require a degree in medicine, suffice it to say that CTS develops from overstraining the muscles and ligaments in your wrist through a constant, repetitive action. And piano playing is a constant, repetitive action.

As you can probably imagine, many a keyboardist and full-time blogger experience CTS during their careers. Unfortunately, many wait until it's too late for a simple remedy. They ignore what starts out as a dull pain in the forearms, wrists, and fingers until it becomes a severe pain whenever the hands are in motion. Severe CTS requires surgery to remedy, but the results aren't always 100 percent successful. As a piano player, you need 100 percent of your hand motion, so don't let any pain go unaddressed.

If you're bothered by pain in your wrists, no matter how minor, consult your physician for ways to reduce or prevent it. Of course, if you've already been diagnosed with CTS, talk with your physician about your piano-playing goals and ask what steps you can take to prevent any further damage or pain. (Your doctor will probably ask how you got interested in the piano, giving you an excellent opportunity to wholeheartedly endorse this book.)

Pedal Power: Getting Your Feet in on the Action

When you play the keyboard, your hands are busy on the keys, and your feet are called upon to work the *pedals* to control other aspects of the music.

Most pianos have two or three pedals, and synthesizers can have even more. Pipe organs often incorporate an entire keyboard of pedals to be played by the feet. I won't go into the details of the pipe organ pedals, but if you play a pipe organ, you can find a whole host of teachers at your disposal to help you figure out the pedals (see Chapter 2 for more on pipe organs).

The various pedals on your instrument allow you to achieve different effects in your music. Most of the time, the composer indicates when to use which pedal, but you should feel free to experiment with the pedals and the interpretations they can bring to your music.

Piano pedals

Most pianos come equipped with three pedals, as shown in Figure 5-10.

✔ **To the far right is the *damper pedal* (or *sustain pedal*).** When you hold this pedal down, the *dampers* — mechanisms that mute the strings — are moved away from the strings, allowing the strings to ring until you release the pedal, the sound gradually fades away, or you fall asleep and fall off the bench. You don't have to use the damper pedal every time you play a note because each key has its own damper. (For more on dampers, turn to Chapter 2.)

Left pedal   Middle pedal   Right pedal

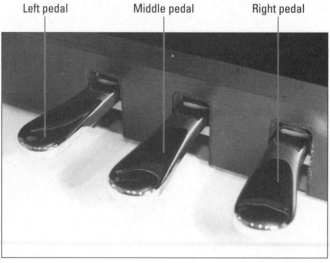

Figure 5-10:
The typical three pedals on a piano.

Photo by Grégory DUBUS/ iStockphoto.com

Most musicians, and even nonmusicians who purport to know something about music, refer to the damper pedal as "the pedal" because it's the most popular and most frequently used pedal.

✔ **To the far left is the *soft pedal.*** This pedal works differently in uprights and grands, but you use it to make your piano sound softer.

The Italian name for the soft pedal is the *una corda.* On grand pianos, pressing down this pedal causes the entire set of hammers inside the piano to shift slightly to the side. When you play on any of the keys with the pedal down, the hammers hit only one string, or *una corda,* instead of the usual three.

✔ **In the middle is the *middle pedal,* or *sostenuto pedal.*** This pedal appears on many pianos, but not all. Unlike the damper pedal, which sustains all notes being played, the middle pedal allows you to sustain a specific note, or group of notes, while you continue playing other notes normally. Simultaneously hold down the middle pedal and play a key on the piano and the sound sustains. Now, quickly play other notes and you'll notice they don't sustain. Pretty cool, right? Well, pretty difficult, too — especially in the midst of playing Rachmaninoff's *Piano Concerto No. 3.* Many piano manufacturers now opt to save money and omit this pedal.

On some upright pianos, the middle pedal is called a *practice pedal* and has an entirely different function: It inserts a layer of felt between the hammers and strings to make the sound much softer and more muffled. This pedal allows you to practice late at night without disturbing others, so you might call it the good neighbor pedal.

To see the pedals in action, head to www.dummies.com/go/piano and watch Video Clip 4.

Digital keyboard pedals

The most common digital keyboard pedals are the sustain pedal (which performs the same function as on an acoustic piano, as explained in the previous section) and volume pedal (which increases or decreases the volume). Nearly every keyboard comes with a plug-in sustain pedal; it doesn't move any dampers or shift any keys because there are no real strings inside a digital keyboard. Instead, the pedal sends an electronic signal to the brain of your keyboard, telling it to sustain the notes or increase or decrease the volume if you're using a volume pedal. (Chapter 2 tells you more about the brain of a digital keyboard.)

Other pedals you can add to your electric keyboard control such things as *vibrato,* which makes the note sound as if it's warbling; program changes; and special effects.

You can sample these various pedals and decide which ones are right for you at your local electric keyboard dealer. The salesperson should be more than happy to show you a whole line of different pedals, hoping that you want to spend even more money than you already are for the keyboard itself. (Chapter 3 has helpful information on shopping for keyboards and accessories.) If you're unsure about extra pedals, hold off on buying them. You can always buy and install them later, when you know that you'll use them. The plug for all pedals and most other accessories is a standard size, making additions a snap.

Part II
Deciphering Squiggles on Paper to Create Sound

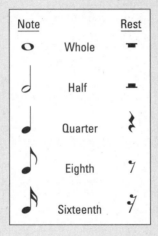

In this part . . .

- Find out how to read notes on — and outside of — the musical staff. Then, transfer that knowledge to play the notes on the piano.

- Recognize different types of bar lines — single, double, repeats, and so on — and how they help you navigate your way through a piece of music.

- Count a range of note and rest values, from whole notes to sixteenths. Learn to automatically know what to do when you see them in notation.

- Navigate common time signatures: 4/4, 3/4, and more, and find out all about how they work and the different types of feels that they lend to music.

- Play a bunch of new songs right away, from "Can Can" to "When the Saints Go Marching In," through a nicely stream-lined approach.

Chapter 6

Reading Lines and Spaces

. . . .

In This Chapter

▶ Figuring out what all those lines, spaces, and marks mean

▶ Fitting all the notes you need on one grand staff

▶ Starting and stopping with bar lines

. . . .

*B*ees buzzing, computers humming, and power tools vibrating are all sounds that can't be easily deciphered and written down on paper. In frustration, humans decide that these noises mean nothing to them and move on with their lives. But people are incapable of being so blasé when it comes to two other types of sound: speech and music. Because this book isn't *Speech For Dummies,* allow me to cut to the chase.

To play music, you have to know what note to play and when. A piano has 88 keys, each sounding a different musical note. (Chapter 5 tells you all about those 88 keys on the keyboard.) With a bunch of lines and dots, a composer tells you which notes to play, which of the 88 keys to press, and how long to play each note. In this chapter, I help you understand how each of these elements is written down in music.

Your Guide to a Piano Score

When you look at a piece of printed music, like "Humoresque" in Figure 6-1, the first thing you may notice are a bunch of dots and circles. These dots and circles represent *notes.* Each written note tells you two essential bits of info:

▶ What key to play

▶ How long to play that key

It shouldn't take you long to notice that the notes are written on either a line or a space above or below a line. Without these lines, the notes are . . . well, just dots and circles.

Figure 6-1:
An example
of music
written for
the piano.

Key:
1. Grand staff (Chapter 6)
2. Treble clef (Chapter 6)
3. Bass clef (Chapter 6)
4. Flat (Chapter 6)
5. Sharp (Chapter 6)
6. Natural (Chapter 6)
7. Bar line (Chapter 6)
8. Final bar line (Chapter 6)
9. Tempo indication (Chapter 7)
10. Quarter note (Chapter 7)
11. Half note (Chapter 7)
12. Whole note (Chapter 7)

13. Sixteenth note (Chapter 7)
14. Rest (Chapter 7)
15. Time signature (Chapter 7)
16. Tie (Chapter 8)
17. Dotted sixteenth note (Chapter 8)
18. Key signature (Chapter 13)
19. Dynamic marking (Chapter 15)
20. Ritardando (Chapter 15)
21. Articulation (Chapter 15)
22. Crescendo (Chapter 15)
23. Decrescendo (Chapter 15)
24. Slur (Chapter 15)
25. Grace note (Chapter 15)

Look a little more closely at Figure 6-1 and you see other familiar musical symbols that are all part of the written-music language. The following sections help you start deciphering that language, starting with the staff and the clef.

Note: Many of the elements of *music notation* (the universally accepted methods and conventions used to write music) are introduced in this chapter, and others are introduced in later chapters. You can, and should, always refer back to this page to remind yourself and reinforce all the elements of music notation. The key in Figure 6-1 tells you which chapter to go to for each element. Feel free to jump ahead and take a peek at any notational element that interests you.

Employing a staff of five lines

Figure 6-2 shows a set of the parallel lines you find in music. Count 'em — you should count five in all. Now count the spaces in between the lines — you should come up with four.

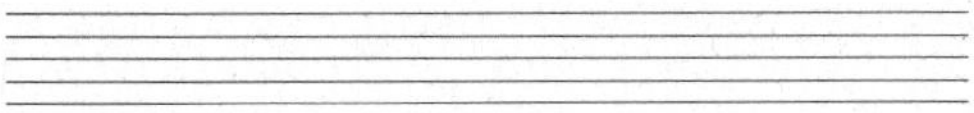

Figure 6-2:
Music's
parallel
lines.

Together, these five lines and four spaces compose a musical *staff.* It's an appropriate name because a composer employs his staff to hold the notes he's writing. And what a staff to have! No complaining, no vacation time, no excuses for tardiness — just some inanimate lines and spaces.

Each line and space represents a specific musical note. The notes are named with the first seven alphabet letters, A-B-C-D-E-F-G, just like the white keys on the keyboard. (You can read more about the letters assigned to each of the keyboard keys in Chapter 5.) Each line and space is also named one of these letters. That way, when you see a note on the G line, you know to play the G key. See how everything is lining up?

Looking at your keyboard, you can see that there are several of each of the seven notes. For example, you see several separate G keys on the keyboard. Obviously, five lines and four spaces aren't enough to accommodate all 88 keys. Before you panic, realize that you have a few more options.

Hanging from a clef

Instead of adding more lines and spaces to accommodate all the occurrences of each of the seven notes, you get a symbol to help out with the job. Think of it as your secret decoder ring, Captain Music Maker. Notice the little squiggly thing at the far left of the staff in Figure 6-3. This ornamental creature is called a *clef* (this one is the treble clef, to be exact).

Figure 6-3:
The treble
clef.

← G line

A clef's sole purpose in life is to tell you the names of the lines and spaces on the staff. If the clef could talk, it would say something like, "For this set of notes, the lines and spaces represent these keys."

Music uses several different clefs, but as a keyboard player you're in luck — you only need to know two of 'em. Think of it as having a clef for each hand.

Treble clef

Generally, the *treble clef* (shown in Figure 6-3) signals notes to be played by the right hand. This clef is also called the *G clef* because it

✔ Looks like a (very) stylized G.

✔ Circles around the second staff line which (not coincidentally) represents the note G.

The G line encircled by the treble clef isn't for just any old G key. It's the G that's closest to the middle of your keyboard (see Figure 6-4 for a guide). After you've found this G, reading the other lines and spaces on the staff is as easy as reciting the alphabet.

If you're close to a keyboard, put a right-hand finger on this G key. (If you're not close to a keyboard, refer to the keys you see in Figure 6-4.) The next white key up (to the right) of the G is represented by the next space up on the staff. According to the E-Z Key Finder in Chapter 5, G stands for "Go back to the beginning of the alphabet," so the next white key on the keyboard and the next space up on the staff correspond to the note A.

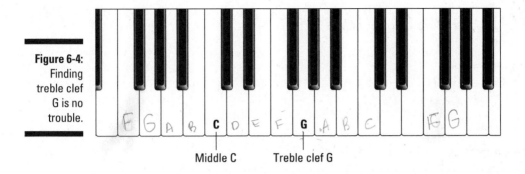

Figure 6-4:
Finding
treble clef
G is no
trouble.

Middle C   Treble clef G

Continue up and down the staff and you get the musical notes you see in
Figure 6-5.

Figure 6-5:
Names for
notes on the
treble clef
lines and
spaces.

E   G   B   D   F

F   A   C   E

Bass clef

Your left hand typically plays the lower notes on the keyboard, which are
also called *bass* notes. (For the record, that's pronounced like *base,* not like
the fish you caught last weekend.)

The rules of equality demand that the left hand get its own clef, too. Meet the
bass clef (shown in Figure 6-6). Like the treble clef, the bass clef surrounds
a particular line that represents a particular note: F. You can remember the
special relationship between the bass clef and the note F by thinking about
the following two things:

✔ The bass clef's two dots surround the staff line that represents the note F.

✔ The bass clef looks like a stylized F (use your imagination).

You can call the bass clef the *F clef* or just think of it as a stylized B (the dots are the humps) for *bass*.

Figure 6-6:
The bass
clef.

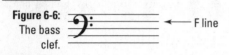

← F line

The bass clef doesn't surround the F just below the treble clef G. Instead, this F is one octave grouping below (or to the left), as shown in Figure 6-7. (See Chapter 5 for more on octave groupings.)

Figure 6-7:
Finding bass
clef F on the
keyboard.

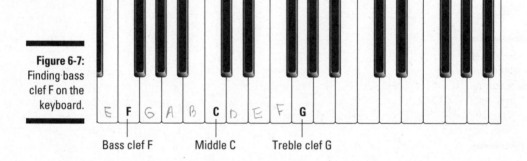

To read the notes on the bass clef, simply start with the F line and travel down (backward) and up (forward) through the alphabet. Figure 6-8 shows you the notes on the bass clef staff.

Figure 6-8:
Names for
notes on the
bass clef
lines and
spaces.

Notice that the bottom line and top space of the treble clef and the bottom line and top space of the bass clef have the same letter name — they're an octave apart. Same goes for the bottom space and top line on each staff. An octave above a note on a space is written on a line, and an octave above a note on a line is written on a space. Figure 6-9 illustrates this point beautifully.

Figure 6-9:
Clues for
reading
octaves.

Accidentals

You may be wondering how these lines and spaces represent the black keys. Chapter 5 explains that the black keys are *sharps* and *flats;* for example, a B-flat is the black key to the left of (or lower than) a B, and an F-sharp is the black key to the right of (or higher than) an F. Instead of adding more lines and spaces to show the sharps and flats, a much simpler approach places these sharps and flats, or *accidentals,* on the same lines or spaces as their "natural" notes but with little symbols to the left of the notes. So B-flat sits on the B line with a little flat symbol (♭) next to it, and F-sharp is written on the F line with a sharp sign (♯) next to it. The *natural* sign (♮) cancels the flat or sharp, returning the note to its natural state, as shown in Figure 6-10.

Figure 6-10:
Notating
accidentals.

Mnemonics help you remember the notes

Having trouble remembering the names of the lines and spaces for each staff (and, consequently, the notes they represent)? Use a *mnemonic,* a word or phrase created from the letter names of these lines and spaces, to help you remember.

You can use the following mnemonics, but feel free to make up your own. Unless otherwise noted, these mnemonics start on the bottom line of each staff and go up:

Treble clef lines (E-G-B-D-F):

- **Traditional (but sexist):** Every Good Boy Does Fine

- **Musical:** Every Good Band Draws Fans

- **Pianistic:** Even Gershwin Began (as a) Dummy First

- **Culinary:** Eating Green Bananas Disgusts Friends

- **Political:** Even George Bush Drives Fast

- **Shameless:** Every Good Book (is a) Dummies Favorite

Treble clef spaces (F-A-C-E):

- **Traditional:** FACE (like the one holding your nose)

- **Musical:** Forks And Chopsticks Everywhere (see Chapter 3)

- **Laundry (start with top space):** Eventually Colors Always Fade

Bass clef lines (G-B-D-F-A):

- **Recreational:** Good Bikes Don't Fall Apart

- **Animal:** Great Big Dogs Fight Animals

- **Musical:** Great Beethoven's Deafness Frustrated All

- **Musical:** Grandpa Bach Did Fugues A lot

- **Painful:** Giving Blood Doesn't Feel Agreeable

Bass clef spaces (A-C-E-G):

- **Musical:** American Composers Envy Gershwin

- **Animal:** All Cows Eat Grass

- **Revenge (start with top space):** Get Even, Call Avon

Read enough of these mnemonics and you'll be hard-pressed to forget them. Of course, if you do happen to forget these helpful tools, simply find the line encircled by the clef and move up or down the alphabet from there, remembering that each line *and* space gets a name.

Double Your Staff, Double Your Fun

Sooner or later, on either staff, you run out of lines and spaces for your notes. Surely the composer wants you to use more of the fabulous 88 keys at your disposal, right? Here's a solution: Because you play piano with both hands at the same time, why not show both *staves* (the plural form of *staff*) on the music page? Great idea!

Grand staff and ledger lines

Join both staves together with a brace at the start of the left side and you get one *grand staff* (it's really called that), as shown in Figure 6-11. This way, you can read notes for both hands at the same time.

Figure 6-11: Isn't this staff grand?

Why all the space between the two staves? Glad you asked. Look at the treble staff in Figure 6-11 and name the notes downward from the treble clef G line. Notice that you only get to E before running out of lines. What to do?

Now find the bass clef F line on the bass staff in Figure 6-11 and name the notes upward. The top line is A. What about the remaining B, C, C-sharp, D, and D-sharp in between A and E, shown in Figure 6-12?

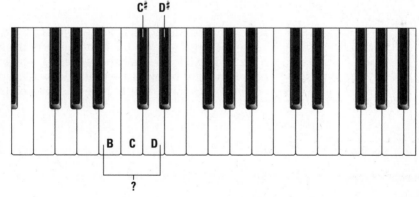

Figure 6-12: Where are the lines and spaces for these little guys?

The solution is the *ledger line.* Ledger lines allow you to notate the notes above and below each staff. Middle C, for example, can be written below the treble staff or above the bass staff by using a small line through the note head, as you can see in Figure 6-13.

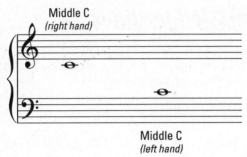

Figure 6-13: Middle C written with ledger lines for both the right and left hand.

If middle C is written with a ledger line below the treble staff, you play it with your right hand; if it's written with a ledger line above the bass staff, you play it with your left hand.

If you're more of a visual learner, try thinking of it this way: The notes written in the middle of the grand staff, or between the two staves, represent notes in the middle of the piano keyboard.

The ledger line represents an imaginary line running above or below the staff, extending the five-line staff to six, seven, or more lines. A grand way to notate all the notes beyond the range of each staff, wouldn't you say? You can, of course, read notes in the spaces between ledger lines just like you read notes in the spaces between the staff lines.

The notes B and D, surrounding middle C, can also be written by using ledger lines. That is, D can either be written below the bottom line of the treble staff, or it can sit on top of the middle C ledger line above the bass staff. Similarly, B can sit on top of the bass staff or below the middle C ledger line of the treble staff. Figure 6-14 illustrates these flexible note positions on the grand staff.

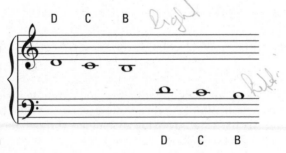

Figure 6-14: Playing the same note with different hands.

Climbing up the staff and beyond

Middle C may be powerful, but it isn't the only note to receive the coveted ledger line award. Other ledger lines come into play when you get to notes that are above and below the grand staff. Notes written above the treble staff represent higher notes, to the right on your keyboard. Conversely, notes written below the bass staff represent lower notes, to the left on your keyboard.

For example, the top line of the treble staff is F. Just above this line, sits the note G. After G, a whole new set of ledger lines waits to bust out.

A similar situation occurs at the bottom of the bass staff. Ledger lines begin popping up below the low G line and low F that's hanging on to the staff for dear life. Figure 6-15 shows a generous range of notes on the grand staff and how they relate to the keyboard.

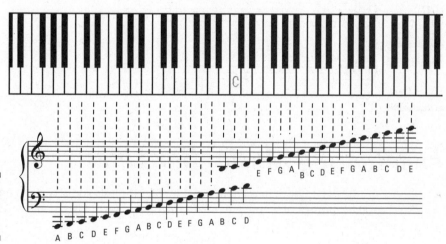

Figure 6-15: Notes on the grand staff.

An octave above, an octave below

Writing and reading ledger lines for notes farther up and down the keyboard can get a little ridiculous. After all, if you were to keep using ledger lines, you'd take up an impractical amount of space, and reading all those lines would become tedious. That's why composers invented the octave, or *ottava* line, which tells you to play the indicated note or notes an octave higher or lower than written. The abbreviation *8va* means play an octave above, and *8vb* means play an octave below. Figure 6-16 shows how these octave lines appear in written music.

Solving the mysteries that lurk between the clefs

The existence of middle C clears up some very big questions about the staves — what I call Staff Line Mysteries:

✔ If it's so important, then why isn't G on the middle line of the treble staff?

✔ Likewise, why isn't F on the middle line of the bass staff?

The answer to both of these mysteries is, of course, that the staff positions of G and F are determined by their distance from middle C. You might say middle C has some power in the musical world.

Figure 6-16: Octave lines.

Punctuating Music: Bar Lines

In addition to horizontal staff lines, music employs some vertical lines to help you keep track of where you are in the music, sort of like punctuation in a written sentence.

A *bar line* divides music into measures, breaking up the musical paragraph into smaller, measurable groups of notes and rests. It helps organize both the writing and reading of music for the composer *and* the performer.

You can find out more about bar lines and measures in Chapter 7, which explains the important function they play when it comes to rhythm. In the meantime, Figure 6-17 shows you how bar lines are written.

Figure 6-17:
Bar lines are vertical lines that divide music into measures.

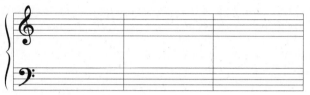

Be prepared to see a few other types of bar lines in piano music. They give you directions on how the music is structured, when and where to repeat, and when to stop. Following are the names of the five types of bar lines and details on what they tell you to do (check out Figure 6-18 to see what each one looks like):

- ✔ **Single:** Go on to the next measure.

- ✔ **Double:** Proceed to the next section (because you've reached the end of this one!).

- ✔ **Start repeat:** Repeat back to this measure.

- ✔ **End repeat:** Repeat back to the measure that begins with a start repeat (or to the beginning if you don't see a start repeat).

- ✔ **Final:** You've reached the end! Stop playing!

Figure 6-18:
The five types of bar lines.

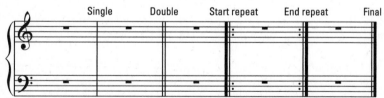

Continuing to Read: Don't Stop

As you read this book, you can instantly see that each page has several lines of text. You don't stop reading when you get to the edge of the page or the end of a line. Instead, your eyes continue to read from left to right, reaching the end of one line and immediately falling to the beginning of the next line. You keep reading until you get to the end of the book, you get to the end of the sentence, or dinner's ready.

Reading music is similar. You play the notes on the staff from left to right. When you get to the end of the staff or the edge of the page, you drop down to the beginning of the next staff, or set of staves, and keep playing until you get to the final bar line. (This process is the same whether you're reading from a single staff or a grand staff.) The arrows along the dotted line in Figure 6-19 show you what I mean. Notice that the appropriate clefs appear on every new line of music.

Figure 6-19:
Keep on
reading,
keep on
playing.

Chapter 7

Joining the Rhythm Nation

In This Chapter

▶ Making some notes last longer than others

▶ Balancing notes with rests

▶ Getting a feel for time signatures

M usic is more than just a series of long, sustained, droning tones. Sure, this description may apply to a few avant-garde pieces — and that stuff bagpipers play — but you probably want to play some songs with melodies and rhythms that make people want to sing and dance.

In this chapter, I show you just how important the timing of your notes is when playing the piano. As they say, timing is everything, and every note in music has a starting point and an ending point. So notes need to have different values that can be counted. You also see how time in music can be measured in other ways: by measuring the rate of the beat to determine the tempo of a song, and by using a time signature to determine the beat pattern of a song.

You'll earn your place in the rhythm nation as you get to know the timely trio — tempo indications, note and rest values, and time signatures — that creates rhythm. This chapter introduces you to these rhythm elements and gives you some practice tunes to play on your keyboard.

Eyeing Tempo: The Beat Goes On

The beat is what you tap your foot to; it's the steady pulse that provides the groove of the music. A fast-paced dance song can get you pumping on the dance floor with a quicker beat, and a slow love song can make you want to sway gently to and fro with your honey in your arms. One of the first things to do when you play music is find out what the *tempo* is. How fast does the beat go? These sections take a closer look at tempo.

Measuring the beat using tempo

Time in music is measured out in *beats*. Like heartbeats, musical beats are measured in beats per minute. A certain number of beats occur in music (and in your heart) every minute. If you're like me, when a doctor tells you how fast your heart is beating, you think "Who cares? I don't know what those numbers mean." But when a composer tells you how many musical beats occur in a specific length of musical time, you can't take such a whimsical attitude — not if you want the music to sound right.

To help you understand beats and how they're measured, look at a clock or your watch and tap your foot once every second. Hear that? You're tapping beats — one beat per second. Of course, beats can be faster or slower. Look at the clock again and tap your foot two times for every second.

How fast or how slow you tap these beats is called *tempo*. For example, when you tap one beat for every second, the tempo is 60 beats per minute because there are 60 seconds in one minute. You're tapping a slow, steady tempo. When you tap your foot two times per second, you're tapping a moderately fast march tempo at the rate of 120 beats per minute.

Composers use a tempo indication and sometimes a metronome marking to tell you how fast or slow the beat is. The tempo indication, shown above the treble staff at the beginning of the music, is a word or two that describes the beat in a simple way: fast, slow, moderately fast, and so on. A metronome marking tells you the exact rate of the beat, as measured in beats per minute. Table 7-1 lists tempo indications and their general parameters using common Italian and English directions.

Table 7-1	Tempos and Their Approximate Beats Per Minute	
Tempo Indication (Italian)	*Translation (English)*	*General Parameters of Number of Beats Per Minute*
Largo	Very slowly (broad)	♩ = 40–60
Adagio	Slowly	♩ = 60–72
Andante	Moderately (walking tempo)	♩ = 72–96
Allegro	Fast, lively	♩ = 96–132
Vivace	Lively, brisk (faster than allegro)	♩ = 132–168
Presto	Very fast	♩ = 168–208

As you learn to read and play music, keep in mind that tempo indications leave a good amount of discretion to the performer and can be followed in ways not limited to the exact rate of the beat.

Get yourself a *metronome,* a handy little device that clicks out the beats at whatever setting you choose, so you don't have to spend all day wondering how to calculate 84 beats per minute. You may have seen some older metronome models, with their mesmerizing, pendulum-style clickers. Newer digital models are about the size of a cellphone. And speaking of cellphones, you can also download metronome applications to your cellphone.

Grouping beats in measures

Think of a music staff as a timeline. (Chapter 6 tells you all about the music staff.) In the same way that the face of a clock can be divided into minutes and seconds, the music staff can also be divided into smaller units of time. These smaller units of time help you count the beat and know where you are in the song at all times.

A three-minute song can have 200 separate beats or more. To keep from getting lost in this myriad of beats, it helps to count the beats as you play the piano. But rather than ask you to count up into three-digit numbers and attempt to play at the same time, the composer groups the beats into nice small batches called *measures* (or *bars*).

Each measure has a specific number of beats. Most commonly, a measure has four beats. This smaller grouping of four beats is much easier to count: Just think "1, 2, 3, 4," and then begin again with "1" in each subsequent measure.

The composer decides how many beats to put in each measure and then marks each measure with a vertical line called a *bar line,* as shown in Figure 7-1. (See Chapter 6 for more on bar lines.)

Why does it matter how many beats are in each measure? Measures help group beats into patterns. These patterns are made up of downbeats and upbeats, which are beats that are emphasized or de-emphasized, respectively. The repeating beat pattern determines a song's *time signature,* which I get into later in this chapter in the section "Counting Out Common Time Signatures."

Figure 7-1 shows a staff with several measures of beats. The slash marks represent each beat. Clap these beats as you count out loud. The first time you try it, don't emphasize any of the beats. The next time, emphasize the first beat of each measure a little more than the other three by clapping louder. Notice how this emphasis adds a little pulse to the overall rhythm, creating a beat pattern.

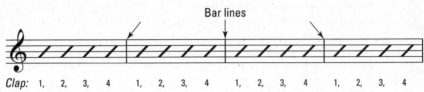

Figure 7-1:
Bar lines
help group
the beats.
Clap to the
rhythm
slashes.

Bar lines

Clap: 1, 2, 3, 4   1, 2, 3, 4   1, 2, 3, 4   1, 2, 3, 4

Serving Some Musical Pie: Basic Note Values

When you listen to music played on the keyboard, or any other instrument for that matter, you hear notes of different lengths. Some notes sound as long as a fog horn; other notes are quite short, like a bird chirping; and others are of a medium length, like the "moo" of a cow. The melody of a song is defined as much by its rhythm — its combination of long-, short-, and medium-length notes — as by the actual pitches. Melody without rhythm is just a nondescript series of musical tones. Rhythm without melody is, well, a drum solo.

Some songs are so well-known that you can recognize them by their rhythm alone. For example, the holiday favorite "Jingle Bells" has a unique rhythmic pattern. After hearing it in every shopping mall and grocery store from November to January each year, you'd probably recognize the song if someone simply clapped the rhythm of the melody.

Piano music uses lots of different symbols and characters. Perhaps the most important symbols to know are those that tell you the length of each note. The unique order and pattern of note lengths make up a song's melodic rhythm.

Each note you play lasts for a certain number of beats or a certain fraction of a beat. If math doesn't exactly thrill you, don't worry: The fractions you use in music are no more complex than the fractions you use when you carve up a fresh pie.

Picture yourself at the ultimate dessert table, staring at hundreds of freshly baked, meringue-topped pies. Now, pretend that each pie represents one measure of music.

Your master chef (the composer) tells you at the beginning of the dessert (music) how many equal pieces to cut each pie (measure) into. Each resulting piece of pie represents one beat. You can eat the whole piece of pie, or just a part of it, depending on how hungry you are (how the music should sound).

Quarter notes: One piece at a time

Most pieces of music have four beats per measure. In essence, your master chef asks you to cut each pie into four equal pieces. When you divide something into four, you get quarters. When you divide a measure into four parts, you also get quarters — quarter notes.

A *quarter note* is represented by a black rounded note-head with one long stem. Because it's so common, the quarter note has become the most popular — and, hence, most recognizable — note in all of music. Look at the notes in Figure 7-2. Recognize them?

Figure 7-2:
Count and
play quarter
notes.

Count: 1, 2, 3, 4   1, 2, 3, 4   1, 2, 3, 4   1, 2, 3, 4

Try playing the quarter note G's in Figure 7-2 on your piano, using your right hand, second finger (that's RH 2). (Chapter 5 tells you about fingering.) Begin by tapping your foot to the beat at a tempo of one tap per second. Count out loud "1, 2, 3, 4." Each time your foot taps the floor, play the next quarter note on the piano. When you reach the bar line, keep playing, tapping, and counting your way through the remaining measures.

Half notes: Half the pie

Returning to the dessert table, if you cut a pie into quarters and you eat two pieces, you end up eating half the pie. Likewise, if you divide a measure of music into four beats and play a note that lasts for two beats, you can surmise that the two beats equal a *half note*.

The laws of stem gravity

You may have noticed that sometimes a note's stem points up and other times it points down. Thanks to the laws of stem gravity, any notes on or above the middle line of a staff point downwards. This applies to all notes with stems. Also notice that up-stems start to the right side of a note-head, and down-stems start to the left of the note-head.

Figure 7-3 shows you four measures with half notes and quarter notes. Notice that a half note looks similar to a quarter note with its rounded note-head and long stem, but the half note's note-head is open (hollow) instead of closed (filled in).

Try playing the notes that you see in Figure 7-3. For every half note, hold the key down for two beats, or two foot taps, before playing the next note. Keep counting "1, 2, 3, 4" to help you know when to play and when to hold.

Figure 7-3:
Save half
for me.

Count: 1,   2,   3,   4   1,   2,   3,   4   1,   2,   3,   4   1,   2,   3,   4

Whole notes: The whole pie

If you eat all four pieces of a pie that has been cut into four pieces, you eat the whole pie. If you play a note that lasts for all four beats of the measure, you're playing a *whole note.*

For obvious oblong reasons that you can see in Figure 7-4, this note is sometimes referred to as a "football." Like the half note, the whole note's note-head is hollow, but its shape is slightly different — more oval than round.

Figure 7-4:
Whole notes
hold out
for all four
counts.

Count: 1,   2,   3,   4   1,   2,   3,   4   1,   2,   3,   4   1,   2,   3,   4

The art of playing whole notes is an easy one — that's why you may hear someone in a band say, "My part's easy; all footballs." Play the notes in Figure 7-4 by holding the key down for four beats, or four foot taps. Keeping the tempo moving along, go across the bar line and immediately play the next measure because a whole note lasts for the *whole* measure. Remember to count all four beats as you play, which helps you maintain a steady rhythm.

Counting all the pieces

After you know how to count, play, and hold the three main note values, try playing Figure 7-5 with a mix of all the different note lengths. Listen to Audio Track 5 at www.dummies.com/go/piano and follow along in the music one time before you play. The song's melody doesn't exactly bring a tear to the eye; it uses the same note throughout to help emphasize the rhythm created by combining the three note lengths.

Figure 7-5:
Mixing up all
the notes.

Faster Rhythms, Same Tempo

As the masterpiece in Figure 7-5 shows, just because a measure has four beats in it doesn't mean that it can only have four notes. Unlike quarter, half, and whole notes (which I talk about in the preceding section), some notes last only a fraction of a beat. The smaller the fraction, the faster the rhythmic motion sounds because you hear more notes for every beat, or foot tap. The following sections examine these faster notes and explain how you can include them in your piano repertoire.

Listen to Audio Track 6 at www.dummies.com/go/piano. Each beat — represented by the steady click of the metronome — is the length of one quarter note, which creates a *quarter-note beat.* However, the shorter note lengths can make the music sound like it's getting faster and faster. Actually, the speed of the music doesn't change at all. Rather, in each successive measure, the length of the notes is a smaller and smaller fraction of the beat. Dividing the beat like this allows you to play more notes in the same amount of time, and it gives the music a slightly different, perhaps more danceable, rhythm.

If you find it difficult to play these smaller note values, simply slow down the tempo by tapping a slower quarter-note beat. This adjustment allows you to play these faster note patterns at a slower tempo, and you can increase the tempo as you become more familiar with the music.

Eighth notes

When you cut the four beats in a measure in half, you get *eighth* notes. It takes two eighth notes to equal one beat, or one quarter note. Likewise, it takes four eighths to make one half note. And it takes eight . . . you get the idea.

A note by any other name

Other English-speaking countries (and a few snobbish music circles in the U.S.) use different names for note values. For example, in the United Kingdom, New Zealand, and Australia, you hear the quarter note referred to as a *crotchet,* the half note as a *minim,* and a whole note as a *semibreve.* Never fear — the notes, by any name, all have the same values.

You can write eighth notes in two different ways, shown in Figure 7-6. By itself, one eighth looks like a quarter note with a *flag*. When two or more eighth notes are present, the flag becomes a *beam* connecting the notes. This beam groups the eighth notes, making it much easier to spot each beat.

Figure 7-6:
Flags on
eighth notes
become
beams.

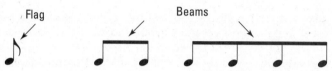

To play the eighth notes in Figure 7-7, count the beat out loud as "1-and, 2-and, 3-and, 4-and," and so on. Every time your foot taps down, say a number; when your foot is up, say "and." When there's a mix of eighth notes and quarter notes, continue counting all the eighth notes of the measure in order to stay on track.

Figure 7-7:
Play and
count the
eighths and
quarters.

Sixteenth notes and more

By dividing one quarter note into four separate parts, you get a *sixteenth note*. Two sixteenth notes equal one eighth note.

As with eighth notes, you can write sixteenth notes in two different ways: with flags or with beams. One sixteenth note alone gets two flags, while grouped sixteenth notes use two beams. Most often you see four sixteenth notes "beamed" together because four sixteenth notes equal one beat. And frequently, you see one eighth note beamed to two sixteenth notes, also because that combination equals one beat. Figure 7-8 shows examples of beamed sixteenth notes plus eighth notes joined to sixteenth notes.

Figure 7-8: Sixteen going on sixteen.

To count sixteenth notes, divide the beat by saying "1-e-and-a, 2-e-and-a," and so on. You say the numbers on a downward tap; the "and" is on an upward tap, and the "e" and "a" are in between. In a measure with a combination of eighths and sixteenths, you should count it all in sixteenth notes.

Sixteenth notes aren't so difficult to play at a slow ballad tempo, but try pounding out sixteenth notes in a fast song and you sound like Jerry Lee Lewis — and that's a good thing!

You could divide the beat even more, and some composers do until there's virtually nothing left of the beat. Figure 7-9 shows that from sixteenth notes you can divide the beat into 32nds, then 64ths, and even 128ths.

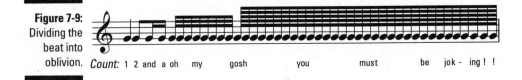

Figure 7-9: Dividing the beat into oblivion.

If you happen to encounter note values smaller than sixteenth notes, simply slow the tempo way, way down and count out the fraction of the beat in a way that makes sense to you. Then gradually speed the tempo back up and try it again.

Listening for the Sound of Silence: Rests

No matter how much you enjoy something, you can't do it forever. Most composers know this and allow you places in the music to rest. It may be resting the hands or simply resting the ears, but rest is an inevitable and essential part of every piece of music.

A *musical rest* is simply a defined period of time in the flow of music when you don't play or hold a note — you play nothing. When you're under a rest, you have the right to remain silent. The beat goes on — remember, it's a constant pulse — but you pause in your playing. The rest can be as short as the length of one sixteenth note or as long as several measures (which is usually the case when you're playing in some sort of ensemble, and you rest while the others continue playing). However, a rest usually isn't long enough to order a pizza or do anything else very useful.

You can use a rest to get ready to play the next set of notes. Don't put your hands in your lap or your pockets. Keep them on the keys, ready to play whatever may follow, and look to the next note or set of notes to guide your hands in your next move.

For every note length, a corresponding rest exists. And as you may have guessed, for every rest there's a corresponding symbol. These sections lay it all out for you.

Whole and half rests

When you see a whole note F, you play F and hold it for four beats. For a half note, you play and hold the note for two beats. (The earlier section "Serving Some Musical Pie: Basic Note Values" covers whole and half notes.) A *whole rest* and *half rest* ask you to not play anything for the corresponding number of beats.

Figure 7-10 shows both whole and half rests. They look like little hats — one off (whole rest) and one on (half rest). This hat analogy and the rules of etiquette make for a good way to remember these rests. Check it out:

- ✔ If you rest for the entire measure (four beats), take off your hat and stay for a while.

- ✔ If you rest for only half of the measure (two beats), the hat stays on.

Figure 7-10:
Hat off for a
whole rest,
and hat on   Whole rest   Half rest
for a half
rest.

These rests always hang in the same positions on both staves, making it easy for you to spot them in the music. A whole rest hangs from the fourth line up, and a half rest sits on the middle line, as shown in Figure 7-11.

Figure 7-11:
Placement
of whole
and half
rests on the
staff.

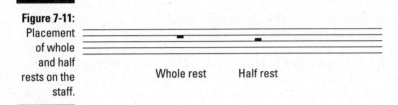

Whole rest   Half rest

To see whole and half rests in action, take a peek at Figure 7-12. In the first measure, you play the two A quarter notes (use your third finger) on beats 1 and 2, and then the half rest tells you not to play anything for beats 3 and 4. In the second measure, the whole rest tells you that you're off duty — you rest for four beats. In the third measure, you put down your donut and play two G quarter notes (second finger) and rest for two beats. Finally, the whole show ends in the fourth measure with a whole note A.

Figure 7-12:
Practice
your whole
and half
rests.

Count: 1,   2,   3,   4   1,   2,   3,   4   1,   2,   3,   4   1,   2,   3,   4

Quarter rests and more

In addition to whole and half rests (refer to the preceding section), composers use rests to tell you to stop playing for the equivalent of quarter notes, eighth notes, and sixteenth notes. Figure 7-13 shows you the five note values in this chapter and their matching musical squiggles.

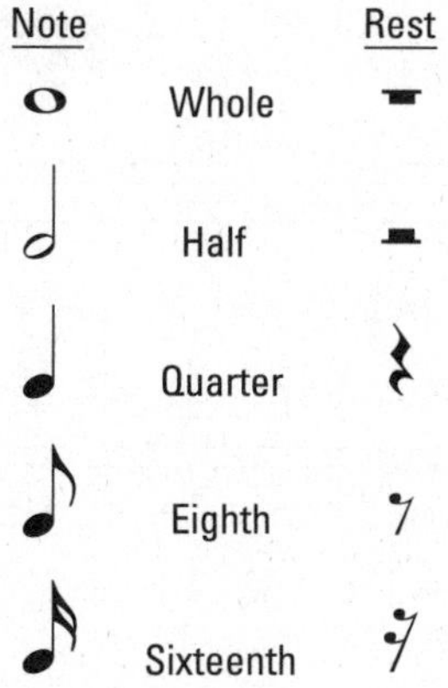

Note		Rest
o	Whole	
	Half	
	Quarter	
	Eighth	7
	Sixteenth	7

Figure 7-13: Notes and their equivalent rests.

You might think of the *quarter rest* as an uncomfortable-looking chair. Because it's uncomfortable, you don't rest too long. In fact, you don't rest any longer than one beat in this chair.

The *eighth rest* and *sixteenth rest* are easy to recognize: They have the same number of flags — although slightly different in fashion — as their note counterparts. An eighth note and eighth rest each have one flag. Sixteenth notes and rests have two flags.

Count all rests just like you count their kindred notes. Quarter rests are easy to count because they last only one beat. Eighth and sixteenth rests can be a bit harder to count simply because they happen faster. Don't be afraid to count out loud; doing so helps you place the eighth rests more precisely and may even cause others to sing along.

Figure 7-14 gives you a chance to count out some quarter and eighth rests. Try clapping the rhythms first, and then play them on your keyboard using the suggested fingering above each note.

To hear the rests incorporated into the music shown in Figure 7-14, check out Audio Track 7 at www.dummies.com/go/piano.

Track 7

Figure 7-14:
Counting
quarter and
eighth rests.

You read sixteenth-note rests when you get into more advanced music. Until then, just remember what they look like (refer to Figure 7-13).

Counting Out Common Time Signatures

In music, a *time signature* tells you the meter of the piece you're playing. Each measure of music receives a specified number of beats. (See "Eyeing Tempo: The Beat Goes On" earlier in this chapter for more information on beats.) Composers decide the number of beats per measure early on and convey such information with a time signature, or *meter.*

The two numbers in the time signature tell you how many beats are in each measure of music. In math, the fraction for a quarter is 1/4, so 4/4 means four quarters. Thus, each measure with a time signature of 4/4 has four quarter-note beats; each measure with a 3/4 meter has three quarter-note beats; and each measure of 2/4 time has two quarter-note beats. Figure 7-15 shows you three recognizable tunes that are written in each of these three time signatures. Notice how the syllable count and word emphasis fit the time signature.

Please keep in mind that 4/4 meter doesn't mean that each measure has only four quarter notes. It means each measure has only four *beats.* These beats may contain half notes, quarter notes, eighth notes, rests, and so on — whatever the composer wants — but all note and rest values must combine to equal no more or less than the top number (or numerator) of the time signature.

Figure 7-15: You can recognize the tunes of three common time signatures.

Common time: 4/4 meter

The most common meter in music is 4/4. It's so common that its other name is *common time* and the two numbers in the time signature are often replaced by the letter C (see Figure 7-16).

Figure 7-16: The letter C is a common way to indicate 4/4 meter.

In 4/4, the stacked numbers tell you that each measure contains four quarter-note beats. So, to count 4/4 meter, each time you tap the beat, you're tapping the equivalent of one quarter note.

To hear an example of 4/4 meter, play Audio Track 8, "A Hot Time in the Old Town Tonight" at www.dummies.com/go/piano. Notice how the beat pattern of 4/4 meter creates an emphasis on beats 1 and 3, which are downbeats (although beat 1 has the strongest emphasis). Beats 2 and 4 are upbeats. In many rock, R&B, and hip-hop songs, the upbeats are accented. As you listen to the track, tap your foot on 1 and 3, and clap on 2 and 4. (I discuss downbeats and upbeats in the earlier section "Grouping beats in measures.")

To play the song "A Hot Time in the Old Town Tonight," skip to the section "Playing Songs in Familiar Time Signatures" at the end of the chapter.

Waltz time: 3/4 meter

In the second most common meter, 3/4, each measure has three quarter-note beats. Of course, this doesn't mean that only quarter notes exist in this meter. You may have one half note and one quarter note, or you may have six eighth notes, but either way, the combination equals three quarter-note beats.

In 3/4 meter, beat 1 of each measure is the downbeat, and beats 2 and 3 are the upbeats. It's quite common, though, to hear accents on the second or third beats, like in many country music songs.

Another name for 3/4 meter is *waltz time* because of the down-up-up beat pattern used for waltzing. Go to www.dummies.com/go/piano and listen to Audio Track 9, "The Beautiful Blue Danube." Notice the emphasis on beat 1 of each measure. Tap your foot on the downbeat, and clap on the upbeats. You could say that 3/4 was probably composer Johann "Waltz King" Strauss's favorite meter.

To play the song "The Beautiful Blue Danube," go to the "Playing Songs in Familiar Time Signatures" section at the end of the chapter.

March time: 2/4 meter

Chop a 4/4 meter in half and you're left with only two quarter-note beats per measure. Not to worry, though, because two beats per measure is perfectly acceptable. In fact, you find 2/4 meter in most famous marches. The rhythm is similar to the rhythm of your feet when you march: "left-right, left-right, 1-2, 1-2." You start and stop marching on the downbeat — beat 1.

Audio Track 10 at www.dummies.com/go/piano is a good example of 2/4 meter. It's a famous dance by Jacques Offenbach called "Can Can." Feel free to march or do the Can Can as you listen.

To play the song "Can Can" on your keyboard, go to the "Playing Songs in Familiar Time Signatures" section at the end of the chapter.

Sorting out the language of rhythm

Using words to describe the rhythmic qualities of music can get tricky. Time signature and tempo are different components that work together to create the rhythmic framework for music. A song in 4/4 and a different song in 3/4 can have the same tempo because tempo tells you the rate of the underlying beat: fast, slow, or exactly at the rate of 120 beats per minute, for example. A fast song and a slow song can share the same time signature — a fast waltz or a slow waltz, for example. The time signature tells you how the beats are organized into measures and how to count the measures. The rhythm of a melody is defined by its unique combination of note values and rests. All other accompanying rhythmic elements (the bass line, chords, drums, requisite tuba solo) combine with these elements and make up the rhythm of a song.

6/8 time

If you notice that a time signature of 6/8 doesn't have a "4" in the bottom (denominator) position, you're no doubt already thinking that it can't be a meter based on quarter notes. If you're thinking that it might be a meter based on eighth notes, you're right on time. 6/8 meter is a grouping of six eighth-notes per measure.

Like the waltz, beats in 6/8 meter are grouped in threes, but there are two groups. The 6/8 meter has an added down-up beat pattern on the first eighth note of each group — beats 1 and 4. Showing the emphasis using italics, you count a measure of 6/8 with one count for each eighth-note beat, as follows: *One,* two, three, *four,* five, six. Beat 1 is a stronger downbeat than 4, so this beat pattern can feel like two broader beats (down-up), each with its own down-up-up pattern within.

Listen to the song "Lavender Blue" on Audio Track 11 at www.dummies.com/go/piano for an example of 6/8 meter. Tap your right foot on beat 1, tap your left foot on beat 4, and clap the upbeats (2, 3, 5, 6).

To play the song "Lavender Blue," go to the "Playing Songs in Familiar Time Signatures" section at the end of the chapter.

Playing Songs in Familiar Time Signatures

The songs in this section are examples of each of the four time signatures covered in this chapter: 4/4, 3/4, 2/4, and 6/8. These are the most common beat patterns in music. In fact, you won't find too many popular songs, folk songs, dance tunes, or lullabies that don't use one of these meters.

You can see that each song has a tempo indication above the starting clef, giving you the chance to feel the beat of the song before you start playing. Use your average walking pace as a guide to a moderate tempo. A fast tempo is the equivalent of walking (or marching) quicker, and you can slow down to an easy saunter to get an idea of a slow tempo. For a tempo indication of "Fast" in 2/4 time, for example, you can start to feel a beat pattern of two beats per measure, one downbeat and one upbeat, at a relatively fast rate. (Refer to Table 7-1 earlier in this chapter for more on tempo indications and their equivalent metronome markings.)

If your skills in reading and playing music on your piano aren't up to playing these melodies yet, don't worry — you get some more help in the coming chapters. For now, feel free to tap your foot on the downbeats and clap on the upbeats. The real goal of this chapter is to get you recognizing note values and time signatures.

If you're ready to give the songs a go, here are some suggestions:

- ✓ **"A Hot Time in the Old Town Tonight":** The half notes that start the melodic phrase of this song mark the downbeats on 1 and 3. Play along with the audio track, and listen for the upbeats (on 2 and 4) played in the accompaniment part.

- ✓ **"The Beautiful Blue Danube":** The melody of this classic waltz really takes you out on the dance floor. Notice the rests that are on beat 2 of most measures. Make sure you release the key after playing beat 1 in these measures, so the rest can give you a nice big upbeat on 2.

- ✓ **"Can Can":** The eighth-note pattern in the melody of this song lets you have fun with the down-up beat pattern. See if you can make a difference between the downbeats and upbeats by giving a bit more emphasis to the eighth notes on the beat and a bit less to those in between (counted as "and").

- ✓ **"Lavender Blue":** The rhythm of the lyrics effectively spells out the 6/8 beat pattern in this song. Count the sixteenth notes in 6/8 time: "1-and, 2-and, 3-and, 4-and, 5-and, 6-and." The sixteenth notes in the first measure are counted, "5-and, 6-and," matching the lyric, "dil-ly, dil-ly."

A Hot Time in the Old Town Tonight

Track 9

The Beautiful Blue Danube

Moderately fast

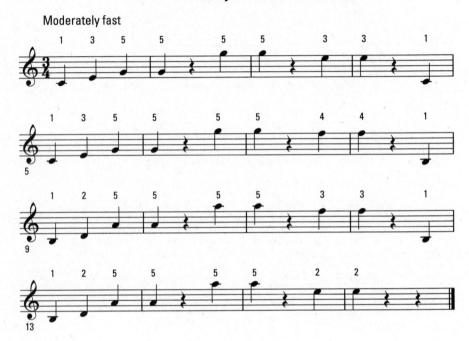

Track 10

Can Can

Fast

Track 11

Lavender Blue

Chapter 8

Changing the Beaten Path

As soon as the music starts, you hear beats as a constant, ever-present force. But you can do a lot more than play a note on every darn one of those beats.

This chapter shows you some ways to play around with the way rhythms interact with the beat, whether that means holding notes longer, playing off or around the beat, or even not playing at all. (For a review of the basics of rhythm and beats, check out Chapter 7.)

Getting a Jump on the Start: Pickup Beats and Measures

You've probably heard the old adage, "Everything starts from nothing." Well, some songs actually begin with rests. That's right: The performer walks out on stage, sits at the piano, and rests for a few beats before hitting a single note. I could give you a long and boring explanation of why some music starts with rests, but instead I just explain pickup beats and measures.

The first two notes of the song "She'll Be Coming 'Round the Mountain" actually fall on beats 3 and 4 of a measure of 4/4 time. (Chapter 7 tells you about time signatures.) These two melody notes are called *pickup notes,* perhaps because they pick up the beat and start the song. (The fancy musical term for pickup notes is *anacrusis.*) How nice of them! To play "She'll Be Coming 'Round the Mountain," you start with a half rest and count "1, 2, She'll be . . .," as shown in Figure 8-1.

Figure 8-1:
Starting with
a half rest.

She'll be com-ing 'round the moun-tain when she comes.

Rather than note a bunch of rests at the beginning, the composer can write a *pickup measure,* which contains only that part of the measure that's played or sung. In other words, the pickup measure eliminates any rests before picking up the tune. Figure 8-2 shows you the notation in a song with a pickup measure.

Figure 8-2:
Instead
of a rest,
this nota-
tion uses
a pickup
measure.

Pickup measure

She'll be com-ing 'round the moun-tain when she comes.

To play and count songs with pickup measures, follow three easy steps:

1. **Note the meter.**

2. **Rest for the number of "missing" beats.**

3. **Play the pickup notes, and away you go.**

Hundreds of songs begin with pickup measures, including "When the Saints Go Marching In" and "Oh, Susannah." Go to www.dummies.com/go/piano and listen to Audio Tracks 18 and 19 to get a feel for these great songs.

If you're ready to play these songs with pickup measures, you can find the music in the section "Playing Songs with Challenging Rhythms" at the end of the chapter.

Adding Time to Your Notes with Ties and Dots

Ties and dots are more than accessories and designs to spice up your wardrobe. In music, they're symbols that add more time or length to your notes. A quarter or half note doesn't quite cut it? Need to play the note a little bit longer? Just throw in some of these value-adding notations to extend the length of your notes. These sections examine these symbols and explain why they're important when you're playing a piano.

Linking notes using ties

Half notes and whole notes last longer than one beat. (Chapter 7 gives you the full scoop on half and whole notes.) But suppose you want to play a note that lasts longer than one measure or a note that lasts for two and a half beats. Of course, music has a solution: a curvy little line called the tie.

The *tie* does just what it sounds like: It ties two notes of the same pitch together, causing one continuous-sounding note. For example, a whole note tied to a quarter note lasts for five beats. Likewise, a quarter note tied to an eighth note is held for one and a half beats. Figure 8-3 shows you a few notes that are tied together, as well as how to count them.

Be careful not to mistake a tie for a slur. They look similar because they're both curved lines, but a tie connects two notes that are the same pitch from notehead to notehead. In contrast, a *slur* connects notes of different pitches. For more about slurs, see Chapter 15.

Extending notes using dots

Another way to extend the length of a note, not to mention to make it look a little fancier, is through the use of a *dot*. A dot on any size note or rest makes that note or rest last 50 percent longer than the note it follows.

Listen to Audio Track 12 at www.dummies.com/go/piano and try to play along with Figure 8-3. When you see two notes tied together, make sure you play the first note and hold it for the combined value of both notes. This example helps you quickly understand the function of a musical tie, other than being a cheesy last-minute gift for your musician friends.

Track 12

Figure 8-3:
Ties that bind notes of the same pitch.

Dotted half notes

A quarter note lasts one beat, a half note lasts two, and a whole note lasts four. You can see that you're in need of a note that lasts three beats — the dotted half note, which gets a total of three beats, as shown in Figure 8-4.

Figure 8-4:
The dotted half note.

Half note (2 beats) + Dot (1 beat) = Dotted half note (3 beats)

This note gets a lot of use in 4/4 and in 3/4 time, where it takes up the entire measure. (See Chapter 7 for coverage of these time signatures and others.) Figure 8-5 shows dotted half notes in action and tells you how to count them.

Count: 1   2   3   4   1   2   3   4   1   2   3   4   1   2   3   4

Figure 8-5:
Dotted half
notes in 4/4
and 3/4 time.

Count: 1 2 3   1 2 3   1 2 3   1 2 3   1 2 3   1 2 3

To listen to a song that incorporates dotted half notes, go to Audio Track 20 and check out the song *Scheherezade* at www.dummies.com/go/piano.

To play a melody with dotted half notes, turn to the section "Playing Songs with Challenging Rhythms" at the end of the chapter for the music to *Scheherezade*.

Dotted quarter notes

When you add a dot to a quarter note, you get a great hybrid note that lasts for one and a half beats. Because of its length, the dotted quarter note is commonly paired with an eighth note in order to finish out the second beat (see Figure 8-6).

Figure 8-6:
A dotted
quarter note
paired with
an eighth.

Count: 1 and 2 and   1 and 2 and   1 and 2 and   1 and 2 and   1 and 2 and

Dotted eighth notes

The dotted eighth note equals one and a half eighth notes, or three sixteenth notes. As you know from Chapter 7, it takes four sixteenth notes to make one quarter note (or one beat). So, a dotted eighth note is often paired with a sixteenth note to make a full quarter-note beat. In this combination, the normal eighth-note beam connects the two notes, and the sixteenth note gets a shortened second beam (see Figure 8-7).

Figure 8-7:
A dotted eighth, a sixteenth, and their beams.

Get some practice reading and playing some dotted notes with the exercise in Figure 8-8. Work on developing the kind of flexible counting system shown in the figure. You count only quarter notes in the first measure, then count out eighth and sixteenth notes for the measures that require that type of breakdown. When you're out of the rough in the last measure, you can go back to counting quarter notes. Just make sure you keep the beat steady!

To hear the music shown in Figure 8-8, listen to Audio Track 13 at www. dummies.com/go/piano.

Track 13

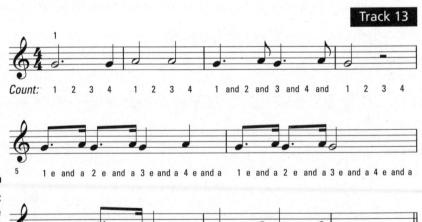

Figure 8-8:
Practice with dotted notes.

To hear an example of dotted notes in a tune you're probably familiar with, listen to "Swanee River" on Audio Track 21 at www.dummies.com/go/piano.

"Swanee River" is a classic example of both dotted quarter notes and dotted eighth notes. Listen to it until you get the feel of the rhythm, and when you're ready to play the song, you can find the music in the later section "Playing Songs with Challenging Rhythms."

Playing Offbeat Rhythms

When you understand note values (see Chapter 7) and ways to extend those values with ties and dots (refer to the previous sections in this chapter), you can expand your rhythmic range with some fancy ways to divide, delay, anticipate, and swing note values. After all, you live in a world filled with rhythm, and most of the music you hear day in and day out is surprisingly rhythmic, thanks to the influence of jazz, blues, and plenty of other folk and popular music from all around the world.

This section expands your musical knowledge with many of the fascinating rhythms you need to know to play your favorite music, whether it's jazz, classical, popular, or folk tunes. Start off with triplets, and then move on to swing rhythms and syncopation.

As you read the following sections about dividing the beat and playing notes off the beat, tap your foot along to the examples. Even when you don't play a note right on the beat, you won't lose the beat.

Triplets love chocolate

Most notes divide a beat neatly by some factor of two. But every now and then, you may want to divide a beat into more than two eighth notes but less than four sixteenth notes. That means playing three notes per beat, aptly called a *triplet*.

The most common triplet pattern is the *eighth-note triplet,* which looks like three beamed eighth notes. To help you spot these triplets quickly, composers add a little number 3 above (or below) the beam. A popular variation on this triplet pattern is the quarter-eighth triplet, which looks like (get this) a quarter note and an eighth note but with a little bracket and a number 3. Figure 8-9 shows you both types of triplets.

Figure 8-9:
Congrats!
You have
triplets.

You can hear an example of these triplets on Audio Track 14 at www.dummies. com/go/piano before you try to play them yourself in Figure 8-10.

To count these triplets, tap your foot and say "1 trip-let, 2 trip-let" or "choc-o-late" for every beat. The most important point is to divide the beat into three equal parts so each syllable gets its fair share.

Track 14

Figure 8-10:
Counting
triplets.

Now try playing the triplets in Figure 8-11. You can hear them played on Audio Track 15 at www.dummies.com/go/piano. Keep thinking "choc-o-late" as you practice playing them until you take a candy bar break.

Track 15

Figure 8-11:
Practice
with triplets.

You can make triplets using other note values, too, but you probably won't have to play them for a while, at least not until you start jamming with your local drum circle. It's worth remembering, though, that with any triplet rhythm, 3 = 2: Three quarter-note triplets equal two quarter notes (two beats), and three sixteenth-note triplets equal two sixteenth notes (half a beat). You play three notes (equally) in the time you would normally play two notes of the same value.

Swing and shuffle time

The beat may go on and on, but music can be quite dull if every note you play is on the beat. By changing up the rhythm a bit and playing some notes off, around, or in between the main beats, your songs take on a whole new life.

I could go on and on expounding the virtues of the *swing feel*. But ultimately, the best way to understand swing is to hear it.

Go to www.dummies.com/go/piano and listen to Audio Track 16 while you look at the four measures of music in Figure 8-12. The eighth notes are played with a swing feel; the notes are the same, but the rhythm has a slightly different, swingin' feel.

Track 16

Figure 8-12: Swing those eighths.

Instead of straight eighth notes played as "1-and, 2-and," you hear a long-short, long-short rhythm. The most accurate way to notate this long-short rhythm is with a quarter-eighth triplet. (See the preceding section for more on triplets.) But rather than write a ton of triplets, the composer gives you a big heads-up along with the tempo indication above the first measure by telling you to "swing," either in plain English or with a little symbol like the one in Figure 8-13.

Figure 8-13:
This notation tells you to swing it.

When you see the swing notation, you should play all the eighth notes in the music as swing eighths. You can still count them as "1-and, 2-and, 3-and, 4-and," but the notes on the beats are longer and the notes off the beats are shorter.

Swing, the classic rhythmic feel, is so popular that it has its own type of bands and dance moves. Listen to some of the music of the big-band era, like the Duke Ellington Orchestra or the Tommy Dorsey Orchestra. They really had the whole world swingin'. Chapters 16 and 17 have more swing, blues, and boogie music for you to play and more tips on who to listen to for great examples of these styles.

You can also hear an example of swing-style eighth notes at www.dummies.com/go/piano. Listen to "By the Light of the Silvery Moon" on Track 22.

To play a song with swing eighths right now, skip to "By the Light of the Silvery Moon" in the section "Playing Songs with Challenging Rhythms" at the end of this chapter.

Shuffle feel has the same long-short swing eighths as swing time, but the shuffle beat is more readily associated with rock and blues-style music. A shuffle feel is characterized by a heavier beat than swing, which is lighter on its feet.

"I've Been Working on the Railroad" is a song with a shuffle feel that you can listen to at www.dummies.com/go/piano. Check it out on Audio Track 23.

To play a song with a shuffle feel, skip to "I've Been Working on the Railroad" in the section "Playing Songs with Challenging Rhythms" at the end of this chapter.

Syncopation

One of the most common forms of playing off the beat is a little rhythmic concept called *syncopation*. To understand syncopation, you have to know about *downbeats* and *upbeats*. (For a refresher, go to Chapter 7.)

Start tapping your foot to a moderate 4/4 beat, and count eighth notes "1-and, 2-and, 3-and, 4-and." Your foot goes *down* on the downbeats and *up* on the upbeats.

Downbeats are the beats that are normally emphasized in a song. But through the miracles of syncopation, you emphasize some (or all) of the upbeats instead. Play those notes a little bit harder, or louder, than the others. For example, the note normally played on beat 3 is played on the upbeat before, and this anticipation naturally emphasizes the upbeat and creates syncopation.

Figure 8-14 shows a two-measure melodic phrase written first to emphasize the downbeat on beat 3, and then transformed into a syncopated rhythm, with the arrows showing the point of emphasis on the upbeat, on "and" before beat 3.

Figure 8-14:
Suddenly
syncopa-
tion by
emphasizing
upbeats.

You can hear how syncopation works with a well-known melody. Listen to Audio Track 17 at www.dummies.com/go/piano while you follow along with the music in Figure 8-15. You'll hear the opening four measures of the classic song "After You've Gone," first without and then with syncopation. Keep your foot tapping the beat throughout the entire eight measures and notice the emphasized notes on the upbeats (when your foot is up). The arrows mark the syncopated notes.

Track 17

Figure 8-15: "After You've Gone," without (top) and with (bottom) syncopation.

You can listen to a syncopated piece of music at www.dummies.com/go/piano. Check out "Limehouse Blues" on Audio Track 24.

If you're feeling the off-kilter groove and are ready to play a syncopated piece, try "Limehouse Blues" in the following section.

If all this talk of syncopation has piqued your interest, turn to Chapter 17, which explores various ways to make a plain vanilla melody into something special with this offbeat rhythm.

Playing Songs with Challenging Rhythms

The songs in this section give you a chance to play music featuring the rhythmic tricks covered in this chapter, from pickup measures to ties and dots to swing eighth notes and syncopation.

Here are a few tips on each of the songs to keep in mind:

- ✔ **"When the Saints Go Marching In":** This song has a pickup measure with a three-beat pickup. The last measure has only one beat in order to make a complete measure. Note that this song also has ties and dots.

- ✔ **"Oh, Susannah":** This song has two eighth-note pickups, which equal one beat and are counted "4-and." Notice how the last measure has only three beats; this is often done to complete the three missing beats in the pickup measure. Taken together, the pickup and last measure equal one complete measure.

- ✔ *Scheherezade:* You find dotted half notes scattered throughout waltzes and other songs in 3/4 meter, like the theme from Rimsky-Korsakov's *Scheherezade*. (Chapter 7 tells you all about 3/4 meter.) Notice that this melody combines the use of ties and dots. The tie simply adds even more time to the dotted half note. For example, in the fourth measure, you hold the note B for four beats.

- ✔ **"Swanee River":** You hear dotted eighth notes in all types of music, but especially in dance tunes. Composer Stephen Foster made good use of dotted quarters as well as dotted eighths in his classic tune "Swanee River." You may want to listen to the track a couple of times before trying to play it yourself.

- ✔ **"By the Light of the Silvery Moon":** The swinging rhythm of the lyrics helps you get the hang of playing swing eighth notes in this tune.

- ✔ **"I've Been Working on the Railroad":** The chug-a-lug train rhythm of this song matches a shuffle feel quite naturally. The eighth notes are swing eighths, but the underlying triplet feel is a bit heavier than in a swing feel.

- ✔ **"Limehouse Blues":** The melody to "Limehouse Blues" has built-in syncopation, and you get lots of practice with this tune: Every other measure has a syncopated note held by a tie into the following measure.

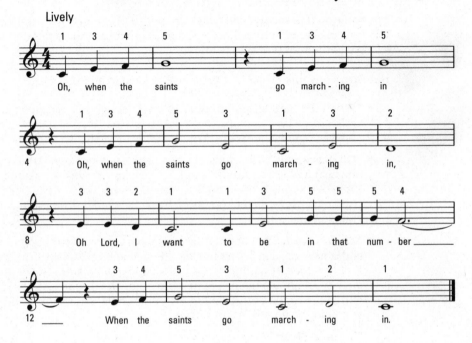

When the Saints Go Marching In

Track 19

Oh, Susannah

Lively

Oh, I come from Al - a - bam - a with a ban- jo on my knee. And I'm

goin' to Lou'- si - an - a my Su - san- nah for to see.

Oh, Su - san- nah, Oh, don't you cry for me 'Cause I

come from Al - a - bam- a with a ban- jo on my knee.

Track 20

Scheherezade

Moderately fast

Swanee River

Track 22

By the Light of the Silvery Moon

Track 23

I've Been Working on the Railroad

Track 24

Limehouse Blues

Moderately fast

Part III
One Hand at a Time

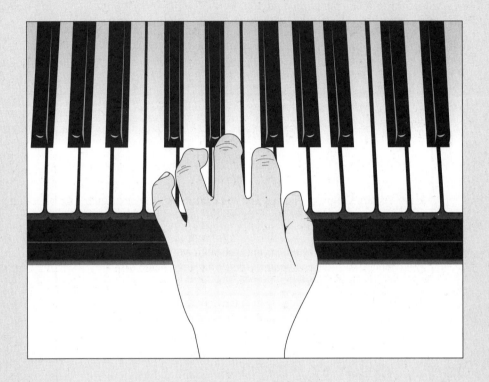

Go to www.dummies.com/extras/piano for some supplemental scales.

In this part . . .

- Continue on the path to piano perfection by mastering melodies like "Ode to Joy" with your right hand.

- Explore scales, both major and minor, and why they're such an important element in music, from warm-up tools to the sources of melodies.

- Build your skills by adding your left hand and playing accompaniment patterns and scales — everything you need to be an excellent solo pianist.

- Shift between positions in both the right and left hands. Learn how to get from Point A to Point B smoothly every time.

- Bring both hands together to play new songs like "The Sidewalks of New York" and "Stars and Stripes Forever" — crowd-pleasers that you can whip out at a party.

Chapter 9

Playing a Melody

• •

In This Chapter

▶ Putting your right hand in the proper position for a melody

▶ Extending positions to reach more keys

• •

*M*elodies create a wonderful transformation in music: They turn a whole bunch of random notes into songs that entertain, please your ear, and sometimes get stuck in your head.

In order to really get the most out of this chapter about melodies, you need to have the following skills under your belt, er, fingers:

✔ Naming all the keys, both white and black (see Chapter 5)

✔ Naming all staff lines and spaces (see Chapter 6)

✔ Counting rhythms and rests, from whole notes to sixteenth notes (see Chapter 7)

✔ Recognizing time signatures (see Chapter 7)

✔ Recognizing pickup measures, ties, and dots (see Chapter 8)

If you're a little shaky on any of these key ingredients, please take a glance at the referenced chapters. Without these fundamentals, attempting to play melodies and songs may lead to frustration.

This chapter helps you get to some recognizable melodies on piano by touching on how your hands fall on the keyboard and then by explaining two common positions: C and G. Because not all melodies stick to these original positions, I also instruct you in shifting and extending positions. You put these techniques to use playing melodies drawn from classical, folk, and Tin Pan Alley styles.

Let Your Fingers Do the Walking

In order to play a melody on the piano, you need to observe the way your hands make contact with the keyboard. If you don't develop comfortable moves, you'll find it hard to reach the notes you need to play — and your playing will look and sound more like Charlie Chaplin than Chopin.

I introduce you to finger numbers in Chapter 5 — think of your fingers as being numbered 1 through 5, with the thumbs being 1. In this book, I refer to your fingers by number and to your hands by abbreviations: RH and LH. So, RH 1 means the thumb on your right hand.

In Figure 9-1, RH 2 plays D. Notice the relaxed but arched position of the hand and fingers. See, too, how the other four fingers are poised and ready to play the next note, whatever it may be. Of course, because it's a drawing, these fingers will never, ever play another note. (Chapter 5 tells you more about how to hold your body and hands at the keyboard.)

With correct hand position and fingering, your fingers literally walk along the keys. Practice enables them to do so with a fluid motion, with you guiding their movements.

Figure 9-1:
Playing a
key.

As you play a melody, your fingers should travel gracefully up and down the keyboard. You aren't typing a letter or playing video games, so there's no need to punch or slap the keys.

Getting into the Right Position

So, you're at the keyboard, your back is supported and straight, the lights are on, and the music's waiting. Where does your right hand go? Good question. You need to get into position.

Position is a common term you hear regarding any musical instrument. Several positions exist for each musical instrument, giving the player points of reference all along the body of the instrument. The keyboard is no exception.

Using effective hand positions is vital to playing the keyboard well. From each designated position, you can easily access certain notes, groups of notes, and chords, and then move to other positions. These sections spell out the positions you need to know when playing your piano.

When you sit down to play, survey the music to get a general idea of the hand positions the piece requires, and look for the hand position for the first notes.

C position

Many easy tunes start at middle C or close to it, so you often find yourself in *C position* at the beginning of a song. C position simply means placing your right-hand thumb on middle C and your other right-hand fingers on the four successive white keys, as shown in Figure 9-2. Put another way, RH 1 should be on C and RH 5 on G with the other three fingers in the middle. If the other three aren't in the middle, something very unusual is going on with your fingers. (Chapter 6 helps you find middle C.)

With your right hand in C position, which is sometimes also called *first position,* play the melody of "Frere Jacques" in Figure 9-3, playing one note at a time. (To make C position easier for you, I chose a tune that's recognizable and has almost all quarter notes.) It may be helpful to just imagine the moves your fingers will make as you listen to Audio Track 25 a couple of times before you attempt to play along.

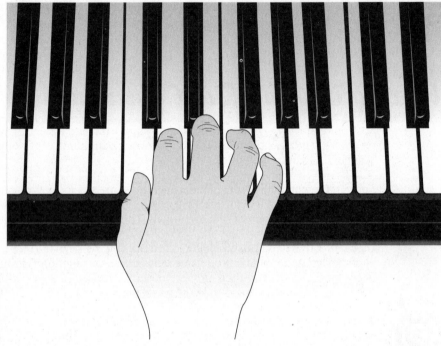

Track 25

Figure 9-2:
Getting into
C position.

Figure 9-3:
The melody
of "Frere
Jacques"
requires the
right hand
to be in C
position.

TIP

Be sure to observe the fingerings (numbers above the notes). These numbers
are called *fingerings* because they tell you which finger to use for each note.
Most players appreciate fingerings because they indicate the best possible
finger pattern for executing the notes. Of course, being the wunderkind that
you are, you may invent other custom fingerings. For now, though, try the
helpful fingerings I provide.

Head to www.dummies.com/go/piano and watch Video Clip 5 that demonstrates the C position on a handful of tunes.

Try another song that uses C position. In "Ode to Joy," the melody begins on RH 3, travels up to RH 5, and then dips all the way down to RH 1. Beethoven, the composer of this piece, was a pianist, so no doubt he knew just how well this melody would play under the fingers. Figure 9-4 shows the opening melody to "Ode to Joy."

Figure 9-4:
The melody
of "Ode
to Joy"
calls for C
position.

To play the full version of "Ode to Joy" right now, skip to the section "Playing Melodies in the Right Hand" at the end of the chapter.

As you can probably imagine, not all melodies use only five notes. Eventually, you must come out of your safe little shell of five white keys, make a move, and extend certain fingers up or down. The following sections guide you through extensions from basic C position.

Thumbing a ride to B

From C position, your thumb can extend down to B. As you play B with your thumb, you simply leave your other fingers exactly where they are.

To play "Skip to My Lou" in Figure 9-5, simply move your thumb one key to the left in measure 3 to play the B.

You can listen to "Skip to My Lou" on Audio Track 26 at www.dummies.com/go/piano.

Good stretch, pinky!

From C position, RH 5 (your pinky) can reach up one key to the right to play A. In the campfire classic "Kumbaya," you anticipate the extension up to A by shifting fingers 2 through 5 to the right from the very start. Notice this shift in the fingerings above the notes in Figure 9-6: Instead of playing D with RH 2, you play E with RH 2, but keep your thumb on middle C. *Note:* "Kumbaya" begins with a two-beat pickup (see Chapter 8 for more on pickup measures).

Track 26

Figure 9-5:
"Skip to My Lou" uses C position but extends your thumb to play B.

Don't take the word "stretch" too literally — you don't want to injure yourself. It's quite alright to allow RH 1 through 4 to move toward RH 5 as you reach up to play A.

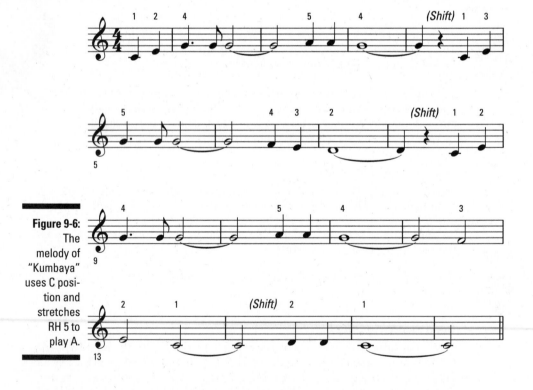

Figure 9-6:
The melody of "Kumbaya" uses C position and stretches RH 5 to play A.

Stretching C position to the limits

In many songs that begin from C position, you shift your fingers or extend RH 5 and RH 1 to play all the melody notes. "Chiapanecas" is one such number. Using the music in Figure 9-7, try to play this Latin American tune as it was meant to be heard: hot and spicy. You may want to listen to Audio Track 27 before attempting it on your keyboard.

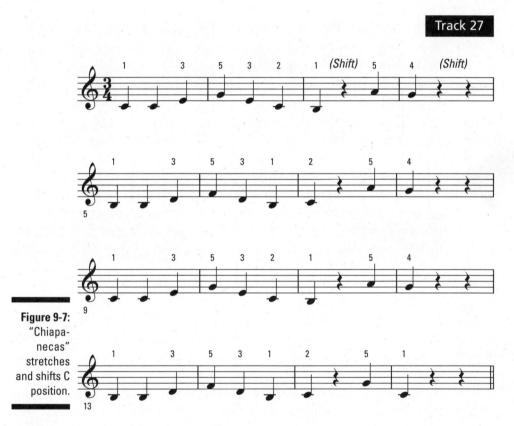

Figure 9-7: "Chiapanecas" stretches and shifts C position.

Check the time signature before you start playing. You don't want to be thinking "1, 2, 3, 4" if the song is in 3/4 time. And, by the way, "Chiapanecas" *is* in 3/4 time.

G position

To get into *G position*, move your right hand up the keyboard so that RH 1 rests on G. (This is the same G occupied by RH 5 in C position.) Figure 9-8 shows you this new position as well as the staff notes you play in it. Notice that RH 5 now rests all the way up on D.

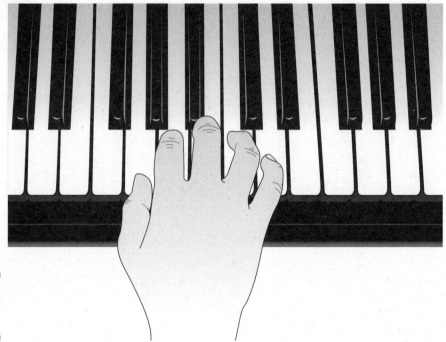

Figure 9-8:
Gee, I like G
position!

The melody to "Little Bo-Peep" fits easily in G position. Give it a whirl by playing the music in Figure 9-9.

Just like in C position, in G position you can extend RH 5 and RH 1 east and west to access E and F, respectively. Try out this extended G position by playing "This Old Man" in Figure 9-10. Watch the fingering in this song and shift your fingers where appropriate.

Figure 9-9: "Little Bo-Peep" is a breeze in G position.

Figure 9-10: "This Old Man" uses G position with some stretching.

Shifting your hand position as you play

Knowing two positions, C and G, is great, but you really only get five or six notes in each position. Shifting your hand to different positions in the same song allows you to play a few more notes. To shift positions in the middle of a song, you just need a bit of planning and practice. One strategy is to simply make good use of a rest in the music to make a move while you have the chance. (The next section covers other methods for movement when the music doesn't provide rests in which to make the change.)

For example, in Figure 9-11 you play the first two measures in G position. During the rest on beat 4 of measure 2, you can move your hand down and get ready to play G in measure 3 with RH 5. Ta-da! You've just shifted to C position.

Figure 9-11:
One song,
two hand
positions.

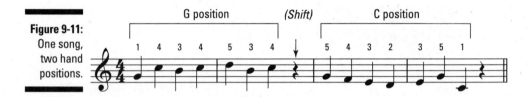

Crossing Your Fingers and Hoping It Works

Shifting positions can be smooth and easy when rests are involved (refer to the previous section), but when the melody doesn't stop, you must find alternative ways to move between positions. The best way is to use a little maneuver called *finger crossing*. Finger crossing is one of those techniques that can be awkward at first, but it has a whopping payoff once you get the hang of it.

Don't try to make your hand, wrist, fingers, or arm do something impossible. You don't want any broken ligaments here. When you cross over or pass under, let your hand and arm follow your fingers with easy, fluid movements. Try to keep your forearm and hand more-or-less perpendicular to the keyboard without any excess twisting.

If you really want to make strides with your technique, feel the unbound freedom that comes with smooth finger crossings, and work on other smooth moves up and down the 88s, check out *Piano Exercises For Dummies* by David Pearl (Wiley).

Crossing over your thumb

Why cross over fingers when you can just move your hand? In C position, the thumb can sometimes extend to play B, but not always. For example, you may need to play B followed immediately by middle C. If you extend and contract your thumb back and forth between these two keys, it sounds clunky. Instead, you cross RH 2 over your thumb to play B, as shown in Figure 9-12.

Figure 9-12: Crossing over your thumb to play more notes.

You can watch your hand on the keys when you cross over or under, but with practice you should easily feel where the keys are without looking. Whether you look or not, it's important to keep a relaxed arch in the hand and avoid twisting your hand as you cross a finger over your thumb.

The well-known "Minuet" from Bach's *Notebook for Anna Magdelena Bach* requires your RH 2 to cross over your thumb. As you can see in Figure 9-13, you shift positions briefly in measures 3 and 11, but the main focus is on the finger cross to B in measures 7 and 15.

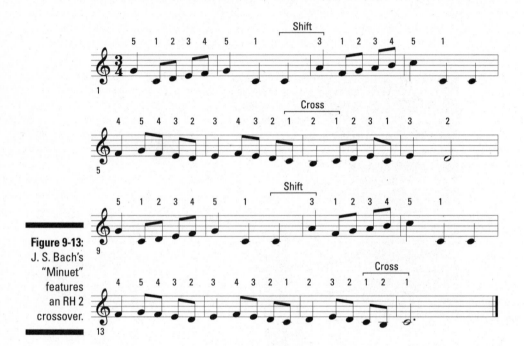

Figure 9-13: J. S. Bach's "Minuet" features an RH 2 crossover.

Passing your thumb under

You can pass your thumb under RH 2 to move to a new position. The song "Row, Row, Row Your Boat" gives you a chance to try out this little switch-o-rama between positions (see Figure 9-14). You start with your right hand in C position (middle C to G), but in measure 3 you pass your thumb under RH 3 to play F, and then you play the G at the beginning of measure 5 with RH 2. You've shifted your hand position with a pass under! You then continue with your hand in this new position. Your hand position will naturally shift downward from the high C in measure 5 as you follow the tune back to C position by measure 6, where you stay to finish the song.

Figure 9-14:
"Row, Row, Row Your Boat" is a classic melody that requires the thumb to pass under.

Go to www.dummies.com/go/piano and watch Video Clip 6 for a bunch of finger-crossing moves.

Playing Melodies in the Right Hand

When you know the techniques for playing melodies in the right hand, you're guaranteed to want to put them to use playing more melodies. Following are four well-known melodies that let you apply the hand positions, position shifts, and finger crossings covered in this chapter:

- ✔ **"Ode to Joy":** You can stay in C position for almost all the melody. In measure 12, you make a shift to reach with RH 1 and play the low G, which is the only note outside of C position.

- ✔ **"Autumn":** Your RH stays in G position for this melody from Vivaldi's *The Four Seasons*. Because of the many repetitions, this melody is a good one for practicing rhythm and counting. (See Chapter 8 to review the dotted eighth-note rhythms in measures 9 through 15.)

- ✔ **"Oranges and Lemons":** This is an English folk song that lets you practice shifting hand positions. Start in C position, move to G position in measure 8, and return to C position in measure 16 to repeat the opening phrase. Remember to make use of the rests to facilitate the position shifts.

- ✔ **"Simple Melody":** Irving Berlin's tune gives you the chance to practice passing RH 1 under RH 2. Not so simple? The song is so catchy you won't mind practicing until the movement feels natural.

Track 28

Ode to Joy

Track 29

Autumn

Track 30

Oranges and Lemons

Moderately fast

Track 31

Simple Melody

Moderately fast

Chapter 10

Scaling to New Heights

In This Chapter

▶ Getting to know scale basics

▶ Building major and minor scales

▶ Playing melodies featuring scales

*H*ave you ever heard the following from your musician friends?

✔ "Scales are boring!"

✔ "Scales are difficult."

✔ "I never play scales."

✔ "The scales in my bathroom read ten pounds more than I actually weigh."

These statements are all questionable, including the last one. Your friends are mistaken: Scales are easy, scales can be fun, and every musician plays scales, and your friend actually put on a few pounds over Spring Break.

You can use scales to do some great things on the piano — like play entire songs. Okay, not all scales are songs. But it's true that all songs are created from scales, be it an entire scale or just a few notes from the scale. Remember the "Do-Re-Mi" song from *The Sound of Music?* The whole darn song is *about* scales, and those kids had fun!

In this chapter, I explain why giving scales a chance is well worth it. Besides using scales to understand the notes in a song's melody, you can use scales to beef up your finger power on the piano. Plus, the more scales you know, the easier it becomes to play the piano.

You've probably heard this a thousand times before now, but it's true: Practice makes perfect. Later in this chapter, I show you several different types of scales. Pick the ones you like and play through them five to ten times a day. This practice warms up your fingers and builds finger dexterity. Think of it like shooting baskets every day before the big basketball game. You wouldn't go out on the court without a little practice, would you?

Building a Scale, Step by Step

Put simply, a musical *scale* is a series of notes in a specific, consecutive order. Major and natural minor scales are the two most common types, and they have the following attributes:

- ✔ They're eight notes long.
- ✔ The top and bottom notes are an octave apart, so they have the same name.
- ✔ The series follows a stepwise pattern up and down, and the name of each note in the scale follows the alphabet up and down.

Each scale gets its own name, like *C major.* A scale derives its name from the following two things:

- ✔ The scale's bottom note, or the *tonic.* For example, a C major scale starts and stops on C.
- ✔ The *stepwise pattern* used to create the scale. Music has two kinds of steps, *half-steps* and *whole-steps,* which are the building blocks of scales. The "major" part of C major means the third note of the scale is a major third above the tonic. (You can find more on intervals in Chapter 12.)

Look at your keyboard or Figure 10-1, and notice that some white keys have a black key in between and some white keys are side by side. On a piano keyboard

- ✔ Two keys side by side (whether black or white) are one half-step apart.
- ✔ Two keys separated by one other key (black or white) are a whole-step apart.
- ✔ Two half-steps equal one whole-step.

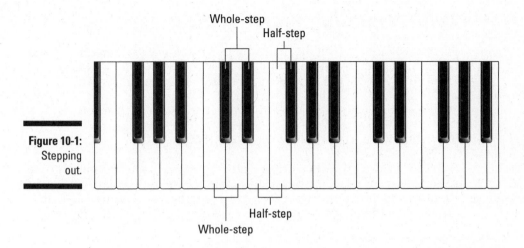

Whole-step

Half-step

Half-step

Whole-step

Figure 10-1:
Stepping
out.

In Chapter 5, I explain how the suffixes *sharp* and *flat* are used to name the black keys. When you measure half-steps up or down, you help define the black keys as sharps and flats. For example, find any D on your keyboard. Move one half-step higher and play the black key to the right, D-sharp. Now play one half-step lower than D, or D-flat.

Knowing some basic facts about scales, you can build any scale starting on any root note simply by applying the correct scale pattern (or combination of whole- and half-steps).

Stepping Up to the Majors

The two scales you most frequently use — and the most famous scales in Western music — are the *major* and the *natural minor* scales. You can make a major and a minor scale starting with any note on the piano. The difference between these two scales is the pattern of whole- and half-steps that you use to build them. (Check out the preceding section if you need to brush up on whole- and half-steps.) These sections take a closer look at major and minor scales.

Major scales have a reputation for sounding happy, and minor scales get the sad rap, but it's really how they're used that counts. Maybe that's why Pachelbel named his famous string quartet piece *Canon in D major* and not *Canon in D happy*. He wanted to make sure it would get played at weddings *and* in sad movies.

Understanding major scales

Every major scale is built the same way. Don't let a scale salesman try to sell you a new and improved major scale — there's no such thing. (Actually, you should turn and run from anyone pretending to be a scale salesman.)

The ascending step pattern used by all major scales on the planet is

Whole-Whole-Half-Whole-Whole-Whole-Half

For example, you can form a C major scale by starting on C and applying this pattern. Play any C, and then play the pattern of whole-steps and half-steps all the way to the next C. Figure 10-2 shows you the way. Starting with C, the layout of the white keys follows the scale pattern exactly, so you play the entire C major scale on white keys only.

Figure 10-2:
The C major scale follows all the white keys.

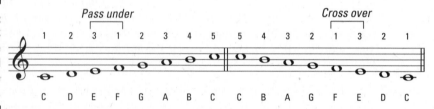

Pass your thumb under and cross over your thumb in the appropriate spots in order to successfully play up and down the scale. See Chapter 9 for more on this finger-crossing business.

When playing most scales up and down, it's important to realize that the scale pattern is exactly reversed on the way down. All you have to do is remember which keys you played going up and then play the same ones in reverse order going down.

Now for something slightly different: Start on G and apply the major scale pattern. When you get to the sixth step, notice that a whole-step up from E requires playing a black key, F-sharp. Figure 10-3 shows you the G major scale in all its glory.

Figure 10-3:
The G major scale employs one sharp: F-sharp.

The tonic note and scale pattern determine which notes will be sharps and which will be flats. G major uses one sharp. How about a major scale that uses one flat? Start on F and apply the pattern, as shown in Figure 10-4, and you've built yourself the F major scale, which incorporates B-flat. (Note the new fingering for this scale pattern.)

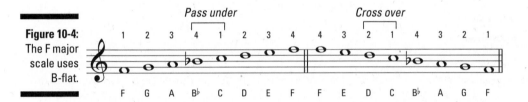

Figure 10-4:
The F major scale uses B-flat.

How do you know it's B-flat and not A-sharp? Excellent question. The easy answer is that in a scale, every letter name has its turn. Because the third note of the scale, or *scale degree,* represents A, it would show nothing but favoritism to call the fourth note A-sharp. So, the fourth scale degree represents B with its flat version, B-flat, which is one half-step higher than A.

Take your newfound major scale knowledge and see how it applies to a portion of a song. "Joy to the World" (see Figure 10-5) opens with a complete descending C major scale and continues with an ascending pattern from the fifth degree of the scale up to the eighth to end the phrase.

Figure 10-5:
A joyful melody made from a major scale.

Track 32

Of course, the composer of a song isn't obligated to use every note from a scale in the melody. The scale is simply a menu to choose from. For example, "The Farmer in the Dell" (see Figure 10-6) is based on the F major scale, but it doesn't use the note B-flat. Listening to Audio Track 33 or playing the song on your piano, I bet you don't even miss the B-flat.

Track 33

Figure 10-6:
A frugal melody needs only five notes of the major scale.

You can play around with the notes of the C major scale by starting on a different note or playing them in a different order. This is what composers do. Instead of a scale, you may end up with a beautiful melody.

Trying a major scale exercise

Practice playing up and down the C major scale with the exercise in Figure 10-7. You can use it to reinforce the scale pattern mentally, perfect your fingering, and improve your finger crossing. Start out playing at a slower tempo, and increase the speed as you become familiar with the notes and the moves.

Figure 10-7:
Building your C major scale chops.

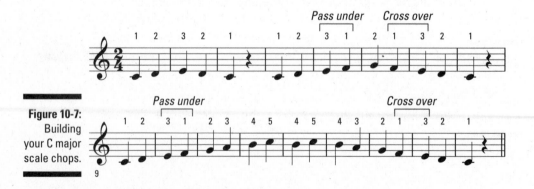

Go to www.dummies.com/go/piano and watch Video Clip 7 for further exploration of the major scale.

Exploring Minor Variations

Allow me to clarify something right away: Minor scales are no less important or any smaller in size than major scales. They just have an unfortunate name. Minor scales come in a few varieties, each of which I discuss in this section.

Like major scales, minor scales have eight notes with the top and bottom (tonic) notes having the same name. But minor scales have their own, unique scale patterns.

Natural minor scales

The *natural minor* scale uses the following ascending stepwise pattern:

Whole-Half-Whole-Whole-Half-Whole-Whole

Sure, it may look similar to the major scale pattern, but this slight rearrangement of half- and whole-steps makes all the difference in the world. The best way to understand the difference is to play and listen to a major and a minor scale side by side. Figure 10-8 shows the C major scale, followed immediately by the C minor scale.

Figure 10-8:
Major and
minor C
scales.

Hear the difference? Try something else: Play the melody in Figure 10-9, where the notes of a C minor scale are plugged into the same rhythms as the original "Joy to the World." Notice the difference in the sound.

Figure 10-9:
"Joy to the World" in C minor.

You can play a minor scale on only the white keys, too. Apply the same scale pattern to the tonic note A, and you get the A natural minor scale. But apply the same pattern to other tonic notes and you encounter some minor scales with sharps (like E minor) and some with flats (like D minor), as you can see in Figure 10-10.

The notes from minor scales make great, memorable melodies, too. Skip to the section "Playing Songs Made of Scales" at the end of the chapter and try "House of the Rising Sun."

Figure 10-10:
So many minors, not enough chaperones.

Harmonic minor scales

The *harmonic minor* scale differs from the natural minor scale (refer to the preceding section) by only one half-step, but in making that slight change, you achieve a scale with a whole new sound. For example, to play the A harmonic minor scale, follow these steps:

1. **Start out playing the A natural minor scale.**

2. **When you get to the seventh note, G, raise it one half-step to G-sharp.**

   This change makes the distance from the sixth to the seventh scale degree one and a half steps and gives the harmonic minor scale its unique sound.

The complete pattern for an ascending harmonic minor scale is

Whole-Half-Whole-Whole-Half-1½-Half

Play and compare the natural minor scale in Figure 10-11 with the harmonic minor scale next to it. Sounds rather exotic, doesn't it? You'll encounter this scale in lots of classical piano music (which you can read more about in Chapter 17).

Figure 10-11:
The A natural minor and A harmonic minor scales.

A minor scale:

A B C D E F G A

A harmonic minor scale:

A B C D E F G♯ A

Melodic minor scales

Another variation on the minor scale is the *melodic minor* scale, which is notable (forgive the pun) because it has a different pattern depending on whether you're going up the scale or coming down. That's right — a chameleon-like scale that ascends one way and descends another. This flexibility is useful when you want the scale to sound, you guessed it, melodic. Try playing the A melodic minor scale in Figure 10-12, and you'll hear that the scale sounds pleasingly melodic going both up and down.

A melodic minor scale:

Figure 10-12:
The A
melodic
minor scale.

Notice that the sixth and seventh degrees of the scale are raised a half-step ascending and are lowered a half-step descending. You probably recognized that the descending scale is identical to the natural minor scale, so only the ascending pattern is really new:

Whole-Half-Whole-Whole-Whole-Whole-Half

Composers sometimes combine scales for a song's melody just to spice things up a bit. In the section "Playing Songs Made of Scales" at the end of the chapter, play "Greensleeves" to hear what I mean.

To review the minor scales, watch Video 8 at www.dummies.com/go/piano.

Trying minor scale exercises

Get some practice with the C natural, harmonic, and melodic minor scales by playing the following exercises (Figures 10-13a, 10-13b, and 10-13c). You can use these as a warm-up along with the C major scale exercise in the previous section.

Using scales any which way you like

Major and minor scales are definitely the most popular scales, but they aren't the only ones. Come on, admit it — you've experimented a little with these scale patterns. Curiosity begs you to insert a half-step in place of a whole-step here and there to hear what happens.

Well, what happens is that you begin to form other scales, venturing into territory neither major nor minor. Some sound great, some sound not so great, and some sound sort of exotic. Creating your own scales is not only acceptable, it's recommended. Fresh new scales inevitably give birth to fresh new melodies and harmonies.

People have experimented with scale patterns since the dawn of music, so go ahead and make up your own scales. Improvise a melody or a bass line using just a few notes of a scale. Write them down on staff paper, tape them to your walls, and decorate your life with scales!

Figure 10-13: Exercising the three C-minor scales: C natural (a), C harmonic (b), and C melodic minor (c).

Showing Your Rebellious Side with Blues Scales

You can hear the *blues scale* in rock, country, jazz, and of course . . . the blues.

This scale is a real rebel, practically throwing the rules of scale building out the window. Of course, there aren't really any hard-and-fast rules for scale building, but this scale is rebellious anyway. Here's how:

✔ It begins with one and a half steps.

✔ It has only seven notes.

✔ It has two half-steps in a row.

The step pattern for this seditious little scale is

1½-Whole-Half-Half-1½-Whole

To try it out, play the scale in Figure 10-14.

Figure 10-14:
Getting the blues.

Steps: W+H   W   H   H   W+H   W

C   E♭   F   F♯   G   B♭   C

Where else have you seen a scale with this much mojo? Not in this book, for sure. But after you know the blues scale, playing it is as addictive as eating peanuts. You can use the notes in the blues scale, or *blue notes,* for all kinds of little riffs and melodies like the one in Figure 10-15.

Figure 10-15:
Using the
blues scale
for a cool
melody.

Playing Songs Made of Scales

In the age-old battle between theory and practice, there's no doubt that practice is more fun. Your efforts to grasp the theory behind scales throughout this chapter will be rewarded by putting them to good use playing the songs in this section.

Here are a few tips on the tunes:

- ✔ **"Danny Boy":** The classic "Danny Boy" uses all the notes from the F major scale, even good old B-flat.

- ✔ **"House of the Rising Sun":** "House of the Rising Sun" is based on the E natural minor scale. Play this song along with Audio Track 35 and you'll hear how a minor (but not less important) melody sounds.

- ✔ **"Greensleeves":** "Greensleeves" uses the A natural minor scale (measures 1–5), the A melodic minor scale (measures 13–16), and the G major scale (measures 17–20). It's just a folk song, but they were some smart folk who wrote it!

Track 34

Danny Boy

House of the Rising Sun

Track 36

Greensleeves

Chapter 11

Hey, Don't Forget Lefty!

In This Chapter

▶ Settling your left hand into position

▶ Playing melodies and scales with the left hand

▶ Exploring left-hand accompaniment patterns

▶ Playing songs hands-together

*W*ant to know an industry secret? Many a pianist who plays with a band never even uses the left hand. Oh sure, you think the left hand is play-ing because it's moving up and down the left side of the keyboard and you're hearing lots of bass lines and chords. But au contraire, mon frére. The bass player fills in the bass notes; the guitarist covers the chords. The not-so-good pianist just fakes it.

Playing the piano with your left hand, or both hands together, is considerably more difficult than just right-hand playing. But you have no need to fake your way through a career. You can show those phonies how a real player does it! In this chapter, I tell you how to get both hands jamming together.

Note: In this chapter, I refer to your fingers with the numbers 1 through 5 (the number "1" represents your thumb; your pinky is "5"). Your right and left hands are abbreviated as "RH" and "LH."

Exploring the Keyboard's West Side

If you consider middle C the middle of the piano, you can think of the keys to the right of middle C as the East Side and the keys to the left of middle C as the West Side. (Turn to Chapter 5 if you need help locating middle C.) It's time to turn and head west.

To explore the lower keys, first acquaint yourself with the bass clef. Chapter 6 has some easy ways to remember the lines and spaces on this oft-neglected staff, but the best way to figure out this staff is to dig in and start playing. You'll soon recognize each line and space by sight, without even thinking about it.

Moving into position

In Chapter 9, I show you two positions for the right hand: the C and G positions. These positions are the same for the left hand except that C position has LH 5 (pinky) occupying the C below middle C, the second space up on the bass clef staff. In G position, LH 5 moves down to G, the bottom line of the staff. Figure 11-1 shows you the proper left-hand placement for C position.

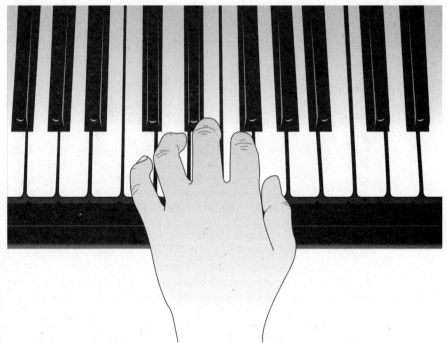

Figure 11-1:
Assume
C position
with the left
hand.

Getting used to the new neighborhood

You have several options for playing with your left hand: You can play scales, melodies, simple one-note harmonies, chords, or just plain cool-sounding accompaniment patterns. (That's not just a sales pitch — they really do sound cool.) I show you single-note harmonies and chords in Chapters 12 and 14, respectively.

For a quick (and stimulating) drill, Figure 11-2 helps limber up the left-hand fingers in C position. Sing or say out loud the name of each note as you play it. Doing this will go a long way in helping you remember the notes on the staff.

Change your life by switching hands

If you aren't left-handed by nature, start using your underappreciated left hand to perform everyday tasks you normally perform with your right hand, such as:

✔ Opening doors

✔ Flipping channels on the TV remote

✔ Steering your automobile

✔ Handing people money

✔ Brushing your teeth

✔ Opening tightly sealed pickle jars

By *consciously* switching hands for a couple of weeks, you *subconsciously* make your left hand stronger, more versatile, and more independent.

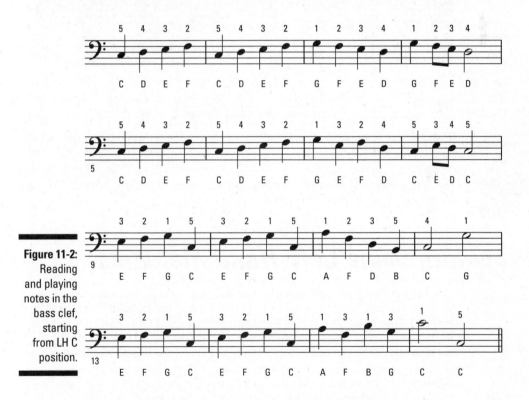

Figure 11-2: Reading and playing notes in the bass clef, starting from LH C position.

Figure 11-3 features a similar workout, but in G position. Again, remember to sing each note out loud. Never mind what those around you think of your ranting and raving — they're just jealous that you can play the piano.

Figure 11-3:
Lower notes
in the bass
clef, starting
from LH G
position.

If you're ready to play songs hands-together, skip ahead to the section "Playing Songs with Both Hands" at the end of the chapter.

Tackling Some Left-Hand Melodies

Sometimes playing a melody with your left hand is nice. You may tire of playing with your right hand, want to hear the melody lower, want to add a little variety to the song, or have an itch that needs a good right-hand scratching. Whatever the reason, playing melodies with the left hand helps familiarize you with the bass clef notes while strengthening your left-hand coordination.

Left-hand melodies are lots of fun, but remember to observe the correct fingerings as you play these classics, "Swing Low, Sweet Chariot" (see Figure 11-4) and "Little Brown Jug" (see Figure 11-5).

Figure 11-4:
Melody
in the left
hand:
"Swing
Low, Sweet
Chariot."

Figure 11-5:
Another
melody
in the left
hand: "Little
Brown Jug."

Head to www.dummies.com/go/piano to watch both of these songs played in Video Clip 9.

Practicing Some South-Paw Scales

They may not be the most exciting things to play, but by working on left-hand scales you unwittingly master the following music essentials:

- Reading the bass clef
- Playing with the correct fingering
- Using nifty patterns and harmonies
- Realizing how much you miss playing with the right hand

Start with some major and minor scales by reading and playing the following scales left-handed. (Chapter 10 tells you all about major and minor scales.) As with right-handed playing, remember to use the correct fingerings as indicated by the numbers above each note. How and when you cross your fingers is very important for obtaining a smooth sound and comfortable left-hand technique.

C, G, and F major

Figure 11-6 shows three major scales for the left hand. You can use the same fingering, both up and down the scale, for all of these. Applying the major scale pattern (see Chapter 10), you play a scale with no sharps or flats (C major scale), one sharp (G major scale), and one flat (F major scale).

A, E, and D natural minor

You use the same fingering pattern in the three natural minor scales in Figure 11-7 as you do in the three major scales in Figure 11-6.

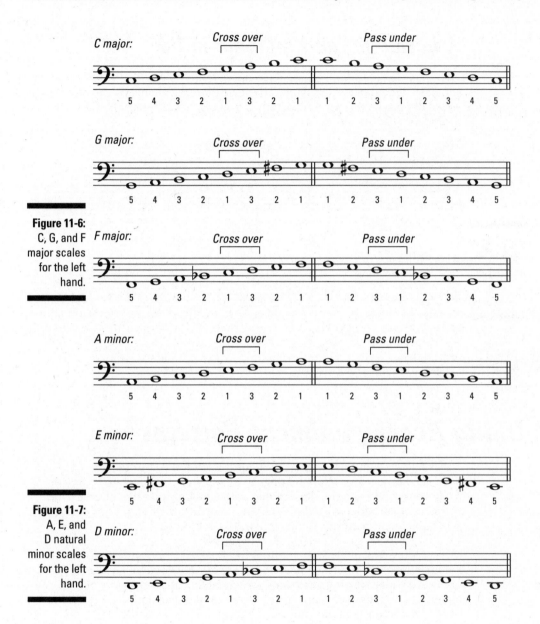

Figure 11-6: C, G, and F major scales for the left hand.

Figure 11-7: A, E, and D natural minor scales for the left hand.

A harmonic and melodic minor

The scales in Figure 11-8 offer a good opportunity to practice your crossovers and pass-unders in the left hand. The scale patterns change at the same point you shift your hand position. Listen for smooth transitions and an even touch throughout each scale.

Figure 11-8:
A harmonic and melodic minor scales.

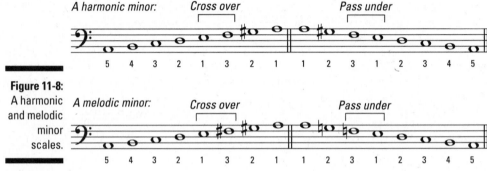

Head to www.dummies.com/go/piano and watch Video Clip 10 for a bunch of left-hand scales being played.

Trying Accompaniment Patterns

Scales and melodies are fine material for the left hand, but they aren't Lefty's main gig. Rather, your left hand begs to be playing *accompaniment patterns* while your right hand noodles around with a melody or some chords. One of the most user-friendly left-hand patterns is the *arpeggio.* (Other jazzier accompaniment patterns are demonstrated in Chapter 14.)

Oh, no! More Italian? Yes, in addition to *pizza, rigatoni,* and *ciao,* the other Italian word that should be part of your everyday vocabulary is *arpeggio.* The word translates to "harp-like," which means absolutely nothing to piano players. However, after many years of bad translations, musicians have come to understand this word as meaning "a broken chord."

Well, nothing's really broken about an arpeggio — it works great. You simply play the notes of a chord one at a time, rather than all at once. (See Chapter 14 for more about chords.)

For more on arpeggios, head to www.dummies.com/extras/piano. You'll find all the tools you need to arpeggiate basic seventh chords.

Three-note patterns

Three-note patterns may be the easiest and most versatile left-hand accompaniment to play, and they conform to the hand really nicely, too. For example, place your left hand on the keys in C position with LH 5 on C, LH 2 on G above that, and LH 1 on middle C. Fits like a glove, right?

The three notes you use for this pattern are the root, fifth, and top notes of the appropriate scale. (Chapter 10 tells you more about roots and scales.) Using the C major scale, for example, the notes are C, G, and C. Now comes the versatile part: The three-note pattern is the exact same in the C *minor* scale. So, you can apply the three-note pattern to major or minor harmonies by playing the root, fifth, and top notes of the scale, as shown in Figure 11-9.

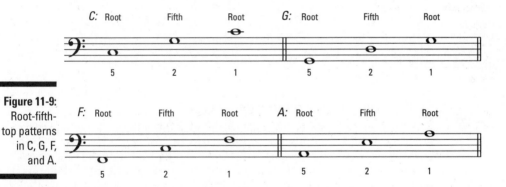

Figure 11-9: Root-fifth-top patterns in C, G, F, and A.

Playing the pattern in quarter notes

The easiest way to start playing this three-note pattern is with a quarter-note rhythm. In 4/4 meter, you play in an "up and back" motion — root, fifth, top, fifth — so that every measure begins with the root note of each arpeggio. In 3/4 meter, you play upwards — root, fifth, top — and then start again with the root for the next measure.

Figure 11-10 demonstrates these three-note patterns with a simple quarter-note rhythm in both meters. The first eight measures show how the pattern works in 4/4, and the next eight measures show how the pattern works in 3/4. The letter names above the staff are chord symbols, which tell you the scale that the pattern is derived from.

Figure 11-10:
Three-note
arpeggios in
quarter-note
patterns.

Cranking up the pattern in eighth notes

Play the three-note pattern using eighth notes for a more energetic, faster arpeggio. You play a full set of root-fifth-top-fifth for every two beats, so that beats 1 and 3 of every measure start again on the root note of the arpeggio. Gently rock your left hand back and forth over the keys until you feel this pattern is second nature to you. These eighth notes in 3/4 meter are slightly different: You can play all six eighth notes in a pattern or modify the pattern to give you time to move to other positions, as shown in Figure 11-11.

Four-note patterns

Adding another note to the three-note pattern (see the previous section) gives you enough notes to make a major or minor chord. For this arpeggio, you add the third note of the scale. The four-note *major* arpeggio uses the root, third, fifth, and top notes of the scale. To form a four-note *minor* arpeggio, you simply lower the third note a half-step. For example, the notes of a C major arpeggio are C, E, G, and C. To make a C minor arpeggio, simply lower the third, E, to E-flat, just like you do in the C minor scale (see Figure 11-12).

Figure 11-11: Three-note arpeggios in eighth-note patterns.

Figure 11-12: Four-note arpeggios based on C.

Playing the pattern in quarter notes

As with the three-note arpeggios, different meters allow you some rhythmic options. Using quarter notes in 4/4 meter, you play up — root, third, fifth, top — once in each measure. Each subsequent measure begins again with the root note. For 3/4 meter, you play up in one measure — root, third, fifth — and hit the top note before coming down in the next measure — top, fifth, third.

Take a gander at the quarter-note patterns in Figure 11-13. Call out the name of each note as you play; hearing yourself helps you recognize the notes.

Try the alternate fingerings in Figure 11-13, shown in parenthesis below the suggested fingerings. Every hand is different, and you may find one of these is more comfortable than the other.

Figure 11-13: Up and down the four-note arpeggios.

Cranking up the pattern in eighth notes

With an eighth-note rhythm, you can have lots of fun exploring different patterns for the four arpeggio notes. Just keep the correct four notes of each scale in mind — root, third, fifth, and top — and play two of them for every beat in the measure. Figure 11-14 gives you a few examples of different patterns.

Figure 11-14: Four-note arpeggio patterns in eighths.

Arpeggio, your friend in need

So, there you sit. It's late. The pianist finishes "My Funny Valentine" and heads off for an overdue coffee break. You decide to impress your friends and quickly steal up to the bench. The room is waiting. You open the songbook atop the piano and — egad! — all you see is a treble staff and chord symbols.

What you see is probably a *fake book* (see Chapter 19 for more on fake books). This is a real songbook, but it only contains the melody and chord symbols, allowing a working pianist to "fill in" the left hand as he or she feels best

suits the situation. Of course, you *aren't* a working pianist and *any* left hand would be suitable for this late-night situation.

First, take a deep breath. Next, open your bag of tricks and pull out some left-hand arpeggios that I tell you about in this chapter. Use the chord symbols — the little alphabet letters above the staff — to locate the name of the lowest note (or root note) of the arpeggio and play away. Pretty soon you'll have friends you never even knew.

To see some of these accompaniment patterns in action, see Video Clip 11 at www.dummies.com/go/piano.

Adding the Left Hand to the Right Hand

No matter how much you enjoy playing melodies with the right and left hands separately, the time comes when you have to get these two great friends together.

See for yourself how you can play the left and right hands together online at www.dummies.com/go/piano in Video Clip 12.

You have several things to keep in mind when you attempt to play songs hands-together:

- ✔ When playing music from the grand staff, read the notes vertically (bottom to top) before moving on horizontally (left to right).

- ✔ Play the song a couple of times with the right hand by itself. Then play the song a few times with the left hand only. When you're confident with the notes for each hand, you can try playing the song hands-together.

- ✔ Play slowly at first and speed up the tempo as you become more comfortable with the song.

- ✔ Be patient and calm.

- ✔ Ask listeners to leave for a while and allow you a chance to practice. Invite them in for the concert after you feel good about your playing.

Sharing the melody in both hands

Start reading from the grand staff by passing a melody between your hands. In Figure 11-15, the melody to "When Johnny Comes Marching Home" starts in the left hand, and the right hand takes over as it climbs into a higher range. Go over the note names once or twice before you play in order to get comfortable recognizing all the notes and switching between the bass and treble clefs. Then you can make an easier transition to the piano.

Track 39

Figure 11-15:
RH and LH
share a
melody.

Melody plus one note

Mozart knew how to have a little fun with music, and it shows in his piece called "A Musical Joke." He takes a simple melody and tries it in a major scale, then in a minor one, and finally settles on the major version. In Figure 11-16, the left hand plays a single-note accompaniment to the melody, making it a good introduction to playing "hands-together," as the saying goes.

Track 40

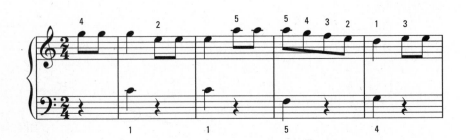

Figure 11-16:
A simple
melody and
accompani-
ment from
Mozart.

Melody plus three-note accompaniment pattern

"On Top of Old Smoky" (see Figure 11-17) gets you working a melody with the right hand and some arpeggios with the left hand. After you get the hang of it, your left hand starts rocking back and forth effortlessly on the arpeggiated patterns.

Track 41

Figure 11-17:
"Old Smoky"
with a three-
note LH
pattern.

If the bass clef gets too intimidating to read, hold your left hand in position for an arpeggio and move LH 5 to each new root note. From each root note you can easily find the appropriate arpeggio notes and go to town . . . or to the top of Old Smoky.

Melody in unison octaves

In the classic "Yankee Doodle" (see Figure 11-18), you try another way of reading from both clefs at once with a double-handed melody. Although the melodies look completely different on the different staves, they're actually the same — you play the same named keys with both hands.

Figure 11-18:
Double the
melody.

Most people have faster note recognition reading the treble clef than reading the bass clef at this stage. For a challenge, look at the note in the bass clef *before* you look at the corresponding note in the treble clef to solidify your bass clef–reading skills.

Playing Songs with Both Hands

You're ready for some two-handed music-making, and you're looking for some tunes that put it all together. You've come to the right place; the songs in this section utilize both hands.

Go to www.dummies.com/go/piano and watch Video Clip 13 to see these songs played.

Here are a few things you need to know in order to play them:

- ✓ **"The Sidewalks of New York":** For this song, you need to be able to read bass clef (see Chapter 6), play a (mostly) one-note accompaniment in the left hand, read sharps, and play in 3/4 time. Oh, and you should enjoy the swaying rhythm, too.

- ✓ **"Stars and Stripes Forever":** You need to know about pickup measures (see Chapter 8), playing in 2/4 time, and playing a left-hand accompaniment pattern with a melody in order to play this tune.

The Sidewalks of New York

Track 43

Stars and Stripes Forever

Bright March

Part IV
Living in Perfect Harmony

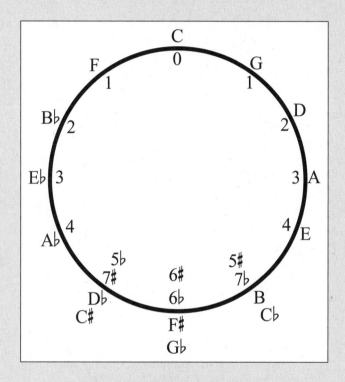

Work through some seventh-chord arpeggios at www.dummies.com/extras/
piano.

In this part . . .

- Discover how to identify intervals — seconds, thirds, fourths, fifths, sixths, and sevenths, the building blocks of harmony.

- Understand how to choose and arrange notes around a melody to create a sense of harmony in any context.

- Break down various keys, both major and minor, and what they tell you about a song, from which sharps and flats are used to which scale the song is based on.

- Arm yourself with a vocabulary of many different chord types — major, minor, diminished, augmented, and more — and, with any luck, the ability to recognize these sounds when you hear them being played.

- Explore the rules behind building chords. That way you won't have to rely on sheet music to make beautiful harmonies, and your playing will sound more complex as a result.

Chapter 12

The Building Blocks of Harmony

In This Chapter

▶ Measuring the distance between two notes

▶ Hearing and playing intervals

▶ Constructing harmony

▶ Harmonizing a melody

*W*hen you listen to music, the melody is usually the first thing to grab your ear. You're less aware of the other notes being played along with the melody to form the harmony of the music.

Without harmony, you would hear one single note at a time. On your piano, you can play more than one note at a time, giving it the coveted distinction of being an instrument capable of harmonizing. Sure, other instruments in a band or orchestra can play collectively to form harmony, but you can harmonize all by yourself with a piano.

Playing many notes simultaneously is the essence of harmony. The notes you choose and how you arrange them around the melody determines the kind of harmony you produce, whether you use many notes or just one note with each hand. Go ahead and try it: Play two, three, four, even ten notes at once. Ah, sweet harmony . . . or a cluttered mess, depending on what notes you play.

Measuring Melodic Intervals

The distance between any two musical notes is called an *interval*. You need to understand the concept of intervals and the notes that make up each interval so that you can identify and select the right notes to build harmonies. But you also use intervals to identify and build notes in a melody. As you play or sing the notes of a melody, the melody can do one of three things: It can stay on the same note, it can go up, or it can go down. When it goes up or down, the question of *how much* leads to the subject of *melodic intervals*.

You measure an interval by the number of half-steps and whole-steps in between the two notes. But because this method involves lots of counting, memorization, and complicated arithmetic, I have an easier solution: Use the major scale as a measuring tape. (Chapter 10 tells you all about whole- and half-steps as well as scales.)

Each major scale contains seven different notes plus the octave — that's eight notes that you can use to name intervals. For example, Figure 12-1 shows the ever-popular C major scale, with the notes numbered from 1 to 8.

Figure 12-1: Numbering the notes of the C major scale.

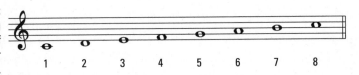

TIP

Pick two notes and count the scale notes (not the piano keys) in between to find the name of the interval. For example, if you play the first note of the C major scale (C) followed by the fifth note (G), you just played a *fifth* interval. If you count the scale notes in between C and G, you get five — C, D, E, F, G. From C to E (the *third* note in the scale) is a *third* interval, and so on. Not much originality in these names, but is this easy or what?

REMEMBER

You don't have to start with the first note of the scale to make an interval of a fifth. This concept of intervals is all about distance. You can build a fifth on the note G by climbing up five scale notes to D. It's easy to check yourself by counting the scale notes in between.

Figure 12-2 shows you the C major scale and its intervals.

Figure 12-2: A family of intervals on the C major scale.

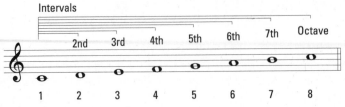

I use the C scale as an example because it's so easy, with no sharps or flats. However, this method of number-naming the intervals works for every single major scale. Simply write out the scale and number the notes from 1 to 8 — it works the same every time.

Interval shorthand

Like scales, intervals come in different varieties: *major, minor, perfect, diminished,* and *augmented.* Knowing these classifications helps you identify and build harmonies for the music you play. For example, if you want to build a minor chord to harmonize with a melody, you must use a minor interval. (Chapter 14 tells you all about building chords.)

Here's your guide to making different types of intervals:

- **Major interval:** Measure a major second, third, sixth, or seventh by matching the second, third, sixth, or seventh notes of the major scale and counting the half-steps from the root note.

- **Minor interval:** You can make a second, third, sixth, or seventh interval minor by lowering its major counterpart a half-step.

- **Perfect interval:** This label applies only to fourths, fifths, and octaves.

- **Diminished interval:** You can make any interval diminished by lowering it a half-step.

- **Augmented interval:** You can make any interval augmented by raising it a half-step.

Musicians use the following abbreviations when discussing intervals:

- *M* for major intervals
- *m* for minor intervals
- *P* for perfect intervals
- *dim* for diminished intervals
- *aug* for augmented intervals
- Numbers for the interval size, as in the number 5 for a fifth

So, when you see *P5,* you know it means a perfect fifth. When you see *M2,* it means a major second. When you see *m6,* it means a minor sixth.

I would be remiss not to point out that intervals can be measured upwards or downwards. That is, when you play a C-G fifth interval, you can say that G is a fifth above C or that C is a fifth below G. So, a *descending* interval is measured from the top note to the bottom note. Likewise, *ascending* means . . . oh, you can figure that out.

In the sections that follow, I explain each interval on the scale and give you an example of a well-known tune that uses the interval. Definitely play each of the examples on your piano. Nothing trains a musician more than playing and hearing at the same time. Put these intervals in your head along with the corresponding tunes, and you won't forget them.

Seconds

The first interval you sing in the celebratory song "Happy Birthday" is a *major second interval,* or *M2*. Go ahead and sing it. "Hap-py Birth-" Stop! On "Birth" you jump up a major second interval. Using the C scale, an M2 is the distance from C to D.

Another song beginning with an M2 is "London Bridge," which you see in Figure 12-3. Every time you play the name of the bridge, you go up and back down a major second. Try it on your piano.

Figure 12-3: "London Bridge" uses major seconds.

You create a *minor second,* or *m2,* simply by making the major second a half-step smaller. In other words, play C to D-flat. Think of an m2 as the famous interval used in the *Jaws* theme by composer John Williams. Figure 12-4 shows you an m2 from Beethoven's ubiquitous "Für Elise." You'd recognize this melody anywhere, and now you can name the opening interval as an m2.

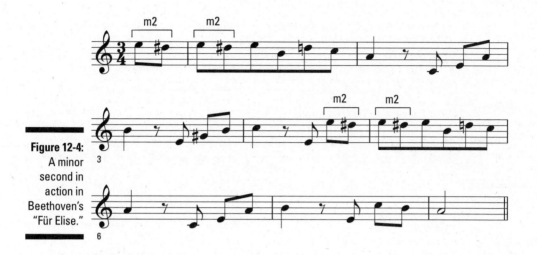

Figure 12-4:
A minor
second in
action in
Beethoven's
"Für Elise."

Thirds

The first four notes of Beethoven's legendary *Fifth Symphony* employ a *major third,* or *M3*. If a composer could copyright an interval, Ludwig van Beethoven would have this one. And if that isn't enough, Beethoven tried to claim the *minor third,* or *m3,* too, by using it in the next four notes of the theme. Play Figure 12-5, a snippet of the *Fifth Symphony,* and you'll forever know major and minor thirds.

Figure 12-5:
Major and
minor thirds
paired
for the
symphonic
theme of
Beethoven's
Fifth.

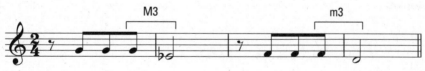

You also hear the M3 interval frequently in spirituals. Figure 12-6 demonstrates this interval in the songs "Amazing Grace" and "Swing Low, Sweet Chariot."

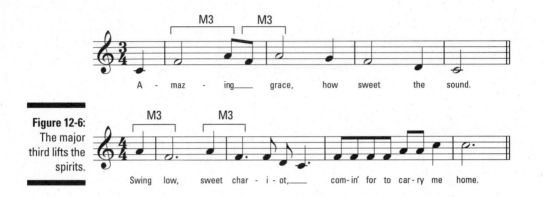

Figure 12-6:
The major third lifts the spirits.

For some reason unknown even to Beethoven, an m3 seems particularly appealing to children. As you see in Figure 12-7, the opening notes of the children's favorites "This Old Man" and "It's Raining, It's Pouring" form an m3, which is smaller than an M3 by a half-step.

Figure 12-7:
A minor interval close to children's hearts.

Fourths and fifths

The fourth interval gets the classification of being perfect when it's five half-steps above or below another note. From C up to F is a *perfect fourth,* or *P4.*

The sound of a P4 is perfect for imparting just about any kind of emotion. Composers use this interval to convey heroism, love, comedy, and even outer space in their melodies. Play and sing the opening notes of "I've Been Working on the Railroad," and you jostle back and forth on a P4 until the lyric "the" ruins the fun, as shown in Figure 12-8.

Figure 12-8:
The perfect
fourth
in (loco)
motion.

You can also remember the P4 interval going down and back up again in the theme of Schubert's *Unfinished Symphony* (see Figure 12-9).

Figure 12-9:
Though
unfinished,
Schubert's
*Unfinished
Symphony*
is still a
perfect
fourth.

Another perfect interval is the *perfect fifth,* or *P5.* Why is this one so perfect? Practically any song ever written has at least one P5 interval somewhere in it. And, hey, it fits the hand nicely: from C up to G is C position. (Chapter 9 explains C position.)

As you play the first two notes of Figure 12-10, you may see stars. Both "Twinkle, Twinkle Little Star" and the theme to *Star Wars* begin with a P5.

Figure 12-10:
A shining
star, the
perfect fifth.

Play a descending P5, from G to C, and you may recognize the immortal classic "Feelings" and the theme from *The Flintstones* TV show. Speaking of classics, the romantic standard "The Way You Look Tonight" also begins with a descending P5 to the words "Some day." The Bach "Minuet" you may have played in Chapter 9 also opens with the descending P5, as you see in Figure 12-11.

Figure 12-11:
A fifth
interval
descending
perfectly.

A handy way to remember perfect fourths *and* perfect fifths is by humming the opening bars of "Here Comes the Bride," in which one interval conveniently follows the other (see Figure 12-12). "Here Comes the Bride" originates in the Bridal Chorus sung in the opera *Lohengrin* by Richard Wagner. You may object to sitting through a three-and-a-half-hour opera just to hear the original, but perhaps you've experienced a wedding ceremony that felt twice as long and didn't have nearly as much beautiful music.

Figure 12-12:
Perfect
fourth and
perfect fifth,
together
forever
in "Here
Comes the
Bride."

Between a perfect fourth and a perfect fifth exists an interval that's exactly half of an octave (see Figure 12-13). From C, count up six half-steps to F-sharp, or G-flat. If you call it F-sharp, you call the interval an *augmented fourth* because it's larger than a fourth but not quite a fifth. If you call it G-flat, the interval is a *diminished fifth* because it's a perfect fifth lowered by one half-step. Many people remember this interval by singing "Maria" from *West Side Story* — the first two notes are an augmented fourth.

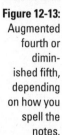

Figure 12-13:
Augmented
fourth or
dimin-
ished fifth,
depending
on how you
spell the
notes.

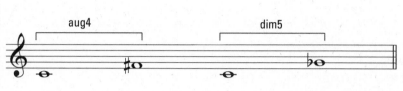

Although you can diminish or augment any interval by lowering or raising it a half-step, the only intervals you diminish or augment in this book and in most beginning-level piano music are fourths and fifths.

Sixths and sevenths

A *major sixth,* or *M6,* interval is the opening interval of "My Bonnie Lies Over the Ocean." "My Bon-" is the M6 interval, from C to A. If you play C to A-flat, you get a *minor sixth,* or *m6.* Figure 12-14 shows you both sixths.

Figure 12-14:
Bonnie's
favorite
intervals —
the major
and minor
sixth.

The *major seventh (M7)* and *minor seventh (m7)* are the last numbered intervals in the scale. You can call up an m7 by singing the first two notes of "Somewhere" from *West Side Story* (matching the first two words of the phrase, "There's a place for us"). Not many songwriters begin a melody with a major seventh interval; perhaps that's why there are few memorable examples.

In any case, it's an important interval to know because the seventh interval helps form a few of the most popular chords in Western music. (Chapter 14 tells you more about chords.) Get to know these two interval sizes and judge for yourself how melodic they are after you play the notes in Figure 12-15.

Figure 12-15:
Seventh
heaven.

Octaves

You may think that the last interval in the scale would be called an eighth. You're partly right. The prefix *octa* means *eight*. The interval of an eighth is called an *octave (P8)*, and is another perfect one at that.

Figure 12-16 shows you a perfect octave, a sound Judy Garland made memorable when she sang "Over the Rainbow" in *The Wizard of Oz*. In the opening lyrics, from "some" to "where" is an octave leap. Another easy way to remember this interval is that both notes have the same name.

Figure 12-16:
Somewhere
over the
octave.

Combining Notes for Harmonic Intervals

In the preceding section, you play each interval as single notes to see and hear the distance between each. But that's not harmony. You have to play the intervals together to get harmony. These sections examine harmonic intervals at a closer level.

Playing two notes together

Figure 12-17 shows each interval — perfect, diminished, augmented, major, and minor — from seconds to an octave. Try playing the notes of each interval at the same time. Notice that the notes in each interval are stacked. When two notes appear stacked, or attached to the same stem, you play them at the same time. You know, in harmony.

They sound perfectly lovely, but how do you use these intervals to create harmony? You can

✔ Add intervals to the right hand under a melody line.

✔ Play intervals in the left hand while the right hand continues the melody.

✔ Do both.

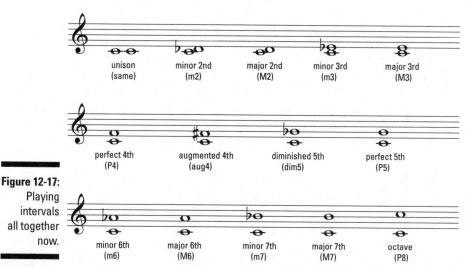

Figure 12-17:
Playing
intervals
all together
now.

To start playing songs with harmonic intervals, skip ahead to the section "Playing Songs with More Harmony" at the end of the chapter.

Adding intervals to the melody

Adding harmonic intervals to the melody really fills out the sound. Figure 12-18 shows the melody of "Aura Lee" as a single-note melody in the opening phrase, followed by the same melody played with right-hand intervals added below the melody for the second phrase. As you play both phrases, listen to the difference this harmony makes.

Figure 12-18: "Aura Lee" is a melody that begs for harmony.

Figuring out how or when to add these intervals to a melody isn't necessary. The composer does that for you and notates these intervals in the printed music you play. But you should understand that all these intervals combine with the melody to make a very harmonic tune. Sure, you could just play the melody by playing only the top note of each group of notes, but your audience will appreciate the extra effort of playing the intervals. Besides, why do you think you have so many fingers?

Of course, if you want to add intervals to a melody yourself, try choosing the interval either a third below or a sixth below the melody note. Take a simple melody like "Yankee Doodle" and add an interval a sixth below each right-hand melody note. You can see how this is done in Figure 12-19.

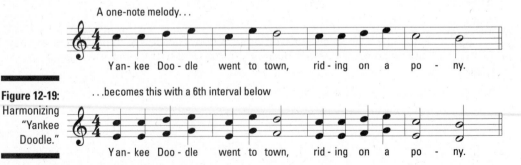

A one-note melody. . .

Yan- kee Doo - dle   went to town,   rid - ing on a   po - ny.

Figure 12-19: Harmonizing "Yankee Doodle."

. . .becomes this with a 6th interval below

Yan- kee Doo - dle   went to town,   rid - ing on a   po - ny.

If you've ever sung in a chorus or even made up a harmony to sing along to your favorite recording, you know that some notes sound good together and some don't. Certain intervals sound more stable, or resolved, than others. The intervals that sound resolved are thirds, fifths, and sixths; seconds, fourths, and sevenths can sound unresolved. (Octaves sound good, of course, because they match the same notes as the melody.) Depending on the context, stable intervals are more *consonant* (harmonious and agreeable), whereas unstable intervals sound more *dissonant* (discordant and jarring).

Harmonizing with the left hand

One of the easiest ways to add harmony to music is to play single notes with the left hand that form intervals when combined with the right-hand melody notes. Often, you simply play one note with the left hand and hold it for several measures as you continue with the melody.

In Figure 12-20, the right hand plays the opening phrase of "America, the Beautiful" while lefty plays single whole notes below. The harmonic intervals are simply moved an octave below, making use of the lower register of the piano and creating a nice, full sound.

Figure 12-20: "America, the Beautiful" with a harmonious, single-note LH part.

You can fill out the sound even more by adding a harmonic interval to the left-hand part, as shown in Figure 12-21. When the left-hand part consists of whole- and half-note rhythms, adding this interval is easy enough.

Figure 12-21:
Adding more
harmony to
the LH part.

In Figure 12-21, the left hand plays stable, resolved intervals (thirds and fifths) except in one place: The unresolved interval of a seventh on beat 3 in measure 3 is resolved to an interval of a third to end the phrase on a more consonant harmony.

Another way to go is to add a harmonic interval below the melody in the right hand, plus add a bass note in the left hand, as shown in Figure 12-22.

Figure 12-22:
Adding har-
mony below
the melody
in the RH
part.

To give a song a little more movement, you can play a harmony part in the left hand that matches the melody note-for-note (see Figure 12-23).

Figure 12-23:
The LH
harmony
matches the
rhythm of
the melody.

And for the ultimate in harmony, make it a four-part style with simple intervals in both hands. Just a couple of notes create a nice, full sound, as shown in Figure 12-24.

Figure 12-24: A full, choir-like harmonic treatment.

Playing Songs with More Harmony

Feeling ready to play songs with more harmony? Each of the following songs explores different ways to use harmonic intervals.

- ✔ **"I'm Called Little Buttercup":** In this song, the left hand plays single bass notes while the right hand plays the melody. The two parts move in different ways, so if you find it difficult to play at first, be patient and practice each hand separately until you feel comfortable with the notes. Then play hands-together.

- ✔ **"Marianne":** You can see and hear the harmonizing power of two-note harmony in this song. It may be helpful to play the melody, right hand only, a couple of times. Then try the left-hand part only. When you're relaxed and confident, put both hands together.

- ✔ **"Aura Lee":** Adding a melodic interval below the melody in your right hand and adding your left hand to the mix is simple to do, and oh so satisfying. If you get lost as you play, just slow down and try each hand separately until you feel like putting them together again. (You may recognize the melody as a song made famous by Elvis Presley. Of course, Elvis used different lyrics — something about loving him tender.)

- ✔ **"Shenandoah":** In this piece, both hands play the same rhythm, with the left hand mirroring the melody with a soothing harmony line. Listen carefully as you play to match rhythms with both hands, just like two voices singing together.

- ✔ **"Auld Lang Syne":** Your left hand isn't limited to single notes or certain intervals. The composer may give you seconds, fourths, or anything else he or she desires. Give both hands a shot at some four-part harmony with this song, which mixes up several types of intervals in both hands. This can't be overstated: Practice each hand separately before putting the two together.

Track 44

I'm Called Little Buttercup

Moderately

Track 45

Marianne

Moderately fast

Aura Lee

Moderately slow

Shenandoah

Track 48

Auld Lang Syne

Moderately

Chapter 13

Understanding Keys

In This Chapter

▶ Finding your music's home key

▶ Interpreting key signatures

▶ Playing songs with key signatures

K eys allow you to drive a car, open doors, and even read maps. Some keys may be frustrating when you misplace them several times a week, but they're still handy and essential tools in life — and in music.

In this chapter, I tell you about musical keys. I'm not talking about the black and white keys you press when you play a keyboard. This is a completely, utterly, totally, wholly different type of key. A *key* is a set of notes that corresponds to a certain scale. (Chapter 10 tells you all about scales.) Keys and scales provide a foundation of compatible notes that composers can use to construct melodies and harmonies.

Homing In on Home Key

A musical key is a song's home. The key tells you several things about a song: which sharps and flats are used (see Chapter 6 to understand sharps and flats), which scale the song is based on (see Chapter 10 for more on scales), which of the scale notes is the song's home note, and much more.

A song has a single home note, and all the other notes used in a song have a relation to that home note based on how far away or near they are to home. So understanding a musical key means also understanding the relationships notes have to one another. A song can be thought of as a musical journey, and understanding where a song goes on its journey is part of the joy of making music.

When a song is *in the key of C*, it means that the song is primarily based on the C major scale, using mostly (or only) notes from that scale for the song's melody and harmony. Throughout the song, your ears get comfortable with notes from the C major scale. If the composer throws in a slew of other notes from another scale (like F-sharp), it's a bit unsettling to your ears. When the song returns to notes from the C major scale, your ears feel at home again.

The real definition of a song's key is not, of course, a song's home. As the musically minded will quickly point out, a song's key is its *tonal center,* meaning the tones of a scale that the melody and harmony of the song are centered around.

A whole ring of keys

Music uses many different keys that are named after the many different notes on your keyboard. In other words, you have a musical key for the notes A, B, C, D, E, F, and G, plus all the sharps and flats.

Each key has its own unique character, look, feel, and sound. A composer uses a particular key to give his or her music the right sound and feeling. I could expound on the differences between the keys for probably another 30 pages, but the best way for you to understand their subtle effects is to listen to the same song written in two different keys. Play "Good Night, Ladies" as you see it in Figure 13-1, which is in the key of C.

Track 49

Figure 13-1: "Good Night, Ladies" in the key of C (major).

You can also play "Good Night, Ladies" in the key of F (see Figure 13-2). Although the *intervals* (the relationship of each note to the next) remain the same, the sound and character of the song change subtly simply by changing keys, in this case moving the song down to the key of F. (To read more about intervals, check out Chapter 12.)

Track 50

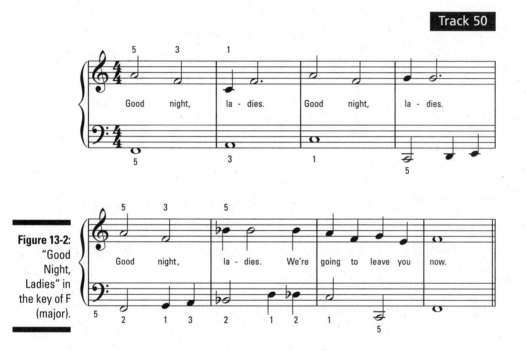

Figure 13-2: "Good Night, Ladies" in the key of F (major).

Composers and performers find keys very, very helpful because they allow musical selections to be modified to fit different performers. For example, if a composer writes a song in the key of G and the melody is too high for a particular singer to sing, the song can be changed to a lower key (like F or E) to accommodate the singer's voice. The composer likes that the overall song isn't affected, only the *range*, which is the highness or lowness of the melody. Changing the musical key of a song is called *transposing*, and it's a frequent occurrence in music.

Using keys to play music

As a performer, recognizing and reading keys is an invaluable skill, more so than just knowing how high or low a song sounds. Understanding keys helps you play better because the key of a song tells you which notes to play or not to play.

For example, if you play a melody in the key of G, you mostly play notes from the G major scale. Your knowledge of scales (see Chapter 10) reminds you that G contains the note F-sharp, so you can expect to play all the Fs in the song as F-sharps.

To conserve ink, composers employ a tool called a *key signature.* Placed just after the clef on every line of music, a key signature allows the composer to

✔ Avoid writing all those little tic-tac-toe symbols next to every sharp in the song.

✔ Avoid writing flats next to every flat in the song.

✔ Instantly tell the performer (that's you!) what key the song is in.

As the music you play becomes more and more complex, believe me when I say that you don't want to see sharps and flats cluttering the music you're trying to read.

Reading key signatures

What does reading key signatures do for you?

✔ It makes reading music easier because you know what notes to expect to play in each key.

✔ It makes playing music more fun because you can start to identify what makes one song different from another if you understand the idea of songs being in a key.

✔ It's a tool to help you remember the music, because you can identify a certain characteristic in the context of the key. For example, if the melody begins on the third note of the major scale and you know what key you're in, you can right away play the first note of the song.

Figure 13-3 shows you two key signatures: one for the key of G and one for the key of F. The first shows a sharp symbol on the top line of the staff, which tells you to play every F as F-sharp. The G major scale contains one sharp, so this must be the key of G. The second key signature uses a flat on the middle line of the staff, telling you to play every B as B-flat. This must be the key of F because the F major scale has one flat, B-flat.

Key of G:

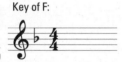

Figure 13-3:
The sign on
the line.

Key of F:

You may think that only Fs on the top line are altered by the sharp in the key signature. Nope! The key signature applies to every F, not just the one on the top line. This, of course, is another time- and ink-saving decision.

The only time the same note is marked with a sharp or flat twice in a key signature is when you have two staves. In this case, you get one key signature on the treble staff and one on the bass staff, as shown in Figure 13-4.

Figure 13-4:
A key
signature for
each hand.

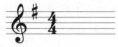

Playing a melody with a key signature is no more difficult than playing a song without one. You just have to remember (with a little help from your friendly key signature) which notes to make sharp or flat throughout. Figure 13-5 features the opening melody to a tune called "Worried Man Blues" in the key of G. When you play, keep in mind that all the Fs are actually F-sharps.

Figure 13-5:
Playing a
melody in
the key of G.

Try the same song in the key of D, which has two sharps. Notice the key signature in Figure 13-6, and remember to play all the Fs as F-sharps and all the
Cs as C-sharps.

Figure 13-6:
Trying
the same
melody in
the key of D.

To play the entire melody of "Worried Man Blues" with the left hand added,
skip to the section "Playing Songs with Key Signatures" at the end of the
chapter.

A key signature tells you instantly which key the song is in. You may be thinking, "Well, if I have to count all the sharps or flats and then figure out which
scale they're in, that's not very instantaneous!" With a little experience, you'll
start to recognize the most common key signatures. Without counting, without playing — without even thinking about it, really — you'll simply glance
at the key signature and know immediately which key the song is in. Most
beginning piano music sticks to the key signatures with few sharps and flats
or none at all.

The Circle of Fifths

Lucky for you, there's a method to the madness of key signatures, an order that starts with no sharps and flats and cycles the ring of keys to all 12 keys. Figure 13-7 shows the *Circle of Fifths* with the letter names for each possible home key, or tonal center. As you travel around the circle, you find each of the 12 keys in the tonal system. The numbers inside the circle tell you how many sharps or flats are in each key signature.

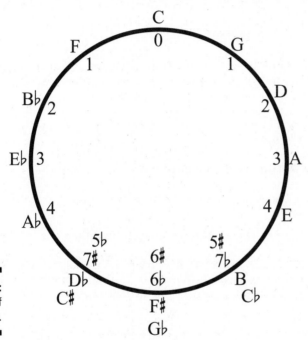

Figure 13-7:
The Circle of
Fifths.

As you check out the Circle of Fifths, note the following important points:

- ✔ Each key is a fifth up from the previous key, circling clockwise. (See Chapter 12 for the scoop on intervals.)

- ✔ The key of C, at the top, has no sharps or flats.

- ✔ The keys on the right half of the Circle are all sharp keys, gaining one sharp at each position traveling clockwise from the top.

- ✔ The keys on the left half of the Circle are all flat keys, gaining one flat at each position traveling counterclockwise from the top.

- ✔ The three keys at the bottom of the Circle can be either sharp *or* flat keys; the composer gets to decide.

Among the marvels of this oracle of tonality, the Circle shows the relationship of the keys to each other. The keys that are neighbors have a lot in common, like seven of eight scale tones. Very often a song travels smoothly to a neighboring key during its musical journey. The keys that are farthest away from each other have little in common, and a musical journey from one side of the Circle directly to the opposite side sounds quite abrupt.

The order of sharps and flats as they're written on the grand staff follows the Circle of Fifths, adding a sharp or flat in the same order as the Circle.

Key signatures with sharps

Suppose you want to play a song on the piano that has two sharps in the key signature. If you look at the Circle of Fifths in Figure 13-7, you can quickly see that the key with two sharps is two positions away from C, so the song is in the key of D.

Eventually you want to be able to know what key a song is in without glancing at the Circle. Here's how:

To read a key signature that contains sharps:

1. **Locate the last sharp (the one farthest to the right) on either the treble or bass clef.**

2. **Move up one half-step from the sharp to find the name of the key.**

For example, if you have two sharps, F-sharp and C-sharp, the last one is C-sharp. Up a half-step from C-sharp is D. The song is in the key of D. Figure 13-8 shows you key signatures for all sharp keys.

Figure 13-8: Sharp keys.

G   D   A   E   B   F#   C#

Naming keys with lots of sharps requires a bit of brain power because note spelling can get tricky. For example, on your piano keyboard the key one half-step up from E is F. Technically, you can also spell F as E-sharp. So, if the sixth sharp in the key signature is E-sharp, you raise it one half-step to determine the correct key, which is F-sharp. You can't determine the key to be G-flat because you would be skipping the letter name F in the sequence of note names, as explained in Chapter 10.

Key signatures with flats

To read a key signature that contains flats:

1. **Locate the next-to-the-last flat (the one that's second from the right) in the key signature.**

2. **The name of that flat is the name of the key.**

For example, if you have three flats in a key signature — B-flat, E-flat, and A-flat — the next to the last one is E-flat, and the song is in the key of E-flat. Figure 13-9 shows all the flat keys.

Figure 13-9:
Flat keys.

F   B♭   E♭   A♭   D♭   G♭   C♭

WARNING!

The one key for which this naming method doesn't work is the key of F. Because it has only one flat (B-flat), there's no such thing as a "next-to-the-last" flat for you to read. So, you must remember that one flat in the key signature means that a song is in the key of F. You can also remember that F is the key with one flat because it's one position before the key of C in the Circle of Fifths, or a fifth below C (count up five note names), so it must have one flat.

Give yourself a hand

An easy way to find the key signature for the most common keys uses mnemonics. All you need are five fingers and a short memory.

The most common keys you play in are C, F, G, D, A, E, and B. The first two are a piece of cake to remember: C has no sharps or flats, and F has only B-flat. For the other five common keys (which happen to all have sharps), follow these steps:

1. **Memorize the order G-D-A-E-B with a simple mnemonic of your choice:**

   Good **D**iamonds **A**re **E**xpensive to **B**uy

Glass **D**oors **A**re **E**asily **B**roken

Grand **D**ivas **A**ren't **E**ver **B**ashful

2. **Count out the keys in order on the fingers of one hand until you get to the key you need.**

   For the key of A, count G, D, A. How many fingers are you holding up? Three. The key of A has three sharps.

The sharps in a key signature always appear in ascending fifths, starting with F-sharp. Thus, the three sharps in the key of A are F-sharp, C-sharp, and G-sharp.

Leaving and returning to the "home" key

No matter what a home looks or sounds like, its basic purpose is to be the place you return to after you've been away. The same applies to keys.

Melodies and harmonies often venture outside of a song's basic key. Jazz musicians in particular lift the music and give it a fresh sound by exploring notes and chords outside of the original key. Composers as far back as you can imagine have used various keys to carry the music to new and unfamiliar places. After such an "out of key" experience, you feel a sense of coming home when the song returns to the original key.

To get a better grasp of this concept of musical travel, check out www. dummies.com/go/piano and listen to a snippet of the song "After the Ball" on Track 51. It begins in the key of G and travels to the key of A for a few measures before returning home to G. Just by listening, see if you can tell when the song leaves the home key and when it returns home to its original key. Then listen to the piece again as you follow along with the music in Figure 13-10.

Track 51

Figure 13-10:
Changing keys and then returning home.

Did you hear it? In measure 5, the music begins to venture outside of the original home key of G, and it starts to return safely and smoothly to the home key of G in measure 9.

To play "After the Ball" in its entirety and with the left hand added, skip to the next section "Playing Songs with Key Signatures."

Playing Songs with Key Signatures

The songs in this section give you a chance to read and play music written with key signatures. Here are some pointers as you prepare to play each piece:

- **"Worried Man Blues":** This is the full version of the song that introduces key signatures earlier in the chapter. Written in the key of G, it has one sharp (F-sharp) to keep in mind as you play. The left-hand part is pretty simple, but you may want to go over the fingering and position changes in the last five measures before you try it hands-together.

- **"After the Ball":** This is also the full version of a song introduced earlier in the chapter. This one illustrates a melody in the key of G that makes a brief sojourn to another key before returning to the home key at the end. Check out the natural sign before the note C in the right hand, in measure 26. This helpful reminder cancels out the C-sharp played two measures before.

Track 53

After the Ball

Chapter 14

Filling Out Your Sound with Chords

. . . .

In This Chapter

▶ Building chords of all types

▶ Translating chord symbols

▶ Inverting the notes of a chord

▶ Playing songs with major, minor, and seventh chords

. . . .

A quick glance through this chapter may have you thinking, "Why do I need to know how to build chords?" Here's one answer you may like: to impress your friends. Wait, here's another: to play like a pro.

Playing melodies is nice and all, but harmony is the key to making your music sound fuller, better, cooler, and just downright great. Playing chords with your left hand is perhaps the easiest way to harmonize a melody. Playing chords with your right hand, too, is a great way to accompany a singer, guitarist, or other performer.

This chapter shows you step-by-step how to build chords and use them to accompany any melody.

Tapping into the Power of Chords

Three or more notes played at the same time form a *chord*. You can play them with one or both hands. Chords have but one simple goal in life: to provide harmony. (Chapter 12 tells you all about harmony.)

You may have encountered chords already in a number of situations, including the following:

✔ You see several musical notes stacked on top of each other in printed music.

✔ You notice strange symbols above the treble clef staff that make no sense when you read them, like F♯m7(-5), Csus4(add9).

✔ You hear a band or orchestra play.

✔ You honk a car horn.

Yes, the sound of a car horn is a chord, albeit a headache-inducing one. So are the sounds of a barbershop quartet, a church choir, and a sidewalk accordion player (monkey with tip jar is optional). Chances are, though, that you probably won't use car horns or barbers to accompany your melodies — piano chords are much more practical.

Dissecting the Anatomy of a Triad

Chords begin very simply. Like melodies, chords are based on scales. (Chapter 10 gives you the skinny on scales.) To make a chord, you select any note and put other scale notes on top of it.

Generally, the lowest note of a chord is called the *root*. The root also gives the chord its name. For example, a chord with A as its root is an A chord. The notes you use on top of the root note give the chord its *type,* which I explain later in this chapter, starting with major and minor chords.

Most chords begin as *triads,* or three *(tri)* notes added *(ad)* together. Okay, that's not the actual breakdown of the word, but it may help you remember what triad means. A triad consists of a root note and two other notes: the intervals of a third and a fifth. (Chapter 12 tells you about all the fun and games involved in intervals.) Figure 14-1 shows you a typical triad played on the white keys C-E-G. C is the root note, E is a third from C, and G is a fifth from C.

Figure 14-1:
This C chord is a simple triad.

You build new chords by altering this C triad in any of the following ways:

✔ Raising or lowering notes of the triad by a half-step or whole-step

✔ Adding notes to the triad

✔ Both raising or lowering notes and adding notes

For example, Figure 14-2 shows you four different ways to change the C triad and make four new chords. Play each of these chords, the intervals of which are marked, to hear how they sound. (Chapter 12 explains these intervals and abbreviations.)

Figure 14-2:
Making new chords from the C triad.

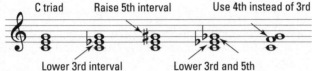

Starting Out with Major Chords

Major chords are perhaps the most frequently used, most familiar, and easiest triads to play. It's a good bet that most folk and popular songs you know have one or two major chords.

You make major chords with the notes and intervals of a major scale. (Chapter 10 provides a field guide to major scales.) You build a major chord by starting out with a root note and then adding other notes from the desired chord's scale. For example, suppose you want to build a G major chord. Play the root note G, and add the third and fifth notes (or third and fifth intervals) from the G major scale on top of the root note.

Major chords, such as the four in Figure 14-3, are so common that musicians treat them as almost the norm. These chords are named with just the name of the root, and musicians rarely say "major." Instead, they just say the name of the chord and use a chord symbol written above the staff to indicate the name of the chord.

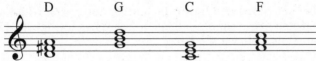
Figure 14-3:
Major chords.

Use fingers 1, 3, and 5 to play major chords. If you're playing left-hand chords (see Figure 14-4), start with LH 5 on the root note. For right-hand chords, play the root note with RH 1.

Figure 14-4:
Major
chords for
lefty, too.

To play a song with left-hand major chords right now, skip to the section "Playing Songs with Chords" at the end of the chapter and play "Down by the Station."

Head to www.dummies.com/go/piano and watch a selection of major chords being played in Video Clip 14.

Branching Out with Minor Chords

Like the major chord, a *minor chord* is a triad comprised of a root note, a third, and a fifth. Written as a chord symbol, minor chords get the suffix *m,* or sometimes *min.* Songs in minor keys give you lots of opportunities to play minor chords.

Don't be fooled by the name "minor." These chords are no smaller or any less important than major chords. They simply incorporate minor thirds, rather than major thirds. Minor chords are to major chords as shadow is to light, the yang to the yin.

You can make a minor chord two different ways:

- ✔ **Play the root note, and add the third and fifth notes of the minor scale on top.** For example, play A as the root note, and add the third note (C) and fifth note (E) of the A minor scale.

- ✔ **Play a major chord and lower the middle note, or third interval, by one half-step.** For example, a C major chord has the notes C-E-G. To play a C minor chord, lower the E to E-flat.

Figure 14-5 shows you several minor chords. Play them to hear how they sound, and then compare these chords to their major counterparts in Figure 14-3.

Just like playing major chords, use fingers 1, 3, and 5 for minor chords. For left-hand minor chords, play the root note with LH 5; for right-hand chords, play the root note with RH 1.

Figure 14-5:
Minor, but not insignificant, chords.

To play "Sometimes I Feel Like a Motherless Child," a minor-key song with lots of minor chords, go to the section "Playing Songs with Chords" at the end of the chapter.

You can see — and hear — some minor chords at work in Video Clip 15 by going to www.dummies.com/go/piano.

Exploring Other Types of Chords

Major and minor chords are by far the most popular chords, but other types of chords get equal opportunity to shine in music. You form the following other chords by altering the notes of a major or minor chord or by adding notes to a major or minor chord.

Tweaking the fifth: Augmented and diminished chords

Major and minor chords differ from each other only in the third interval. The top note, the fifth interval, is the same for both types of chords, so by altering the fifth interval of a major or minor chord, you can create two new chord types, both triads.

An *augmented chord* contains a root note, a major third (M3) interval, and an *augmented fifth* (aug5), which is a perfect fifth (P5) raised one half-step. Think of an augmented chord as simply a major chord with the top note raised one half-step. Figure 14-6 shows several augmented chords.

Figure 14-6:
Augmented chords raise the fifth one half-step.

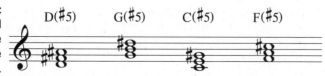

When writing the chord symbol, the suffixes for augmented chords include +, *aug,* and ♯5. I like to use ♯5 because it actually tells you what to do to change the chord — to raise the fifth.

A *diminished chord* contains a root note, a minor third (m3) interval, and a *diminished fifth* (dim5), which is a perfect fifth (P5) interval lowered one half-step. Figure 14-7 gives you a selection of diminished chords.

Figure 14-7:
Diminished chords lower the fifth one half-step.

Note the suffix used to signal a diminished chord in the chord symbol: *dim.* You may also see the suffix *dim* in the chord symbol, as in *Fdim,* or a small, raised circle following the chord symbol, as in Figure 14-7. (Table 14-1, later in this chapter, offers a helpful guide to chord symbols.)

You may find it easiest to use fingers 1, 2, and 4 for augmented and diminished chords played with the right hand. For the left hand, try 5, 3, and 2.

Figure 14-8 shows you an example of how you may encounter diminished and augmented chords in a song. The melody is the last phrase of Stephen Foster's "Old Folks at Home." Take these new chords for a spin and see how they subtly affect a song's harmony.

Figure 14-8:
Augmented and diminished chords in "Old Folks at Home."

Waiting for resolution: Suspended chords

Another popular type of three-note chord, although it's technically not a triad, is the *suspended chord*. The name means "hanging," and the sound of a suspended chord always leaves you waiting for the next notes or chords.

The two types of suspended chords are the *suspended second* and the *suspended fourth*. Because of their abbreviated suffixes, these chords are often referred to as the *sus2* and *sus4* chords; you see them written as *Csus2* or *Asus4*, for example. Here's how you create them:

✔ **A sus2 chord** is comprised of a root note, a major second (M2) interval, and a perfect fifth (P5) interval.

✔ **A sus4 chord** has a root note, a perfect fourth (P4), and a P5 interval.

The sus4 is so popular that musicians often just call it the *sus chord*. So, when the bandleader says to play "a sus chord on beat 1," that probably means to play a suspended fourth. If in doubt, do ask for clarification, though.

Figure 14-9 shows you some of these suspenseful chords.

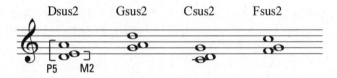

Figure 14-9: Suspended chords.

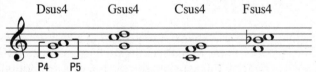

What's being suspended, exactly? The third. A suspended chord leaves you hanging, and its resolution comes when the second or fourth resolves to the third. This doesn't mean that all sus chords have to resolve to major or minor triads; actually, they sound pretty cool on their own.

Fingering suspended chords is pretty easy. For the right hand, use fingers 1, 2, and 5 for sus2 chords; use fingers 1, 4, and 5 for sus4 chords. For the left hand, use fingers 5, 4, and 1 for sus2 chords; use fingers 5, 2, and 1 for sus4 chords.

Play along with Figure 14-10, and listen to how the chord that follows each sus chord sounds resolved.

Figure 14-10:
A little
suspension
tension.

Visit www.dummies.com/go/piano to watch the grab bag of three-note chords demonstrated in Video Clip 16.

Adding the Seventh

Adding a fourth note to a triad fills out the sound of a chord. Composers often use chords of four notes or more to create musical tension through an unresolved sound. Hearing this tension, the ear begs for resolution, usually found in a major or minor chord that follows. At the very least, these tension-filled chords make you want to keep listening, and to a composer, that's always a good thing.

The most common four-note chord is the *seventh chord,* which you build by adding a minor seventh above the root note of a triad. Played on the piano by itself, the minor seventh may not sound very pretty, but it sounds good when you add it to a triad. In fact, the result is one of the most common sounds in Western music. You'll be amazed at how many great songs use seventh chords.

Each of the four types of three-note chords introduced earlier in this chapter — major, minor, augmented, and diminished — can become a seventh chord. Simply adding a seventh interval (the seventh note of the scale) on top of any of these triads makes that chord a seventh chord.

The basic seventh chord uses the *minor seventh* interval, which is the seventh note up the scale from the chord's root but lowered one half-step. For example, if the root note is C, the seventh note up the scale is B. Lower this note by one half-step and you get a minor seventh above the C, B-flat.

The four-note chords shown in Figure 14-11 are all seventh chords. The chord symbol is simple and easy: It's an Arabic numeral 7 placed after the triad symbol.

Figure 14-11: There's nothing plain about these seventh chords.

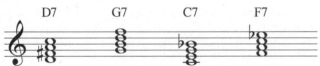

The suffixes used by seventh chords are placed *after* the triad type's suffix. For example, if you add a minor seventh to a minor triad, the suffix *7* comes after *m,* giving you *m7* as the full chord type suffix for a minor seventh chord.

To play seventh chords, use fingers 1, 2, 3, and 5 in the right hand. You may want to use RH 4 instead of RH 3 for certain chords, when the chord shape feels natural with RH 4. With the left hand, play the root note with LH 5 and the top note with LH 1.

To play Brahms's "Lullaby," featuring seventh chords in the left hand, skip to "Playing Songs with Chords" at the end of the chapter.

Watch Video Clip 17 at www.dummies.com/go/piano for a performance of this piece, along with a little demonstration of seventh chords.

Reading Chord Symbols

When you encounter sheet music or songbooks containing just melodies and lyrics, you usually also get the little letters and symbols called *chord symbols* above the staff, as shown in many of the figures in this chapter. Knowing how to build chords from chord symbols is an extremely valuable skill. It equips you to make a G diminished chord, for example, when you see the chord symbol for one, *Gdim*.

A chord's symbol tells you two things about that chord: *root* and *type*.

- ✔ **Root:** The capital letter on the left tells you the chord root. As with scales, the root note gives the chord its name. For example, the root of a C chord is the note C.

- ✔ **Type:** Any letter and/or number suffix following the chord root tells you the chord type. Earlier in this chapter, I explain suffixes like *m* for minor and *7* for seventh chords. Major chords have no suffix, just the letter name, so a capital letter by itself tells you to play a major triad.

Music written with chord symbols is your set of blueprints for what type of chord to construct to accompany the melody. For any chord types you may come across in your musical life (and there are plenty of chords out there), you build the chord by placing the appropriate intervals or scale notes on top of the root note. For example, *C6* means play a C major chord and add the major sixth (A); *Cm6* means to play a C minor chord and add the major sixth.

Figure 14-12 shows the tune "Bingo" with its chord symbols written above it in the treble staff. The notes in the bass staff match the chord symbols and show you one way to play a simple chord accompaniment in your left hand.

Track 55

Figure 14-12: Transforming chord symbols into notes on the staff.

Play the chord with the melody note that's directly below the chord symbol. The chord lasts until you see a chord change at the next chord symbol. So if you see a C chord at the beginning of measure 1, like in "Bingo," play it on beat 1. If there isn't a chord change, like on measure 5, you can play the C chord again, or not — your choice.

To play a song with chord symbols right now, skip to the section "Playing Songs with Chords" at the end of the chapter and work through "Scarborough Fair."

You may encounter many curious-looking chord symbols in the songs you play. Table 14-1 lists the most common and user-friendly chord symbols, the variety of ways they may be written, the chord type, and a recipe for building the chord. *Note:* The examples in the table all use C as the root, but you can apply these recipes to any root note and make the chord you want.

Table 14-1   Recipes for Constructing Chords

Chord Symbol	Chord Type	Scale Note Recipe
C	Major	1-3-5
Cmin; Cm	Minor	1-♭3-5
Caug; C(♯5); C+	Augmented	1-3-♯5
Cdim; Cdim.; °	Diminished	1-♭3-♭5
Csus2	Suspended second	1-2-5
C(add2); C(add9)	Add second (or ninth)	1-2-3-5
Cm(add2); Cm(add9)	Minor, add second (or ninth)	1-2-♭3-5
Csus4	Suspended fourth	1-4-5
C(♭5)	Flat fifth	1-3-♭5
C6	Sixth	1-3-5-6
Cm6	Minor sixth	1-♭3-5-6
C7	Seventh	1-3-5-♭7
Cmaj7; CM7; C△7	Major seventh	1-3-5-7
Cmin7; Cm7; C-7	Minor seventh	1-♭3-5-♭7
Cdim.7; Cdim7	Diminished seventh	1-♭3-♭7
C7sus4	Seventh, suspended fourth	1-4-5-♭7
Cm(maj7)	Minor, major seventh	1-♭3-5-7
C7♯5; C7+	Seventh, sharp fifth	1-3-♯5-♭7
C7♭5; C7-5	Seventh, flat fifth	1-3-♭5-♭7
Cm7♭5; CØ7	Minor seventh, flat fifth	1-♭3-♭5-♭7
Cmaj7♭5	Major seventh, flat fifth	1-3-♭5-7

Figure 14-13 shows you exactly how to make a chord from a recipe in Table 14-1. The recipe of 1-3-#5-7 is applied to three different root notes — C, F, G — to illustrate how chord-building works with different root notes and thus different scale notes. By the way, the resulting chord is called a Cmaj7#5 because you add the seventh interval and sharp (raise one half-step) the fifth.

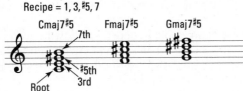

Figure 14-13: Building a chord from a chord symbol.

Playing with Chord Inversions

When you play a chord with the root on the bottom, or the lowest note, you're playing the chord in *root position*. But you don't always have to put the root on the bottom of the chord. Thanks to certain civil liberties and inalienable rights, you're free to rearrange the notes of a chord any way you like without damaging the chord's type. This rearrangement, or repositioning, of the notes in a chord is called a *chord inversion*.

How many inversions are possible for a chord? It depends on the number of notes the chord contains. In addition to the root position, you can make two inversions of a triad. If you have a four-note chord, you can make three inversions.

Putting inversions to work

Why would you want to rearrange a perfectly good chord? Play the left-hand chords in Figure 14-14, and notice how much your left hand moves around the keyboard.

Figure 14-14: Traveling back to your roots.

Constantly jumping around to all the chords in Figure 14-14 can become tiring, and it doesn't sound very smooth, either. The solution is to use inversions. Play Figure 14-15, and notice the improvement. You play the same chords as in the previous exercise, but you don't move your left hand up and down the keyboard.

Figure 14-15:
There's less effort in these chord inversions.

TIP

Making a song easier to play is just one reason you may choose to use chord inversions. They also help you with the following:

- ✔ **Drawing attention to the top note:** Most of the time, you hear the top note of a chord above the rest of the notes. You may want to bring out the melody by playing chords with melody notes on top.

- ✔ **Chord boredom:** Root position chords get boring if used too frequently, and inversions add some variety to a song.

- ✔ **Smoother chord progressions:** Each song has its own progression of chords. Inversions help you find a combination of chord positions that sound good to your ears.

Flipping the notes fantastic

Any triad has three possible chord positions: root position, first inversion, and second inversion. *Root position* is just like it sounds: The root goes on the bottom, as shown in Figure 14-16.

Figure 14-16:
Root position grabs chords by the roots.

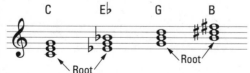

For the *first inversion,* you move the root from the bottom to the top, one octave higher than its original position. The chord's third moves to the bottom. See Figure 14-17 for examples of first inversions.

Figure 14-17: First inversions put the thirds on the bottom and the roots on top.

The *second inversion* puts the third on top (or one octave higher than its original position). The fifth of the chord is on the bottom, and the root is the middle note of the chord. Figure 14-18 shows you some second-inversion chords.

Figure 14-18: Second inversions put the roots in the middle.

Use the exact same process to invert four-note chords. The only difference is that another inversion is possible when you have four notes: the *third inversion.* It's easy enough to guess what you do: Keep inverting the chord until its seventh, or fourth note, is on the bottom, and the three notes that were previously below are up above. Figure 14-19 illustrates this process with G7 and C7.

Figure 14-19: Seventh chords and their third inversions.

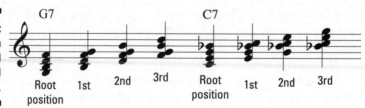

Experiment with these inversions on various types of chords so that when you're playing from a fake book, you know which inversions of which chords work best for you. (Chapter 19 explains what fake books are.)

To play a song with chord inversions, play "Red River Valley" in the next section.

Playing Songs with Chords

The songs in this section give you some experience adding chords to familiar songs. As you play the selections, try to identify the chords in the left hand and match them to the chord symbols written above the treble staff. First locate the chord root, then the third, fifth, and seventh (if included). If you notice any chord inversions, see how they affect the chord progression and melody.

- ✔ **"Down by the Station":** This song lets you play a few chords of the major type with your left hand.

  If you play along with Audio Track 56 at www.dummies.com/go/piano, you'll hear both the chords and the melody. You can play the left-hand part by itself until you get comfortable with the shape of the chords in your hand. Then add the melody.

- ✔ **"Sometimes I Feel Like a Motherless Child":** This spiritual gives you practice playing minor chords and a couple of major chords, too. It also has some chord inversions, so if you need to brush up on inversions, review the previous section.

- ✔ **"Lullaby":** You find all kinds of seventh chords in all kinds of music, from classical to pop. Johannes Brahms's famous "Lullaby" is an example of how seventh chords can create a little harmonic variety. Just don't let it lull you to sleep.

- ✔ **"Scarborough Fair":** This song is in a minor key — D minor. (To find out more about major and minor keys, see Chapter 13.) It gives you a chance to play chords in your left hand based on the chord symbols. If you have trouble building the chords, review the sections on major and minor chords earlier in this chapter. The bass clef staff is left open for you to write in the notes of each chord.

- ✔ **"Red River Valley":** This song calls for lots of chord inversions. It has triads and seventh chords along with first, second, and third inversions and a few garden-variety root position chords. Notice how the left hand plays half-note chords, with a few quarter-note changes in important places. You have the opportunity to change the inversion of a chord when the chord symbols are infrequent, like in this folk song.

Track 56

Down by the Station

Moderately

Track 57

Sometimes 1 Feel Like a Motherless Child

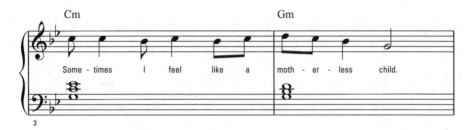

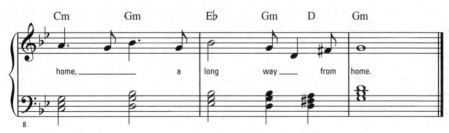

Track 58

Brahms

Lullaby

Moderately slow

Track 59

Scarborough Fair

Track 60

Red River Valley

Part V
Technique Counts for Everything

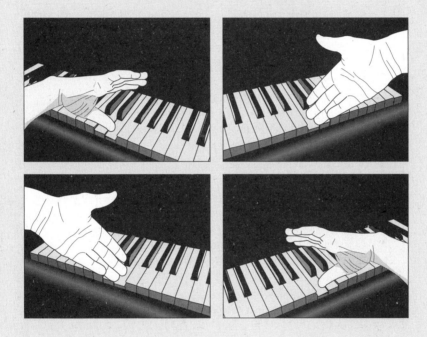

Look at www.dummies.com/extras/piano for additional tidbits and helpful advice for playing your piano.

In this part . . .

- ✔ Dress up your music with dynamics and articulations — staccatos, accents, and more. Find out how to use the pedals judiciously and add musical ornaments to your songs to make them sound fresh and lively.

- ✔ Work on great left-hand patterns, intros, finales, key changes, and bass lines — the same types of sounds heard on everything from classic country-and-western recordings to the great Motown songs.

- ✔ Get the scoop on different styles of music — everything from classical and country to jazz and rock. Uncover all about the blues, which is such an important part of virtually all popular styles.

- ✔ Discover new songs and patterns in a range of these styles. You'll become a musical chameleon in the process.

Chapter 15

Dressing Up Your Music

*P*laying the right notes and rhythms of a song is important, but how you play is even more important. Feeling, technique, and passion all make a performance worth listening to. Dressing up the music and making it your own takes more than just playing the notes. And throwing in a few special effects doesn't hurt, either.

Dazzling effects and techniques in your music keep the audience listening, sometimes even on the edges of their seats. With a little practice, all the effects that I discuss in this chapter are easy. And when you add them to the right spots in the music, your playing comes alive and you sound like a real pro.

Playing Dynamically

How loud you should play depends 5 percent on what the composer wants and 95 percent on how close your neighbors live. The composer usually requests that certain notes be played at certain volumes. Your neighbor demands that all notes be played in a soundproof box. These varying degrees of volume give the music a different dynamic. And that's exactly what volume levels are called in music: *dynamics*.

As with TVs, car stereos, and crying babies, the world of volume has a wide range: from very soft to very loud. Composers are quick to realize this and tell performers exactly where to play in the volume spectrum. Of course, to make things a bit fancier, all dynamics in music are usually indicated by Italian words.

Starting with basic volume changes

When you talk about volume, you say something is loud or soft. This kind of description is always a good starting point. From there you can explain *how* loud or *how* soft. Music uses the same principle: You start with two little Italian words, *piano* (soft) and *forte* (loud), to describe the volume of notes.

In Chapter 2, you find out that your instrument, formally known as the *piano-forte,* derives its name from the ability to play soft and loud. Why the name has been shortened to "soft" probably has something to do with cranky landlords.

By writing *piano* or *forte* under a melody line, a composer tells you to play certain notes soft or loud. Many years and inkwells later, abbreviations for these words are now the norm. You see soft and loud marked simply as *p* and *f,* written in fancy, stylized fonts.

When you see a dynamic marking, whatever the requested volume may be, you continue to play at this volume level until you see a new dynamic marking.

Try basic dynamics out with a tune. Figure 15-1 has two phrases from "Hickory Dickory Dock" marked *piano* and *forte.* Bring out the dynamic contrast as you play it.

Figure 15-1:
Dynamic
contrasts of
piano and
forte.

Widening the range

If soft and loud were the only volume levels available, home stereos would have just two volume buttons, not a turning knob. But, as you know, anywhere you turn the volume knob gives you a variety of volume levels: "kind of soft," "not very loud," you name it. Rather than keep track of some more highly descriptive but multi-syllable Italian words, you need remember only one abbreviation for the in-between volumes: *m,* which stands for *mezzo* (medium). Place this word before *piano* or *forte,* and you get two more shades of volume.

For extreme volumes like "very soft" and "insanely loud," just throw a few more *p*'s or *f*'s together. The more you have, the more you play. That is, *pp* means "very soft" (no jokes, please). The written word isn't *piano-piano*, however. Instead, you use the Italian suffix *-issimo,* loosely translated as "very," and you end up with *pianissimo.* The symbol *ff* would be "very loud," or *fortissimo.*

Gather all of these words, abbreviations, and suffixes together and you get the list of dynamic ranges shown in Table 15-1.

Table 15-1	Dynamic Markings	
Abbreviation	*Name*	*How the Note Sounds*
ppp	Pianississimo	Almost inaudible
pp	Pianissimo	Very quiet
p	Piano	Soft
mp	Mezzo piano	Not too soft
mf	Mezzo forte	Kinda loud
f	Forte	Loud
ff	Fortissimo	Very loud
fff	Fortississimo	Ridiculously loud

Making gradual shifts in volume

Two dynamic symbols that you encounter quite often are those that tell you to gradually play louder or gradually play softer. These symbols look kind of like bird beaks. A bird gets louder as it opens its beak and softer as it closes its beak. So, with this marvelous Audubon analogy, check out Figure 15-2 and see if you can tell what the chicken scratches mean.

To gradually play louder is a *crescendo;* to gradually play softer is a *decrescendo* or *diminuendo.* Composers opposed to using the bird beak symbols in their music write out these long Italian words or use the abbreviations *decres.* and *dim.*

Figure 15-2:
Indications
of gradual
volume
changes.

Whether they appear as words, abbreviations, or symbols, these instructions are almost always preceded and followed by dynamic markings that tell you to play from volume A gradually to volume B. Maybe the composer wants you to gradually go from very soft *(pp)* to very loud *(ff)*, or perhaps the music indicates a subtle change from mezzo piano *(mp)* to mezzo forte *(mf)*. Whatever the case, it's up to you to decide exactly how to play these volume changes.

Sometimes the composer asks you to increase and then decrease the volume for sort of an up-and-down effect. Many musicians call this dynamic marking, shown in Figure 15-3, a *hairpin* because of how it looks.

Figure 15-3:
Get loud,
get soft, get
dynamic.

To play more dynamics right now, skip to the "Dressing Up Your Songs" section at the end of the chapter and play "Polovtsian Dance."

If you want a dynamics demonstration, head to www.dummies.com/go/piano and watch Video Clip 18.

Why even bother with volume changes? Why not just play everything really loudly so everyone can hear? This approach works fairly well for some heavy metal guitar anthems, but with piano music the subtle degrees of volume show off your ability to convey emotion in your playing. Sure, you may not make anyone cry with a crescendo, but at least your efforts enhance the mood.

Articulating the Positive

Don't feel reprimanded when I tell you to articulate when you play. I'm simply referring to the way you play each note. The various ways to play a note are called *articulations* and are often referred to as *attacks*. But because I'm a lover and not a fighter, you can go with the former term, because it's less combative. These sections get you up to speed on articulations.

Interpreting articulation symbols

Articulations come in all shapes. Each one is represented by a symbol that tells you how to play the note: accented, long, short, and so on. You can change the entire sound and style of a song by changing even just a few articulations. Table 15-2 shows you the symbols that composers use to indicate the various articulations.

To add these articulations to music, the composer just places the appropriate symbol right underneath or right above the note.

Table 15-2		Musical Articulations
Symbol	**Name**	**How to Play the Note**
•	Staccato	Short
—	Tenuto	Long
>	Accent	Hard
∧	Accent (Housetop)	Harder
>•	Accent with staccato	Hard and short
≥	Accent with tenuto	Hard and long

In addition to the symbols in Table 15-2, which apply to only one note, composers use an articulation marking that applies to a group of notes. In music, a *slur* is a curved line over two or more notes of different pitches that indicates that the notes should be played *legato,* or connected in a smooth manner. Think of playing the notes within a slur as if someone with a beautiful voice is singing them.

Be careful not to mistake a *tie* for a *slur*. A slur is applied to notes of different pitch and often groups many notes in a melodic phrase. A tie is also a curved line, but it connects one note-head to another note-head of the same pitch. (See Chapter 8 for more on ties.) Slurs start and end near the note-head or the stem, as shown in Figure 15-4, a bit of "O Sole Mio."

Figure 15-4: Notes grouped by a slur (played smoothly) and notes tied (held for the combined value of both notes).

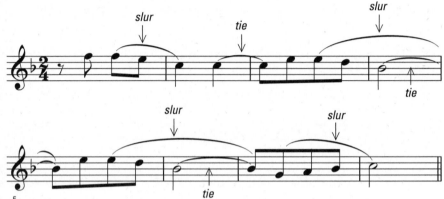

The power of articulation

If you play music without articulations, you can forget about pleasing your audience. Listening to music without articulations is like suffering through a speech given in a monotone voice. Boring.

To understand the importance of articulation, try playing a bit of the melody of "Camptown Races" using articulation markings (see Figure 15-5). Then play it again without the articulations — just ignore them. You should be able to tell that the tune has more verve and personality with articulations than without.

Figure 15-5: Giving a melody some individual character with articulations.

If a piece of music doesn't already have articulations, choose articulations that you think may fit the music and apply them. Pencil in your own articulations and see how the music sounds your way. It's not like you're changing the melody, just the style. Of course, following the composer's articulations (when they exist) is always your best bet for achieving the sound and style the composer intended — if that's your goal.

To play a complete version of "Camptown Races" with more articulations right now, skip to the section "Dressing Up Your Songs" at the end of the chapter.

You can see the power of articulations harnessed in Video Clip 19 at www. dummies.com/go/piano.

Controlling the Tempo

Just like you can shade your music with dynamics, you can make subtle variations to the tempo of the music you play. Chapter 7 tells you that the tempo marking at the beginning of a song tells you how fast to play the song. As a rule of thumb, your goal should always be to keep steady time without unintentionally slowing down or speeding up. (Chapter 7 also tells you about metronomes and how they can help you keep a steady beat.) But there are times when you *do* intend to slow down or speed up. Time in music is flexible in this way: You can change tempo very slightly or quite dramatically when the music calls for it.

Not surprisingly, musical words and symbols exist to tell you what to do and how much to do it. And just like the dynamic markings, the words are usually in Italian. The three most important indications you need to know are:

- ✔ **Accelerando:** When the composer wants you to pick up some speed, you'll see this word or its abbreviation, *accel.* It means accelerate!

- ✔ **Ritardando:** When the composer wants you to slow down, you'll see this word or its abbreviation, *rit.*

- ✔ **Fermata:** The symbol ⌒ stands for *fermata.* When you see it, pause or hold the note(s) under the fermata and stop counting time. There's no rule governing how long you should hold a fermata — the composer intentionally leaves this to the performer's discretion. A good starting point is to hold the note(s) under the fermata for twice as long as its written value.

Figure 15-6 shows the melody to "For He's a Jolly Good Fellow," which illustrates these tempo changes. In a typically playful rendition of the song, you naturally slow down and hold the highest note, and maybe speed up for the final phrase.

Figure 15-6:
Playing
around with
tempo.

Putting the Pedal to the Metal

In Chapter 5 I talk about the number and kinds of pedals that come with acoustic and digital pianos. These sections tell you a bit more about how to use these pedals to assist the dynamics and articulations when you play, adding to the ways you can dress up your music.

Using the damper pedal

When piano players talk about using the pedal, they usually mean using the *damper pedal,* which is the one on the right as you sit at a piano. Because the damper pedal allows the notes to sustain after your fingers release the keys, it's often called the *sustain pedal.*

There are a few different ways to indicate when to put the pedal down, when to lift the pedal, and when to make a quick up-down pedal change. As Figure 15-7 shows, the abbreviation *Ped.* tells you when to put the pedal down. Keep the pedal down until the asterisk or the end bracket of the pedal line. A notch in the pedal line indicates a pedal change: Lift your foot enough to allow the pedal to clear, and then press the pedal down immediately again.

Figure 15-7:
Pedaling
indications.

The best way to learn how to pedal is to just try it out as you play. Although all damper pedals have the same function, each instrument can have its own pedal personality, and just like you adjust to the accelerator and brake system of a car, you have to try out a damper pedal to get a good feel for it.

The most important thing about pedaling is simply not to overuse it. Things can get blurry in a hurry, and for the listener, a song with too much pedal can become the aural equivalent of runny makeup. Listen carefully to the music as you play to hear it as others hear it.

At its most basic function, the damper pedal connects one melody note or chord to the next where there would be a break in the sound without using the pedal. Play Figure 15-8, and use the pedal to connect the first note of the melody to the second, and so on. Then play the excerpt again without the pedal. You'll hear that the two-note phrases don't sound nearly as smooth as the first version because you have to lift your hands to move to the next note, resulting in breaks between the notes within a slur.

Use the pedal to help your music sound more smooth *(legato)*, hold a note or a chord for a long time, or give your music a more resonant quality.

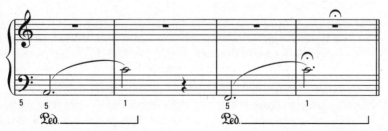

Figure 15-8:
Use the
damper
pedal to
connect
notes
melodically.

Getting the hard facts on soft-pedaling

When the composer wants you to use the soft pedal, which is on the far left as you sit at the piano, you see the indication *una corda.* (Chapter 5 explains how the *una corda* pedal works.) When you see the indication *tre corda,* you release the soft pedal.

You can use the soft pedal anytime you like, of course, to play quietly or to create a hushed atmosphere or an intimate feeling. Try it out on the lullaby "All Through the Night" in Figure 15-9.

Figure 15-9:
Create a
soft sound
with the soft
pedal.

Eyeing the middle pedal

Depending on the kind of piano you're playing, the middle pedal can have two different functions.

- ✔ **The sostenuto pedal:** The traditional grand piano has a pedal that acts like a damper pedal for only the note or notes your fingers are playing when you press the pedal down. For example, you play a big bass note, put the middle pedal down, and then noodle some staccato upper-register filigree, with the bass note sounding throughout thanks to the sostenuto pedal.

- ✔ **The practice pedal:** Many upright pianos have a practice pedal in between the soft pedal and the damper pedal. This pedal mutes the strings, allowing you to hear what you play but softening the sound quite a bit. The practice pedal has a notch at the opening where you can lock the pedal into position with your foot as you play with the muted setting.

Touching on Grace Notes

The term *grace note* sounds pretty fancy, but grace notes are actually a very simple effect that can make your music sound more complex. A grace note is a note that you play just slightly before a real note. In my opinion, it should be renamed a *graze* note because your finger just grazes the grace note before playing the real note.

Grace notes are written in a number of different ways. Figure 15-10 shows you the most common types of grace notes. A single grace note looks like a small eighth note with a slash through it. Think of the slash as meaning "cancel the rhythmic value." Multiple grace notes look like small sixteenth notes. You play them very quickly, too, so that it sounds like you're rolling into the main note.

Figure 15-10:
Amazing grace notes, how sweet the sound.

 You don't always have to play grace notes super-fast. The character and effect of a grace note are determined by the tempo and style of the music. The idea is to use a grace note to give its main note a little lift.

 To hear some grace notes in action, listen to Audio Track 61 at www.dummies. com/go/piano as you follow along with the music to the rousing classic "Pop! Goes the Weasel," which is just bursting with grace notes (see Figure 15-11).

Grace notes are a common feature of blues, jazz, country, and classical piano music styles, which you can read more about in Chapter 17. Heck, you can use grace notes anywhere you like. The best grace notes are those that are a half-step or a whole-step away from the full melodic note, but feel free to try ones that are even farther apart. Beginning a song's melody with a grace note is an excellent idea, especially if the song is in the jazz or blues style.

 If you're still not sure how to play a grace note, be sure to watch Video Clip 20 at www.dummies.com/go/piano.

Figure 15-11:
This weasel
pops with
the help of
some grace
notes.

Tackling Trilling

If you've ever heard the sound of a piccolo twittering high above the band in a John Phillip Sousa march, you've heard the effect of a trill. What sounds like a very elaborate trick for the piccolo player is actually a very simple procedure of alternating between two notes in rapid succession. The same holds true for trills in piano music.

What does a trill sound like? (You mean the piccolo metaphor isn't good enough for you?) A trill sounds like a bunch of 32nd or 64th notes, as shown in Figure 15-12. (For more on 32nd and 64th notes, flip to Chapter 7.) Trills add a certain classical finesse to your playing style. (Chapter 17 tells you all about the classical style of music.)

Figure 15-12:
What a trill
sounds like.

To save the time and ink required to write all those darn beams, composers use a shorthand symbol for trills: They write a *tr* above the trilled note. You know, "tr" as in the first two letters of the word "trill." Sometimes, music isn't so complicated.

Generally speaking, a note is trilled upward to the note a whole-step above the main note. However, sometimes a composer wants a downward trill or even a half-step trill, and he or she writes the specific note to be used in the trill in one of several ways (see Figure 15-13).

Figure 15-13: Simon says, "Trill this note."

(Trill C to D)   (Trill C to C#)   (Trill C to B)   (Trill C to D)   (Trill C to B♭)

In addition to the *tr* abbreviation, the composer can write a sharp or flat sign, which tells you to trill to the note's sharp or to the note's flat. Another way of notating the trill is to write the specific trilled note as a small, stemless note-head in parentheses next to the original note.

To play some trills yourself, skip to the section "Dressing Up Your Songs" at the end of this chapter and play "Trumpet Voluntary."

Check out www.dummies.com/go/piano to watch some trills in Video Clip 21.

Don't wait for the composer to give you permission to trill — add 'em yourself. Find a note that you think would sound good played as a trill and write *tr* above it. Half notes and whole notes are usually the best note lengths to trill because they're long enough to allow you time to get those fingers fluttering. Experiment with half-step and whole-step trills in different directions.

Dazzling Your Audience: Gliss

A *glissando* (also known as a *gliss*) is a fast slide across several keys on the keyboard. There's nothing quite like starting and ending a song with this effect.

To try a right-hand gliss, put your thumb on a high C note and drag your thumb nail down across the keys very quickly all the way to the bottom of the keyboard. Cool, huh?

Figure 15-14 shows you how composers notate this effect, which is generally with a wavy line and the abbreviation *gliss* going from the starting note in the direction of the gliss. For example, if you see a wavy line going up from C, play the note C and slide up the keyboard. Sometimes the specific ending note is shown at the other end of the wavy line; other times, it's up to you to decide where to stop.

Figure 15-14:
Gliss me, gliss me, now you gotta kiss me.

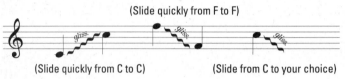

(Slide quickly from F to F)

(Slide quickly from C to C) (Slide from C to your choice)

When the composer specifies both the beginning *and* ending notes of the gliss, all I can advise is to practice, practice, practice. Starting on a specific note is easy, but stopping on the right note is like trying to stop a car on a dime. Sometimes you can use your other hand to play the final note if it's not busy playing something else.

Depending on the direction of the gliss and the hand you use, different fingers do the job. Figure 15-15 shows you the correct hand positions for each glissando:

- ✔ **Downward with right hand:** Gliss with the nail of your thumb (RH 1), as shown in Figure 15-15a.

- ✔ **Upward with right hand:** Gliss with the nail of your middle finger (RH 3) and perhaps a little help from RH 4, as shown in Figure 15-15b.

- ✔ **Downward with left hand:** Gliss with the nail of your middle finger (LH 3) and perhaps a little help from LH 4, as shown in Figure 15-15c.

- ✔ **Upward with left hand:** Gliss with the nail of your thumb (LH 1), as shown in Figure 15-15d.

After raking your fingers across the keys several times, you may begin to curse when your fingers start hurting. In that event, you're using the wrong part of your finger to gliss; when done properly, a glissando shouldn't hurt. Make sure you're using your *fingernail,* and above all, don't play a gliss with your fingertips. Not only can this cause a blister (ouch!), but the squeaking sound is worse than nails on a chalkboard!

Try playing a downward and an upward gliss in Figure 15-16, a Jerry Lee Lewis–inspired number.

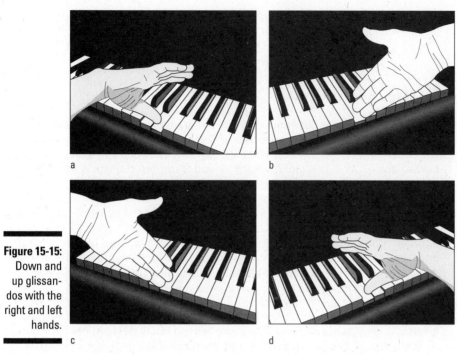

Figure 15-15:
Down and
up glissan-
dos with the
right and left
hands.

Figure 15-16:
Use an RH
gliss to
begin and
end a song.

The effect of a glissando is altogether powerful, energetic, and just plain rock-ing, as you can also see in Video Clip 22 at www.dummies.com/go/piano.

Trembling Tremolos

As I explain earlier in the chapter, a trill occurs when you flutter your fingers very quickly between two notes that are close together, either a half-step or whole-step apart. So, what do you call fluttering between two notes that are farther apart? Well, you call it whatever you want, but the world of music calls it a *tremolo*.

To play a tremolo, pick an interval — anything larger than a whole-step — and alternate playing the two notes as quickly as possible. (Chapter 12 covers intervals.) Like a trill, a tremolo sounds as if you're playing a bunch of 32nd or 64th notes. But unlike the notation for a trill, which just puts *tr* above one note, the notation for a tremolo actually shows you both notes that your fingers rumble between.

In Figure 15-17, you see that the two notes of a tremolo have the same note length. At first glance, it looks like there are too many beats in each measure of this notation, but the three diagonal lines between the notes signal that this is a tremolo and therefore the two notes share the note length. You only count the beats of the first note.

Figure 15-17:
Tremolo
notation.

You can also play tremolo chords. All you do is break the chord into two parts: a bottom note and the remaining top notes. Shake the chord into a tremolo by alternating between the two parts as quickly as possible. Tremolo chords may look intimidating, but if you can play the chord, you can play the tremolo. (Chapter 14 acquaints you with chords.)

Figure 15-18 gives you a chance to play a few tremolo chords. For the first measure, put your hand in position for a G major chord and rock between the top notes (B and D) and the bottom note (G) very quickly. Move to the next measure and do the same with a second inversion C chord, and so on.

Figure 15-18:
Tremolo
chords.

Go to www.dummies.com/go/piano and watch Video Clip 23 to solidify your
understanding of the tremolo.

Working under the hood

In the 20th century, many composers and pianists became bored with the normal sounds of a piano. No longer satisfied by the effects of trills, glissandi, and tremolos, these brave pioneers started tinkering around under the piano lid.

Try it yourself. Open your piano lid and pluck the strings with your fingernail. Now try a gliss across all the strings while holding down the sustain pedal. The sound is mysterious and a bit creepy.

Composers like Henry Cowell and John Cage didn't stop there. They began writing pieces that incorporated these sounds, asking the player to pluck certain notes on the inside of the piano. And you think playing the black and white keys is hard! Pushing the limits even further, a phenomenon called *prepared piano* became quite popular (and still is) with modern composers. A myriad of new sounds were created by inserting various objects between the piano strings — screws, yarn, pillows, and so on.

I don't advise trying prepared piano at home because hardware between the strings can damage your expensive piano. If you really want to experience these sounds the right way, check out the following recordings:

✔ *The Banshee,* **Henry Cowell:** Among other things, you hear strumming or plucking of the piano strings.

✔ *Airplane Sonata,* **George Antheil:** A number of strange piano effects are evident in this eclectic piece.

✔ *Tabula rasa,* **Arvo Pärt:** The piano part is prepared with screws between the strings.

✔ *The Firm Soundtrack,* **Dave Grusin:** This piece uses all types of things on the piano, including a violin bow playing across the strings.

Tremolo chords come in handy when playing rock 'n' roll, especially as part of a band. A tremolo turns the otherwise dull task of playing straight chords into a sizzling rhythmic romp.

To play a song with tremolos right now, skip to the next section and play "Also Sprach Zarathustra."

Dressing Up Your Songs

This section lets you cut loose with the dynamics, articulations, ornamentations, and other fancy techniques that let you dress up your music. For each song, I note a few tips and the techniques they use. Let 'er rip!

- ✔ **"Polovtsian Dance":** This haunting melody by Alexander Borodin is perfect for adding some dynamic shading. Follow the volume indications and hairpins, and get as much as you can out of the *pianos* and *fortes*.

- ✔ **"Camptown Races":** Go hog-wild with the articulation markings on this song. Define each and every staccato, tenuto, and accent to give the song a strong shape.

- ✔ **"Trumpet Voluntary":** Each trill starts on the note D, played with RH 2, and trills upward to E (the next highest scale tone), played with RH 3. Alternate very rapidly between these two notes while counting the number of beats required for the trill, a dotted quarter note. The squiggly line following the *tr* tells you how long to keep trillin'.

  Listen to Jeremiah Clarke's famous "Trumpet Voluntary" at www.dummies. com/go/piano on Audio Track 64 to get an idea of how it should sound. Then try it yourself.

- ✔ **"Also Sprach Zarathustra":** Tremolos of any size sound great played by either hand. Probably the most popular left-hand tremolo is the octave tremolo. Stretch your hand over a C octave and let this interval rumble in a familiar melody. You may recognize this piece as the theme to the movie *2001: A Space Odyssey*.

- ✔ **"Quiet Sunset":** Follow the damper pedal indications when you play this piece to create smooth connections between melody notes and between successive chords. Practice pedaling from one note to the next during the melodic phrases and from one chord to the next during the chordal phrases, and listen for smooth, unbroken lines.

Track 62

Polovtsian Dance (Stranger in Paradise)

Moderately

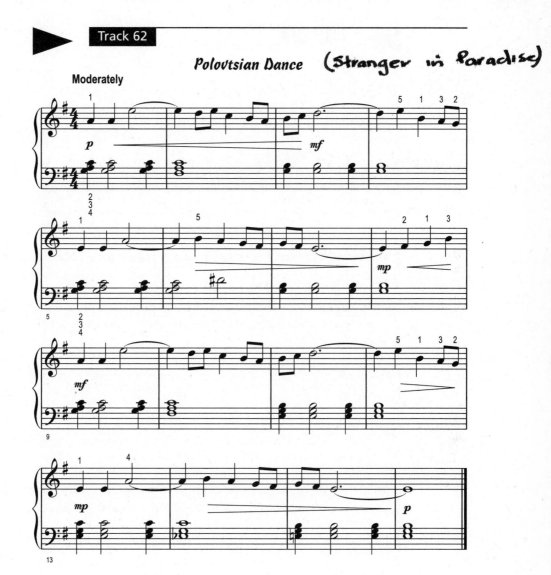

Track 63

Camptown Races

Moderately fast

Track 64

Trumpet Voluntary

Moderately

Track 65

Also Sprach Zarathustra

Moderately slow

Track 66

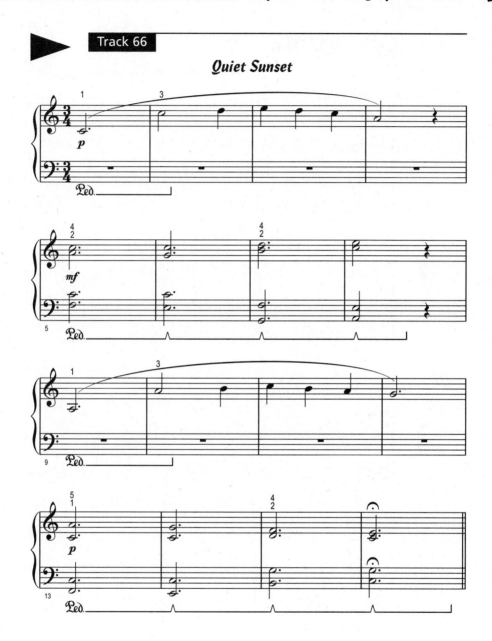

Quiet Sunset

Chapter 16

Great Grooves

In This Chapter

▶ Mastering accompaniment patterns for your left hand

▶ Finding new ways to begin and end a masterpiece

*W*ant to make even a simple song like "Row, Row, Row Your Boat" into a showstopper? This is the chapter for you. I help you apply a handful of tricks and techniques to just about any song you encounter in your piano career. Whether it's an attention-grabbing intro or finale, a cool accompaniment pattern, or just a nice little riff thrown in, the tricks in this chapter help you to spice up your music.

If after you read this chapter you feel like you need even more playing tools and tips, Chapter 17 tells you how to play songs in different styles, including classical, rock, blues, and jazz.

Great Left-Hand Accompaniment Patterns

One of the most important tools for your bag of tricks is a good supply of left-hand accompaniment patterns. Any time you're faced with playing straight chords or even playing melodies from a fake book, you're left to your own resources to supply an interesting-sounding bass line. (See Chapter 19 for more on fake books.)

Fret not — I'm here to help. This section gives you excellent and professional-sounding left-hand patterns that you can apply to just about any song you come across. Each of these patterns is versatile — applicable to both 3/4 and 4/4 meters — not to mention user-friendly.

Practicing these patterns again and again is important to master the right notes and the way each pattern feels under your fingers. After a while, though, you can ignore the printed music and just try to feel the pattern: the distance between the intervals, the shape of the chord, the rhythm, and so on. The more comfortable you are with the pattern, the more easily you can apply it to any key, any chord, and any scale.

Fixed and broken chords

A chord-based approach, whether played straight or with arpeggios, serves as an excellent introduction to left-hand accompaniment. (Turn to Chapter 14 for more on chords and arpeggios.)

Start with the basic chords and find inversions that work well for you without requiring your left hand to move all over the keyboard. (Chapter 14 tells you all about inversions.) Also experiment with various rhythmic patterns. For example, try playing quarter-note chords instead of whole-note chords. Or try a dotted quarter- and eighth-note pattern.

In Figure 16-1, the left hand plays a simple chord progression with several different rhythmic patterns. Run through these a few times and decide which rhythmic pattern works, sounds, and feels best to you.

Track 67

Figure 16-1:
Left-hand
chords
in varied
rhythm
patterns.

You can change the texture and add some variety with a constant arpeggiated pattern in the left hand. For every chord symbol in Figure 16-2, use the root, fifth, and octave notes of the chord's scale to form an up-and-down pattern throughout the song. This pattern works for fast or slow songs.

Track 68

Figure 16-2: Root-fifth-octave patterns are easy to play and sound great.

To play a song using the left-hand accompaniment in Figure 16-2 right now, skip to the end of the chapter and play "Love Me Like You Used To" in the section "Playing Songs with Left-Hand Grooves."

Chord picking

Left-hand *chord picking* is a style best suited to country music (which you can read more about in Chapter 17). But even if you aren't a fan of that genre, you can apply this pattern to just about any song you like.

Chapter 14 tells you that most chords are made up of a root, a third, and a fifth. You need to know these three elements to be a successful chord-picker.

To play this pattern, break a chord into two units: the root note and two top notes. Play the root note on beat 1 and the top two notes together on beat 2. To make it sound even more impressive, do something a little different on beat 3: Play the fifth of the chord by itself but one octave lower, as you see in Figure 16-3, which shows you four measures of this pattern with four different chords.

Figure 16-3:
Practice chord picking with four different chords.

Now try playing this pattern in the piece "Picking and Grinning" (see Figure 16-4). After you get the feel of this bouncy rhythmic pattern, you won't even need to look at your hands. Your pinky will find the two alternating bass notes because they're always the same distance from the root note.

Track 69

Figure 16-4: Left-hand chord picking in "Picking and Grinning."

Octave hammering

This easy (if tiring) left-handed groove is really fun and easy if your right hand is just playing chords. But if you're playing a melody or something more complicated than chords with your right hand, this pattern may not be a practical choice.

To hammer out some octaves, you simply prepare your left hand in an open *octave position,* with your pinky and thumb ready on the two notes, and make sure your wrist is loose enough to bounce a bit with the appropriate rhythm. When the chord changes, keep your hand in octave position as you move directly to the next set of octaves. You can play the octaves using any rhythm that sounds good to you — try whole notes, half notes, even eighth notes, depending on the rhythmic character of the song.

"Octaves in the Left" (see Figure 16-5) lets you roll out some octaves.

Track 70

Figure 16-5: Hammer out octaves in "Octaves in the Left."

As you become more familiar with harmony, you can add to these left-hand octave patterns with octaves built on the notes of the chord. For example, the octaves in "Jumping Octaves" (see Figure 16-6) move from the root note to the third interval note to the fifth interval note for each right-hand chord.

Track 71

Figure 16-6: Build octaves on different chord notes in "Jumping Octaves."

Bouncy rock patterns

In addition to slamming octaves, a nice rock 'n' roll-sounding bass pattern may use other intervals drawn from scale notes. (Chapter 12 explains intervals in great detail.)

You can create a great bass pattern using the octave, fifth, and sixth of each chord. Try this high-energy accompaniment along with "Rockin' Intervals" (see Figure 16-7). You can modify the pattern to fit a two- or one-measure pattern in 4/4 meter. After a few times through, your hands will know what to do, and you can apply the pattern to any major chord.

The great Chuck Berry made the locomotive-sounding pattern demonstrated in "Berry-Style Blues" (see Figure 16-8) very popular on the guitar. It was only a matter of time before some trailblazing pianist adapted this guitar pattern to the piano. All you have to do is alternate between playing an open fifth and an open sixth on every beat.

Melodic bass lines

Some left-hand patterns are so widely used that they're better known than the melodies they accompany. "Bum-ba-di-da" (see Figure 16-9) is one such pattern that was made famous by Roy Rogers in his show-closing song "Happy Trails." All you need are three notes from each chord's scale: the root, fifth, and sixth. Play them back and forth, over and over.

To check out a good sampling of these great grooves, watch Video Clip 24 at `www.dummies.com/go/piano`.

To play a song with the bum-ba-di-da bass line right now, jump to the later section "Playing Songs with Left-Hand Grooves" and play "Country Riffin'."

Another melodic left-hand pattern played by every pianist from novice to pro is the "boogie-woogie" bass line. It doesn't even need a melody. This bass line uses notes from a major scale but lowers the seventh note of the scale a half-step (also called a *flatted seventh*) to give you that bluesy sound.

Track 72

Figure 16-7:
A driving
left-hand
pattern
with the
octave, fifth,
and sixth
intervals
in "Rockin'
Intervals."

Track 73

Figure 16-8:
Open
intervals
that chug
along in
"Berry-Style
Blues."

Track 74

Figure 16-9:
Mosey along with the bum-ba-di-da bass pattern.

For each new chord in the boogie-woogie bass line (see Figure 16-10), you play the following scale notes up the keys and then back down: root, third, fifth, sixth, flatted seventh.

Track 75

Figure 16-10:
A boogie-
woogie
pattern that
never goes
out of style.

Applying Great Intros and Finales

A good pianist should always be able to begin and end a piece in an interesting way. You can join the ranks by filing away some stock intros and finales
(sometimes called *outros*) you can apply to any piece of music at any given
time. An intro or finale is your time to shine, so milk it for all it's worth.

Few things are more fun than playing a great intro or finale. Heck, some of
them sound great alone, without a song attached.

Most of the intros and finales in this section are geared toward popular music. When it comes to classical music, the composer usually gives you an appropriate beginning and ending. Of course, if you really want to fire up Chopin's *Minute Waltz,* you can always add one of these intros.

You can add the intros and finales in this section to virtually any piece of music. Just follow these steps:

1. **Check the song's style.**

   Each intro and finale has a different style or sound. Consider the style of the song you're playing and choose an intro that works best with it. For example, a rock 'n' roll intro may not sound very good attached to a soft country ballad. But, then again, anything's possible in music. (Chapter 17 guides you through many musical styles.)

2. **Check the song's key.**

   All the intros and finales you find in this book are written in the key of C. If the song you want to play is also in the key of C, you're ready to go. If not, adjust the notes and chords of the intro and finale you choose to correspond with the song's key by using the helpful hints shown with each intro and finale.

3. **Check the song's first chord.**

   All the intros transition easily into the first chords or notes of a song, provided that the song begins with a chord built on the first tone of the scale. (Chapter 14 explains these types of chords.) For example, if the song you're playing is in the key of C and begins with a C major chord, any of the intros here work perfectly because they're written in the key of C. If your song starts with a different chord, use the hints provided with each intro to adjust the chord accordingly.

4. **Check the song's last chord.**

   Like intros, you can tack all these finales onto the end of a song if the song ends with a chord built on the first tone of the scale (and most songs do). For example, if the song you're playing is in the key of C and ends with a C major chord, you'll have no problem with one of these finales because they're written in the key of C. If your song ends with a different chord, you need to adjust the finale to the appropriate key.

Adjusting the intros and finales into different keys involves a lot of transposing work. If you're just starting out with the piano, only apply these intros and finales to songs in the key of C. (This book includes many such songs.) When you're ready to apply an intro or finale to a song of a different key, check out which note of the scale it starts on and try to match the interval patterns in the new key.

The big entrance

When a singer needs a good intro, you need to be able to bring it. The audience has a tendency to talk between songs, so it's your job to shut 'em up and announce the start of the new song. Playing a few bars of show-stopping, original material really gets things hopping and leaves them begging for more.

The "Get Ready, Here We Go" intro

The intro you see in Figure 16-11 is bound to grab the audience's attention. It has been used in just about every style of music, from vaudeville to ragtime to Broadway. Hear it once and you'll never forget it. Play it and you'll be hooked. Just keep repeating the measures between the repeat signs, or *vamp*, until you're ready to start the melody. (Chapter 6 talks about repeat signs and what they do.)

Track 76

(Vamp)

Figure 16-11: Intro #1.

The "Rockin' Jam" intro

You can knock some socks off with a rock 'n' roll intro like the one in Figure 16-12. The triplets are tricky, but you can play this one fast or slow. A slower-tempo version works well with a blues song, and a fast version is good for . . . well, a fast rockin' song. This intro also contains grace notes, which you can read about in Chapter 15.

The "Sweet Ballad" intro

When a slow ballad is next on the set list, the intro in Figure 16-13 works well. The left-hand part sets up a root-fifth-octave pattern introduced in the earlier section "Fixed and broken chords." The right-hand part makes use of parallel sixths, moving sweetly down the scale.

Track 77

Figure 16-12:
Intro #2.

Track 78

Figure 16-13:
Intro #3.

The "Killing Time" intro

Sometimes you need to repeat an intro over and over. Perhaps you've forgotten the melody. Perhaps you're waiting for divine inspiration. Or maybe you're waiting for the singer to decide to join you. Whatever the case, you can easily repeat an intro like the one in Figure 16-14 until the time comes to move on. Simply play the first four measures over and over until you're finally ready. You're simply vamping on a G7 chord, which leads you (and the preoccupied singer) into the key of C when you're both ready.

Track 79

Figure 16-14:
Intro #4.

The "Saloon Salutations" intro

When you're just tinkering around in a piano lounge, perhaps all you need is a few bars of honky-tonk style piano, like the ones in Figure 16-15. Notice how effective the grace notes (measure 1) and tremolos (measure 2) are in this intro. (Chapter 15 tells you more about grace notes and tremolos.)

Exit, stage left

The band is building up to the final chord, and it's time for the big finish. The singer belts the last lyric, and it's up to you to drop the curtain. Quick! Grab a handful of these finales and you're sure to receive an encore request.

The "I Loved You, You Left Me" finale

The finale shown in Figure 16-16 is a simple but effective ending, perhaps even a tear-jerker when played with the right emotion. You certainly wouldn't want to use this as an end to a rocking song like "Burning Down the House," but it fits nicely with any major-key ballad (like the one you introduced with Intro #3 in Figure 16-13).

Figure 16-15:
Intro #5.

Figure 16-16:
Finale #1.

The "Let's Load Up the Bus" finale

After a classic rock hand-jam, something like the finale in Figure 16-17 finishes the song with the appropriate amount of flair. The triplets take you down the C blues scale. They should be played as smoothly as possible, so feel free to slow down the tempo until you conquer the correct fingering. And make sure to really punch that last chord! (Chapter 8 gives you tips on playing the triplets you find in this finale, and Chapter 10 has more on blues scales.)

Track 82

Figure 16-17:
Finale #2.

The "Last Call" finale

The triplets in the finale of Figure 16-18 give this closer a distinctive feel that works best with a blues or jazz piece. It has the sound of winding down to a halt.

In this finale, you play the notes of chords C, C*dim.*, Dm7, and C again. You can easily transpose and attach this finale to a song in any key by applying the correct chord types and breaking them up. For example, in the key of G, the chords are G, G*dim.*, Am7, and G. (Chapter 14 explains how to build chords.)

Track 83

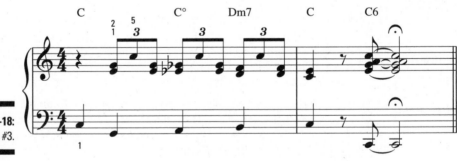

Figure 16-18:
Finale #3.

The "Shave and a Haircut" finale

Everyone knows it. Everyone loves it. I'm talking about the ever-famous "Shave and a Haircut" closer. Figure 16-19 shows you this all-time classic in all its glory. You can play this finale with unison octaves, so the name of each scale note is indicated in the middle of the grand staff. With this information, you can have a shave and a haircut in the key of your choice.

Track 84

Figure 16-19: Finale #4.

Playing Songs with Left-Hand Grooves

The songs in this section put together the techniques introduced in this chapter: left-hand accompaniment patterns and intros and finales. You can enjoy the songs on their own and also use them as examples of how to apply these tools to your own songs.

- ✔ **"Country Riffin'":** This little ditty is easy on the fingers but even easier on the ears. The bum-ba-di-da bass line sets the groove and the "Last Call" finale brings the song home. With a sauntering feel that will lighten the mood, it's sure to be a crowd-pleaser.

- ✔ **"Love Me Like You Used To":** This song combines a left-hand accompaniment pattern from earlier in this chapter with an intro and finale. The left-hand part sets the root-fifth-octave arpeggiated pattern to a slow-tempo groove that supports the entire song.

Track 85

Country Riffin'

Love Me Like You Used To

Moderately slow

Chapter 17

Perusing the Aisle of Style

Do an online search and you'll find countless recordings of the classic song "Stardust," each by a different artist — Willie Nelson, Hoagy Carmichael, Louis Armstrong, Bing Crosby, Rod Stewart, Melissa Manchester, John Coltrane — the list goes on and on. Each artist took the same song and recorded it in his or her own way, making it sound almost entirely different. This just goes to show you that there are literally hundreds of different ways to interpret a piece of music, each way offering its own sound and feel, which is known as style.

In this chapter, I introduce you to many different styles of piano and explain what each style has to offer. Then I show you how to apply each of those styles to a song. When you get the different styles under your skin, try applying them to your favorite tunes. Hey, maybe you can be the first artist to record "Stardust" on piano with a cha-cha/hip-hop groove.

Taking Aim at Classical Music

Some people think of *classical* music as old, intellectual, sometimes boring music written by a bunch of dead guys who wore wigs. This may be true (except for the "boring" part), but the sound and feel of classical music is unique. You, too, can apply the sound and feel of classical music to your songs, even ones written in this century.

Here's a list of the musical tools you need in order to add that classical sound to your music:

✔ Trills (see Chapter 15)

✔ Arpeggios (see Chapter 14)

✔ Scales (see Chapter 10)

✔ Octaves (see Chapter 12)

✔ A curly powdered wig (to look like Mozart)

Figure 17-1 is an excerpt from a classical piano piece by Mozart called *Sonata in C*. Notice the use of arpeggios in the left hand and the trills scattered throughout in the right hand. Then, after introducing the cute little melody, what does he give you? Scales!

Figure 17-1:
Excerpt from
Mozart's
Sonata in C.

Composers like Liszt and Grieg wrote some very dramatic and loud piano music. For example, the opening bars of Grieg's monumental *Piano Concerto* begin with loud, descending octaves, as shown in Figure 17-2. (This piece makes important use of dynamics, which you can read about in Chapter 15.)

(8va means to play these notes one octave higher than written)

Figure 17-2: Excerpt from Grieg's *Piano Concerto.*

But classical composers could also do soft and sweet, and one way they sweetened their sound was by rolling their chords. Liszt, for example, loved to end his odes with a beautiful, soft chord, rolled gently from the bottom note to the top. The squiggly line next to the chords in Figure 17-3 gets you ready to roll.

To play a piece with rolled chords by Liszt right now, skip to the end of the chapter and play "Album Leaf" in the section "Playing Songs in Favorite Styles."

Classical pianists to check out

Legends in the classical piano world: Vladimir Horowitz, Alicia de Larrocha, Artur Rubinstein

On today's classical piano playlist: Martha Argerich, Evgeny Kissin, Lang Lang

Figure 17-3:
Rolling to
a romantic
close.

"Rolled chord" squiggly lines   Played like this:

Playing the Blues

The *blues* is a style of music all its own. Heck, it even has its own scale (which
you can read about in Chapter 10). In this section, you don't apply the blues
style to an existing song, but rather create your own blues from scratch.
That's right: You get to be a composer.

Whether your dog left you or your boss has done you wrong, playing the blues
is as easy as counting to 12. These sections look at the wide array of blues.

Clues for the blues

Two important elements in the blues are form and rhythm. When you have
these down, add a few more essential elements, like grace notes or tremolos.
Then you can make any of your songs sing the blues.

To play the blues, you use the following elements:

- 12-bar form (see the next section "12-bar ditties")
- Swing or shuffle rhythm (see Chapter 8)
- Seventh chords (see Chapter 14)
- Tremolos (see Chapter 15)
- Sad story to tell (everybody's got one)

12-bar ditties

Most blues uses a widely recognized structure called the *12-bar form,* aptly named because each musical phrase of the song is 12 measures long. The 12-bar blues has a chord sequence that repeats over and over, usually with different lyrics and perhaps some melodic variation, until you genuinely feel sorry for the storyteller.

Melody notes, rhythms, and lyrics may differ from one 12-bar phrase to the next, but the chords usually stay the same. The chords most often used in the 12-bar form are all seventh chords; they are as follows:

- ✓ **The I7 chord:** Chord with the first scale note as its root note
- ✓ **The IV7 chord:** Chord with the fourth scale note as its root note
- ✓ **The V7 chord:** Chord with the fifth scale note as its root note

These three chords appear in the same order and for the same number of measures every time the 12-bar phrase is repeated. (Seventh chords are introduced in Chapter 14.)

To play your own 12-bar blues, just follow these easy instructions, playing with either hand or both hands. When you have the chord progression memorized, try playing the chords with the left hand while your right hand plays a simple melody, riff, or blues scale.

1. **Play a I7 chord for four measures.**
2. **Play a IV7 chord for two measures.**
3. **Play a I7 chord for two measures.**
4. **Play a V7 chord for one measure.**
5. **Play a IV7 chord for one measure.**
6. **Play a I7 chord for two measures.**
7. **Repeat Steps 1 through 6 until you have your audience singing with you.**

Figure 17-4 shows an example of 12-bar blues that uses chords only. They may be just chords, but you should still play them with conviction.

Track 87

Figure 17-4:
The 12-bar
blues.

Changing it up

All blues players realize that the same chords over and over can become repetitive (to both audience and musician), so they substitute other chords within the 12-bar form. For example, try a IV7 chord in measure 2 and play a V7 chord in measure 12 as a turnaround, as shown in Figure 17-5.

To play some mo' blues right now, head to the section "Playing Songs in Favorite Styles" at the end of the chapter and play — what else? — "Playin' the Blues."

Go to www.dummies.com/go/piano to watch this piece on Video Clip 25.

Figure 17-5: Chord substitutions for the blues.

Rockin' around the Keys

Hop in your time capsule and travel to a time when Elvis was still king, The Beatles didn't have solo careers, and avocado green was a popular appliance color. *Rock 'n' roll* burst onto the music scene in the 1950s and 1960s with a pair of swinging hips and masses of screaming groupies.

The big names in rock freely acknowledge their debt to the blues artists. Rock 'n' roll wouldn't be possible without the 12-bar blues, which provided the structural framework for many hit songs of the '50s, '60s, and beyond. The following sections bring you up to speed on what you need to know to play some rock 'n' roll.

Rocking ingredients

Pull out your bag o' tricks and find the following musical ingredients to make any song rock:

- ✔ Rockin' intervals (see Chapter 16)
- ✔ Glissandos (see Chapter 15)
- ✔ Chords (see Chapter 14)
- ✔ Lots and lots of pyrotechnics for your elaborate stage show (plus lights, makeup, big hair, a smoke machine — all the necessities)

Slamming and jamming

Jerry Lee Lewis practically invented the classic rock piano sound. For this style, all you need is an opening glissando, fast chords, and lots of energy.

Pour these elements into the 12-bar blues form and you're ready to roll. Figure 17-6 shows a rockin' bass line that follows a typical blues chord progression in the key of C. (See the earlier section "Playing the Blues" for more on blues chords.)

Track 88

Figure 17-6:
Lefty provides the rockin' bass line.

Solid rock pianists to check out

Legends of rock piano: Keith Emerson, Billy Joel, Elton John

On today's rock piano playlist: Bruce Hornsby, Tori Amos, Ben Folds

To play a fast-paced, chord-slamming rock 'n' roll song right now, hightail it to the "Playing Songs in Favorite Styles" section at the end of the chapter and play "Classic R&R."

Head to www.dummies.com/go/piano and watch Video Clip 26 that shows this song being played.

You're a Little Bit Country

Before there was rock 'n' roll, there was country. This style often sounds relaxed, lyrical, simple, and grassroots-ish, but it ain't afraid to rock, roll, and rumble. Artists like Keith Urban, Carrie Underwood, Shania Twain, and others put all kinds of musical influences in their country music, including elements of rock, blues, and even jazz. Influences aside, though, the folks in Nashville still call it country. Read these sections for the lowdown on country music.

Country-style cooking

To enhance your musical dish with the tastes of country on the piano, add some of these stylistic flavorings:

- Intervals (see Chapter 12)
- Grace notes (see Chapter 15)
- Tremolos (see Chapter 15)
- Bum-ba-di-da bass line (see Chapter 16)
- A ten-gallon hat, a pair of boots, and maybe even a nice and shiny belt buckle (purchased from a local Western store)

Finger-pickin' good

Figure 17-7 shows a nice, relaxed-sounding slice of the country music style. The right-hand intervals are unique in that the melody notes are actually on the bottom while the top notes stay the same. Grace notes and tremolos peppered throughout also give this example the feeling of an Old West saloon.

Figure 17-7: Good ol' country music.

To see and hear this song, head to www.dummies.com/go/piano and watch Video Clip 27.

The left-hand accompaniment pattern is challenging, so practice each hand separately until you can confidently put them together. After this inspiring tune, you may find yourself adding a saddlebag to your piano bench.

Country keyboarders to check out

Country piano legends: Ray Charles, Floyd Cramer, Jerry Lee Lewis

On today's country piano playlist: Jimmy Nichols, Michael Rojas, Catherine Styron Marx

---

Pop! Goes the Piano

Arguably, every song on the radio is a popular song because few radio stations play songs that listeners don't like. Country, rock, rap, Latin, and many other styles of music are popular with one audience or another. But most people know the term *pop* (short for "popular") to be the category for Top 40 songs and superstar ballads by such artists as Beyoncé, Justin Timberlake, Prince, and a multitude of others.

Pop music can be rhythmic, romantic, nostalgic, funky, sad, and about 1,000 other adjectives. In this section, you concentrate on the one style of pop music perfectly suited to the piano: the slow and smooth-sounding pop ballad. These sections give you everything you need to know about pop music.

Popular picks

To play a pop ballad, you need a small arsenal of musical ornamentations, including the following:

- Right-hand intervals (see Chapter 12)
- Chord arpeggios (see Chapter 14)
- Damper pedal (see Chapter 15)
- Dimmer switch (essential for setting the right mood)

Topping the charts

To add a little pop romance to any song, take a simple melody and add the ever-so-sweet sixth below each right-hand melodic note. (Chapter 12 sheds light on intervals.) The new melodic line should look like the one in Figure 17-8. For some reason unknown to many a trusted and frustrated musicologist, the sixth adds an element of romance to a melody.

Popular pop piano personalities to check out

Legends of pop piano: Billy Joel, Elton John, Laura Nyro

On today's pop piano playlist: Norah Jones, Regina Spektor, Lady Gaga, Sara Bareilles

Take a melody from this . . .

Figure 17-8:
Romancing
the sixth
tone.

. . . to this

This trick of adding the sixth may look difficult, but it's not. All you do is find the sixth below the first melody note and freeze your hand in that position. Your pinkie always plays the top note and your thumb always plays the bottom interval note. As you play up and down the melody, your hand lands on the correct interval every time.

For a demonstration of this nifty strategy, watch Video Clip 28 at www.dummies.com/go/piano.

Soul Searching

Talk about a broad category of music! *Soul* can encompass anything from *R&B* ("rhythm and blues") to *gospel, hip-hop,* and *rap.* Such soulful styles have been made popular by artists like Stevie Wonder, Aretha Franklin, and Otis Redding, and can feature a lot of wonderful piano playing. It's also great for dancing, although I don't recommend grooving too much while sitting at the piano. These sections give the lowdown on soul.

Saving your soul

Danceable soul music requires danceable rhythms, so have the following rhythmic concepts in your repertoire before strutting over to the keys:

- ✔ Syncopation (see Chapter 8)
- ✔ Right-hand intervals (see Chapter 12)
- ✔ Dotted eighth-sixteenth pattern (see Chapter 8)
- ✔ Disco ball (rent from your local party supply outlet)

Motown sounds

In the 1960s, Motown Records had a stable of artists specializing in the R&B sound. So popular were these artists that their style became known as the Motown sound. But don't think the 1960s are gone; you can add the Motown sound to any of your favorite songs.

Using a left-hand pattern with a syncopated rhythm, play Figure 17-9. Pretty soon you'll be hearing the Temptations doo-wopping right along with you.

Go to www.dummies.com/go/piano to watch this song in Video Clip 29.

Funky sounds goin' round

Soul and R&B styles often incorporate elements of *funk* — you know, like James Brown, Chaka Kahn, or George Clinton. Heavy syncopation with dotted eighth-sixteenth rhythmic patterns provides the funky feel for this funky sound. Play Figure 17-10 with a little attitude.

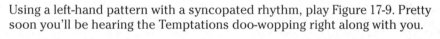

R&B ivory ticklers to check out

Soul legends at the piano: Herbie Hancock, Billy Preston, Stevie Wonder

On today's R&B piano playlist: Alicia Keys, John Legend, Brenda Russell

Track 89

Figure 17-9:
Motown
syncopation.

Figure 17-10:
Funky
patterns.

To play a song with funky rhythms and syncopation right now, groove on to the last section of this chapter and play "Motown Is My Town."

All That Jazz

If there's one particular music style that embraces all that the piano can do, it's *jazz*. Celebrated by many as America's greatest art form, jazz is king when it comes to interesting chord harmonies, changing rhythms, and improvisation. Legendary jazz pianists like Thelonious Monk, Bill Evans, Art Tatum, Bud Powell, and many others have taken these elements and added them to classic songs to make them jazzier. The following sections examine jazz music and explain what you need to know.

Jazzing it up

The great jazz pianists use tried-and-true musical tricks to freshen things up. Borrow these tricks yourself:

- Chord substitutions (see the section "Substituting chords" later in this chapter)
- Swing rhythm (see Chapter 8)
- Syncopation (see Chapter 8)
- Knowledge of scales (see Chapter 10)
- Knowledge of chords (see Chapter 14)
- Nickname like Duke, Bird, or Dizzy

It's up to you

It's time to be creative. Improvisation is perhaps the most important element of jazz music. It can be *literal improvisation,* where you (the performer) make up your own rhythms and riffs, or *implied improvisation,* where the music is originally written in a way that just sounds as if it were composed spontaneously.

The easiest way to improvise is by changing the rhythm of a melody. For example, take the simple quarter-note melody of "Yankee Doodle" and transform it into a swingin' jazz tune by adding swing eighth notes, syncopation, and a well-placed rest now and then to keep things cool (see Figure 17-11).

Track 90

Figure 17-11:
"Yankee Doodle" swings.

See a performance of this song and more on Video Clip 30 when you visit www. dummies.com/go/piano.

Great jazz players to check out

Jazz piano legends: Bill Evans, Thelonious Monk, Art Tatum

Jazz piano iconoclasts: Dave Brubeck, Chick Corea, Keith Jarrett

Jazz piano workhorses: Ahmad Jamal, Marian McPartland, John Lewis

On today's jazz piano playlist: Geri Allen, Brad Mehldau, Jason Moran

Substituting chords

Few jazz compositions use the standard major and minor chords throughout. In fact, few jazz pianists play the original chords written in a song. Instead, they break the rules and substitute new chords to liven up otherwise simple melodies.

Figure 17-12 is the well-known children's song "Merrily We Roll Along." As you play it, notice the simple chord progression of C-G7-C.

Figure 17-12: "Merrily" with standard chords.

Even "Merrily We Roll Along" can sound not-so-childish with the use of *chord substitution.* The idea is to find a more interesting chord progression from I to V7 to I. Try the following options:

- ✔ **Use major scale tones for chord roots.** Move up the scale from C to G7, building triads on each successive scale note, as in Figure 17-13.

- ✔ **Use black and white keys for new chord roots.** Move up in half-steps, building chords on each new root note, as in Figure 17-14.

- ✔ **Move up in fourths.** Start a chord pattern in measure 2 by playing an Em7, then move up a fourth and build a seventh chord on each new root note, as shown in Figure 17-15.

Figure 17-13: "Merrily" jazz variation #1.

Figure 17-14: "Merrily" jazz variation #2.

Figure 17-15: "Merrily" jazz variation #3.

To play a jazz-style tune with rhythm and chord substitutions right now, groove on to the next section and read through "Billy Boy Swings."

Playing Songs in Favorite Styles

Have some friends over one night and give them a concert they'll never forget. This section offers enough tunes to please any music lover, no matter his or her preferences. And who doesn't like piano music, as long as you're having fun?

Here are some tips for each song, with the stylistic characteristic each song features:

- ✔ **"Album Leaf":** Start out with a nice romantic piano piece to get the audience warmed up when you take the stage — or sneak in from the coat closet. This piece has a few gorgeous rolled chords; take your time rolling the chords, and use a little pedal to bring out the resonance of each one.

- ✔ **"Playin' the Blues":** This composition follows the 12-bar blues structure and features bluesy seventh chords and a two-note tremolo at the end. Take it slow, swing those eighths, and feel the steady rhythm as your left hand marks out the beats.

- ✔ **"Classic R&R":** Play this one with abandon and no one will believe that you haven't been playing the piano your whole life. There's a bass riff played by the left hand, and the hard-driving right-hand chords are equally important to the overall sound. This piece makes a great piano solo, but you can also play it with your guitarist friend who has just finished reading *Guitar For Dummies,* 2nd Edition, by Mark Phillips and Jon Chappell (Wiley).

- ✔ **"Motown Is My Town":** Time to get all funky with your bad self. Don't be surprised if your audience starts groovin' to your beat. This selection uses lots of syncopation; to brush up on your syncopated rhythms and articulations, check out Chapters 8 and 15.

- ✔ **"Billy Boy Swings":** This well-known tune gets a jazzy, rhythmic melody and chord substitutions that make you sound like a jazzer who's ready for more gigs. Make sure you keep counting, and give all the rhythms their crisply defined articulations.

Track 91

Album Leaf

Slowly

Track 92

Playin' the Blues

Track 93

Classic R&R

Track 94

Motown Is My Town

Moderately fast

Track 95

Billy Boy Swings

Part VI

The Part of Tens

the part of tens

For ten additional practice-session tips, go to www.dummies.com/extras/piano.

In this part . . .

- ✔ Make the most of your practice time so that you're primed for any performance, whether it's public or private.

- ✔ Explore the world of piano outside of this book by finding music in new places and sharing your music with others.

- ✔ Discover sources for sheet music, reference and method books, and other supplemental materials.

- ✔ Do your due diligence when looking for a piano teacher by asking key questions guaranteed to weed out the duds as the best instructors rise to the top.

Chapter 18

Ten Ways to Improve Your Practice and Performance

In This Chapter

▶ Making the most of your practice time

▶ Preparing for a good performance

*I*n this chapter, you discover how to maximize your practice time and make learning and growing more enjoyable. And if you get the itch to perform for your friends and loved ones or the world at large, check out the tips in this chapter on preparing for your time in the spotlight.

Go to www.dummies.com/extras/piano for ten additional tips to make practicing easier.

Be Comfortable at All Times

Before you start practicing, take a second to make sure everything feels good. Adjust your chair or bench so that you're comfortable and sitting at the right height. Make sure you have enough room to move your arms comfortably. See that you have adequate lighting and the music (or this book) in front of you is well-lit. If you're playing a digital keyboard, check that the volume is adjusted to approximate the volume level of an acoustic piano.

Reading music and concentrating on finger and hand movement can distract you from noticing the tension building in your body. Check in with yourself periodically as you practice. Anything sore or tight? Take breaks often; get up from the piano bench and stroll around. Do some stretches and give your body a break from piano posture.

Shut Off the Distractions

You live in the age of distraction, which means you're probably a multi-talented multitasker. But you do yourself a big favor by taking the time and space to concentrate on music and nothing else. You use your brain, eyes, ears, hands, and feet when you play the piano, and that's not even considering all the heart and soul that also go into it.

If the distractions come from elsewhere (as in housemates, neighbors, or flying insects), investigate ways to minimize these distractions. Maybe there's a certain time of day that you can set aside to practice when you're home alone and the neighbors are usually out of the house. Maybe there's a new bug spray on the market.

Make a Schedule and a List

When you've figured out the best time to practice, schedule it into your week so that time doesn't get eaten up by unforeseen chores and obligations. Be selfish: This is for you.

Make a list of what you're working on as far as your playing goes, and what you'd like to get done. Divide up your time so that you get to everything on the list, allowing some flexibility for a little give and take. You may be surprised at how much playing you can get done in a short period of time when you focus on the skills and pieces that need your attention.

Practicing the same thing over and over isn't always best. Practicing the same mistakes over and over only reinforces the mistakes in your mind and in your muscles. Practice different things, and move on when you get tired or start making careless mistakes. There's always tomorrow.

Get into Deconstruction

When you get to that point when it feels like you're not making any headway on a piece you've been practicing, take a minute just to look over the music. Identify the different sections of the piece; many sections are separated by double bar lines, repeats, and key changes. Find the repeated phrases, and think about how you may play them differently to give more personality to the song. Find the important changes in tempo or dynamics that you can highlight or reinforce.

Figuring out the form of a song can be fun! Label each section with a letter, number, or some other creative name, and behold the structure of the musical composition. Play the deconstructed song in your head and give your hands a break while you renew your desire to play.

Use a Metronome

This is a very simple tip that you'll get from any teacher because almost everyone has a tendency to either rush or slow the tempo when learning a piece with some difficult passages: Use a metronome to help you stay in tempo. Play along with the metronome, and locate phrases where the tempo goes astray when you play — that's where you need more practice.

Use the metronome creatively. Don't play *only* with it on. Use it at first to set a tempo that works for a whole piece or the section that you're working on. Adjust the speed to challenge your control. Play a song once with the metronome and once without. It's a great tool to have.

Rehearse Your Dress Rehearsals

Each time you plan to perform, set up a dress rehearsal — even for the most informal performances. Playing through your program lets you think through the process from beginning to end and discover things you never think about during regular practice time. As part of your rehearsal, consider what you're going to wear, keeping in mind the temperature, the venue, and your comfort. Make sure you have plenty of energy, and prepare some water if you think you'll need it. Practice your entrance and exit, and practice acknowledging the audience in an appropriate way.

Play through all your pieces in the order you plan to play them. You may find some transitions are harder or easier because of what comes before or goes after. Take plenty of time to regroup between pieces. And if possible, rope someone into listening to your rehearsal and providing feedback.

Know Your Performance Piano

If you're not going to perform on your own piano, find a way to play through your pieces on the performance piano. Different sounds, different key action, a different bench, and different surroundings can all be distracting when you're trying to concentrate.

If you're playing on a digital keyboard, do a sound check. Get all the necessary equipment set up; make sure cords, amplifiers, and speakers all work; and have someone sit where the audience will be sitting to make sure the volume is comfortable and the sound is clear. Get all the tech stuff done *before* your performance so you're confident your gear will perform as well as you do.

If You Memorize . . .

There's no need to memorize your music if you don't want to. Most listeners will be very impressed that you know how to read and play music. But if you do memorize your music, go ahead and test out the strength of your memory. Most performers will tell you that a memory slip is at the top on their lists of things they want to avoid. Play your memorized pieces for anyone who will listen, and play in different places and on different pianos. Play the music a bit slower and a bit faster than you plan to play in the performance. If you find some weak spots, give them a little extra attention before the big gig.

Preempt Post-Performance Syndrome

You deserve to feel proud and satisfied after you give a performance, so set yourself up for success. Get to know the range within which you'll perform (your best and your worst). Trust that your performance will be somewhere within this range, most likely toward the middle, and that makes it a successful performance. If you rehearse well, you'll avoid the worst-case scenario because you'll have improved some of the problem spots.

If you've had moments of practice when you think you really sound great, accept that you may not feel quite that good after a performance. Prepare for a realistic outcome so that you can feel proud and move forward with achieving the next level of play.

Smile and Take a Bow

Congratulations! You've accomplished something that most people only dream about and have given your audience the gift of music. Smile for yourself and smile for your audience. Take a bow, leap up in the air and punch the sky, introduce the rest of the band, throw your scarf out into the audience, or descend below the stage on a platform in a cloud of smoke. You're a piano star, after all.

Chapter 19

Ten Ways to Supplement This Book

Although this book certainly provides you with a basic understanding of how a piano works and how to start playing, it simply can't provide you with absolutely everything you need to know about the piano.

In your pursuit of eternal piano prowess, you may think, "What now?" This chapter gives you a few ideas of where to go from here — with one major exception. Hiring a piano teacher is such an important option that it merits its own section: Chapter 20.

Working through Method Books

If you're not ready to hire a piano teacher, an excellent resource for the beginning musician is a good *method book*.

A method book is an instructional book or series designed to teach you how to play a musical instrument in a strategic, proven, *methodical* manner. Countless volumes of these books exist, each featuring its own "method to the madness," whether old-fashioned or new-and-improved.

Like any series of how-to books, piano methods come in all shapes, sizes, and skill levels — from beginner to advanced. After reading *Piano For Dummies*, 3rd Edition, you should be ready for an intermediate-level method.

You can find rock methods, classical methods, jazz methods, country methods — the list is endless. Pick one that's right for you and, most important, one that looks fun and interesting.

Although no book can replace a live, human teacher, method books offer an inexpensive, viable option for continuing to master the piano. To get you started, the following method and exercise books are worth checking out:

- *FastTrack Keyboard Songbook 1 and 2,* by Blake Neely and Gary Meisner (Hal Leonard)

- *Francis Clark Library for Piano Students,* by Francis Clark (Warner Bros.)

- *Hal Leonard Student Piano Library,* by Barbara Kreader, Fred Kern, Phillip Keveren, and Mona Rejino (Hal Leonard)

- *The Jazz Piano Book,* by Mark Levine (Sher Music Co.)

- *Piano Exercises For Dummies,* by David Pearl (Wiley)

- *You Can Teach Yourself Piano,* by Matt Dennis (Mel Bay)

Using Reference Books

In music stores, libraries, and online, you find literally thousands of *music reference books,* sometimes called *supplementals,* about the piano. Books exist on everything from the history of keyboards to building your own piano (good luck!).

Don't be fooled: Reference books don't teach you how to play. They should be used *in addition to,* not instead of, a method book or teacher. Use reference books to help you further understand a concept introduced by your method book or teacher. For example, when you first start to play chords (see Chapter 14), you may want to buy a chord dictionary.

You can find reference books on music theory, harmony, chords, scales, songwriting, the lives of the great composers, musical terms, orchestration, grooves, styles, and much more. Here are some excellent choices for starting a library:

- *1000 Keyboard Ideas,* edited by Ronald Herder (Ekay Music, Inc.)

- *The Art of the Piano,* by David Dubal (Amadeus Press)

- *The A to Z of Foreign Musical Terms,* by Christine Ammer (E.C.S. Publishing)

- *Blues Riffs for Piano,* Ed Baker (Cherry Lane Music)

- *Chord Voicing Handbook,* by Matt Harris and Jeff Jarvis (Kendor Music, Inc.)

- ✔ *Color Your Chords,* by David Pearl (Cherry Lane Music)
- ✔ *Complete Book of Modulations for the Pianist,* by Gail Smith (Mel Bay)
- ✔ *Five Centuries of Keyboard Music,* by John Gillespie (Dover)
- ✔ *The Great Pianists: From Mozart to the Present,* Harold C. Schonberg (Simon & Schuster)
- ✔ *Guide to the Pianist's Repertoire,* by Maurice Hinson (Indiana University Press)
- ✔ *Keyboard Chords & Scales Book (FastTrack Series),* by Blake Neely and Gary Meisner (Hal Leonard)
- ✔ *Pocket Music Dictionary* (Hal Leonard)

Buying Music to Play

You're learning to play the piano for one simple reason: to play music. Okay, so maybe you're also learning piano to impress your friends, but after you achieve the first goal, the second naturally just happens.

Unless you're playing strictly by ear, you need some music to read. Enter the concept of *printed music.*

Types of printed music

Thanks to five centuries worth of composers, you have a wealth of printed music from which to choose. Generally, you find it in three packages:

- ✔ **Sheet music:** Single songs printed on two or more pages, folded or stapled together.
- ✔ **Folios:** Collections of various songs, packaged together for a specific marketing reason.
- ✔ **Classical books:** Some classical pieces are very long and require an entire little book to hold one piece.

For example, suppose you want to learn the song "Hallelujah," written by Leonard Cohen, after hearing a recording by Cohen, John Cale (whose version is on the *Shrek* movie soundtrack), k. d. Lang, Jeff Buckley, or Rufus Wainwright. You can purchase a digital download of the song on sheet music websites, buy the published sheet music of the song from a music store, or get it in a folio of songs from the film *Shrek.*

Folios are great values. At the time of this writing, sheet music sells for around $4.95 for one song, whereas a folio sells for around $21.95 and may have 10 to 50, or even 100, songs. However, chances are that if you're looking for a really new song, it will only be available as sheet music.

Arrangements and transcriptions

Printed music, whether sheets or folios, comes in many different formats called *arrangements.* Arrangements allow the publisher to release the song for several skill levels and for various keyboard instruments. It's the same song, but the publisher has arranged the notes and chords to suit your needs.

For example, you may want to play a very easy version of a song on your digital keyboard or an advanced piano solo version on a grand piano. Both formats are available. And, of course, you can also find other arrangements of the same song for different instruments and voices.

After you master a song, it's fun to try playing other arrangements of it, for instance, 18 different versions of "Yankee Doodle," ranging from plain vanilla to rock 'n' roll. Your local sheet music dealer can help you find the arrangement and style you want.

Fake books

A *fake book* is actually a real book. This is the music industry term for a printed music book or folio that gives you only the melody line, lyrics, and chord symbols of a song. Compared to a piece of sheet music that has both hands written out and fully harmonized, the fake book merely acts as a road map of the song, allowing you to play the melody, sing the lyrics, and create your own left-hand accompaniment with the noted chords. (Chapter 16 gives you some great left-hand accompaniment ideas.)

Working pianists love fake books because they can take a request, flip to the song (usually printed in its entirety on one single page), and improvise their own version of the song. It's even better if a pianist is accompanying a singer because a fake book's streamlined form makes it easy to *transpose* (or change keys) a song on the spot to accommodate the singer's range and repeat the whole song or just a certain section. And that's why you put the little tip jar on your piano!

Here are some excellent fake book options:

- *The Classical Fake Book* (Hal Leonard)
- *Fake Book of the World's Favorite Songs* (Hal Leonard)
- *All the Right Changes,* by Dick Hyman (Ekay Music)
- *The New Real Book Vol. 1–3* (Sher Music)
- *The Real Little Ultimate Fake Book* (Hal Leonard)

Where to buy printed music

Printed music used to be easy to buy at your local music store. Unfortunately, music stores have become few and far between, which is a sad thing for those who fondly recall thumbing through the stacks of sheet music and scores at the neighborhood music store. More and more, people turn to the Internet for an easy way to buy sheet music.

If you're lucky enough to have a local music store that carries instruments and sheet music, please consider supporting it — it's an institution to be treasured.

The web is a wonderful resource for just about anything. You can find free sheet music for public domain titles as well as sheet music to purchase online. Simply search the title of a song or a composer's name along with "sheet music," and you'll find what you need with a few clicks of the mouse. You may want to start your search at the following websites:

- **8notes:** www.8notes.com
- **Burt & Company Discount Music Supply:** www.burtnco.com
- **EncoreMusic:** www.encoremusic.com
- **Frank Music Company:** www.frankmusiccompany.com
- **Online Sheet Music:** www.onlinesheetmusic.com
- **Musicnotes:** www.musicnotes.com
- **Public Domain Music/Royalty Free Music:** www.pdinfo.com
- **Sheet Music Archive:** www.sheetmusicarchive.net
- **Sheet Music Direct:** www.sheetmusicdirect.com
- **Sheet Music Plus:** www.sheetmusicplus.com

You can also contact any of the following publishers to request catalogs or browse their offerings online:

- ✓ **Alfred Publishing Co., Inc.:** website www.alfred.com
- ✓ **Carl Fischer Music:** website www.carlfischer.com
- ✓ **BMG:** website www.bmg.com
- ✓ **Hal Leonard Corporation:** website www.halleonard.com
- ✓ **Mel Bay Publications, Inc.:** website www.melbay.com
- ✓ **Music Sales Group:** website www.musicsales.com
- ✓ **Sher Music Company:** website www.shermusic.com

Many university libraries offer their collections online, and these collections are a valuable resource for out-of-print and public domain music.

Gigging with Others

Nothing teaches music better than playing music. After a while, you may feel in the mood for collaboration. Lucky for you, the concept of piano duets, ensembles, and bands came along.

In any city, college, or university, you can easily find other musicians who simply love to play together, and I'm not talking about playing video games.

Piano duets

Find a friend, sibling, parent, or teacher to share the piano bench with you and play the lower or upper part of a duet. Many songs are available in duet form, where each player gets his or her own printed music showing which part of the piano to play. But playing a duet is not a race; you start, stop, and play the song together.

When you find somebody to play duets with, look into the wealth of music published for piano duets. The duet repertoire includes everything from Beethoven, Tchaikovsky, Schubert, and Stravinsky to folk music and popular songs. There are arrangements of ballet scores and symphonies as well as music for piano players of all levels.

Chamber groups

Many ensembles require a pianist. In the world of classical music, a piano trio features a piano and two other instruments — typically a violin and a cello. In the world of jazz, a quartet may include a piano, drums, bass, and saxophone. Find friends who need a third or fourth wheel, and climb onboard.

Virtually every major composer has written specifically for trios, quartets, and other size ensembles, so the repertoire of pieces you and your friends can play is endless.

Bands

With you on keyboard, all you need is a drummer, bassist, guitarist, and maybe a singer, and you've got yourself a band. Whether you're just having fun in the garage or actually pursuing gigs, playing in a band can be fun and rewarding.

Everyone in a band should be on an equal playing field. Having band members with similar playing proficiency as you (not much better or much worse) helps to keep those intra-band rivalries to a minimum.

As you and your band or ensemble improve, invite friends to come hear you practice. Play songs that your audience wants to hear, or make up your own. When you're convinced that you're really good, solicit interest from local venues — bars, restaurants, hotels, bridge clubs — and play for a bigger crowd. Create a band website and get your music up online. A hobby can easily become a career if you work at it hard enough.

Checking Out the Masters

Many of the great composers of classical and romantic eras were also keyboard players — some of them better known for their playing ability than for the music they wrote. Whether they used a piano, harpsichord, or pipe organ, these old masters managed to find a set of black and white keys to suit their styles.

Johann Sebastian Bach

Regarded by many as the forefather of Western music — not to mention that he was the actual father of many musicians — German musician Johann Sebastian Bach (1685–1750) learned to play the violin under the tutelage of his father. After his parents died, Bach moved in with his big brother, who taught him to play the organ. At the age of 18, Bach got a job as a church organist. This job didn't last long — the church said he improvised too much. He took a job at another church in Weimar, where he had to compose a new piece for the choir and organ every month. Thankfully, that church didn't discourage Bach's improvisations, thus giving the world many much-loved masterpieces. These include two volumes of preludes and fugues, called *The Well-Tempered Clavier,* which remain a touchstone of piano music.

Ludwig van Beethoven

One of the greatest composers who ever lived, German-born Ludwig van Beethoven (1770–1827) was also a piano virtuoso. His playing and original piano pieces were in high demand throughout his career. Unlike many other composers, he became a celebrity during his lifetime. He changed the rules of music and shocked the public, but people still lined up to buy his next piano sonata. Although Beethoven was opposed to naming his sonatas, his publisher insisted that he do so. Names like *Moonlight* and *Appassionata* sold sheet music by the bundle.

Johannes Brahms

The piano music of Johannes Brahms (1833–1897) may have been influenced by Brahms's experience playing the piano in the saloons of Hamburg, Germany, as a young man. You can hear a connection to the real world through his melodies and dance rhythms. He wove together melodic, harmonic, and rhythmic elements and took them to the peak of artistic expression. Even his "easier" pieces are a challenge, but they're well worth the practice. Brahms's piano music is incredibly satisfying both to listen to and to play.

Frederic Chopin

Almost all of Frederic Chopin's music is centered on the piano, and many lovers of piano music name Chopin (1810–1849) as their choice of music to take when stranded on that mythic desert island. He revolutionized the technical possibilities of piano playing but never let that get in the way of a sublime tune. Once you start listening, you'll be hooked on Chopin's whole catalog, from piano concertos and études to mazurkas and nocturnes.

Franz Liszt

Hungarian Franz Liszt was taught piano by his father and began to exploit his talents when he was only 9. Young Liszt (1811–1886) toured constantly and never even received a formal education.

A reputation for theatrical and awe-inspiring concerts produced a huge demand for Liszt's music and an enormous fan club (not to mention a nice-sized ego). He's rumored to have once played so hard that he broke a piano string! *Lisztomania* became a cultural phenomenon, and although no Liszt action figures survive, he did leave the world a bizarre relic: a plaster cast of his hands made upon his death.

Wolfgang Amadeus Mozart

Perhaps the most famous child prodigy, young Austrian Wolfgang Amadeus Mozart turned to his father for lessons. At the age of 5, Mozart (1756–1791) began composing — not just piano pieces, but full-scale symphonic works. He had an amazing memory and infallible ear for music, which allowed him to play entire sonatas perfectly after hearing them only once. His father proudly paraded his son's talents in front of nobility all across Europe with a road show that lasted 14 years. Mozart's piano concertos are regarded today as some of the most important pieces in the keyboard repertoire.

Sergei Rachmaninoff

A Russian-born musician, Sergei Rachmaninoff enjoyed huge success as a composer, conductor, and solo pianist. He also had huge hands, which didn't hurt his playing. Rachmaninoff (1873–1943) built his own solo repertoire, writing intricate, very difficult compositions. Among these was the famous "Prelude in C-sharp minor," which was an enormous hit. Long before the movie *Casablanca,* audiences would cheer, "Play it again, Sergei!" when he played this prelude. He later referred to this popular piece as the "It" prelude. Even today, Rachmaninoff's "Piano Concerto No. 3" is regarded as among the most difficult piano concertos ever written.

Attending Live Concerts

Get out and hear live music that's available to you. Support your local musicians and music venues; without them the most important connection of all — between performer and audience — is lost. If you have a symphony orchestra in your city, buy a ticket. If not, it's worth driving to the closest town that does have one. The orchestra is sure to invite at least one pianist to appear as guest soloist each season; to see and hear a pianist live is wholly different from listening to a recording.

Listening at home gives you the most important part of the performance but not the entire picture. *Watching* a pianist play, you gain insight into playing habits, posture, finger dexterity, intensity, emotions, and overall skill. You subconsciously take this knowledge home with you and apply it to your own playing technique.

If you aren't into classical music, find a jazz club, go to a hotel bar, visit a shopping mall during the holidays, or attend a concert for a band that includes piano. Just find live piano players and watch them play.

Listening to Recordings

Buy them or borrow them — just get your hands on some CDs that you like and listen, listen, listen! Chapter 17 can point you toward some pianists who play the styles you like.

Listening to other pianists gives you insight into the quality of your own playing as well as stylistic ideas you can borrow to liven up your performance. Plus, being inspired is always motivating.

Perusing record stores

It used to be you could find a record store on nearly every major street in every major city — not so anymore. Still, some record stores and bookstores selling CDs survive, and it's always nice to look through a good collection and find something new or exciting.

It pays to patronize record stores with in-store listening, allowing you to sample any CD in the store for as long as you like before you ever let a dime fall from your pocket.

If you can't find it, order it. Store clerks can always order something the store doesn't have in stock, if you want to buy it. They're happy to do the work for you, find what's available and what's out of print, and provide more information on the recording or pianist.

Shopping online

Avoid the traffic, stay in your pajamas, and shop for music from the comfort of your own home. That's right: The Internet has many sites for ordering music. You can order a recording and have it sent to you, or you can download the songs directly to your computer. Most of the following vendors even allow you to listen to a sample of the recording before purchasing.

- **Amazon:** www.amazon.com
- **Amoeba Music:** www.amoeba.com
- **Barnes & Noble:** www.barnesandnoble.com/u/Music-CDs-New-Releases-Reviews-Box-Sets/379003222/
- **CD Baby:** cdbaby.com
- **CD Universe:** www.cduniverse.com
- **iTunes:** www.apple.com/itunes
- **MusicStack:** www.musicstack.com
- **Tower Records:** www.tower.com

Visiting the library

Libraries aren't just for books. Visit your local library and check out its CD collection — literally. That's why it's there.

When a record store fails to locate an out-of-print CD, a library is the place to go. You may not be allowed to take these hard-to-find recordings home, but you'll still get a nice comfortable listening room.

Exchanging music with friends

A time-honored way to build a collection is to swap recordings with friends. With the old barter routine, chances are you can temporarily double the size of your collection.

Exploring Piano Sites on the Web

Among the many music-specific sites on the Internet is a plethora of piano and keyboard web pages. The following sites are some of the best in both content and entertainment value:

- ✔ **The Kennedy Center ArtsEdge:** `www.artsedge.kennedy-center.org`
- ✔ **The Piano Education Page:** `www.pianoeducation.org`
- ✔ **Piano Technicians Guild:** `www.ptg.org`
- ✔ **Piano World:** `www.pianoworld.com`

One of the truly amazing developments of recent years is being able to see video performances by the world's great musicians on video sharing sites such as `www.youtube.com`. You can hear almost all the great pianists of the last 100 years, watch how they move, check out their techniques, and enjoy the never-ending variety of interpretations of your favorite piece.

In addition to web pages, many newsgroups center on the topics of pianos, performance, digital keyboards, MIDI gear, audio recording, and more. Subscribe to any of the following newsgroups (usually without charge) and make friends who care about what you care about:

- ✔ `www.pianosociety.com`
- ✔ `www.pianostreet.com`
- ✔ `www.synthzone.com`

Enjoying Pianos on the Big Screen

Hollywood has produced many, many movies that prominently feature the piano or a piano player. Whether it's a mute woman who speaks through her piano or a deaf composer who can't hear his, filmmakers sure can make a dramatic story out of 88 keys.

Check out these fine films featuring the piano:

- ✔ *Thirty-Two Short Films About Glenn Gould* (1993): One of these films is less than one minute long; the other 31 give you insight into this reclusive and mysterious virtuoso performer.
- ✔ *Amadeus* (1984): It's about that Mozart guy.

✔ ***The Art of Piano:*** This documentary includes performances by the piano giants of the 20th century, including Claudio Arrau, Glenn Gould, Vladimir Horowitz, Sergei Rachmaninoff, and Artur Rubinstein.

✔ ***Art Tatum: The Art of Jazz Piano:*** This documentary about the great jazz pianist includes performances, interviews, and rare footage.

✔ ***Casablanca*** (1942): Bogart didn't say "Play it again, Sam" to a tuba player!

✔ ***The Competition*** (1980): Amy Irving and Richard Dreyfuss are pianists competing for the same prize and falling in love.

✔ ***The Fabulous Baker Boys*** (1989): Jeff and Beau Bridges play duet cocktail pianists in search of a singer. They find one in Michelle Pfeiffer, who manages to slink across a piano like no other.

✔ ***Five Easy Pieces*** (1970): Jack Nicholson is a piano player with five easy pieces to play.

✔ ***Immortal Beloved*** (1995): Gary Oldman plays Beethoven, and Beethoven plays his *Moonlight Sonata.*

✔ ***Impromptu*** (1991): This film dramatizes the story of Chopin's love affair with author George Sand.

✔ ***Madame Sousatzka*** (1988): Shirley MacLaine plays a reclusive but passionate piano teacher in London.

✔ ***The Pianist*** (2003): Adrien Brody won an Oscar for his role playing the famous Polish pianist Wladyslaw Szpilman, who struggles to survive Nazi tyranny in Warsaw during World War II.

✔ ***The Piano*** (1993): Holly Hunter plays a mute woman who expresses herself through her clarinet . . . no, wait, I mean her piano.

✔ ***Piano Grand: A Smithsonian Celebration*** (2000): In 2000, the Smithsonian celebrated the 300-year history of the piano with a memorable museum show. This film of the event features top-tier pianists performing a live concert at the Smithsonian.

✔ ***Shine*** (1996): Geoffrey Rush plays David Helfgott, who practices Rachmaninoff's concerto so much that he goes a little loco.

✔ ***Song Without End*** (1960): According to this film, in the height of Lisztomania, Franz has an affair with a countess and ponders giving up performing. Oh, the humanity!

✔ ***Thelonious Monk: Straight, No Chaser*** (1988): This documentary about the great jazz legend features footage shot during his 1968 sessions and tour.

Realizing You're Not Alone

I thought it would be fun to give you a sample list of famous people who also play (or played) the piano. Now you know that you're not alone in your quest for piano perfection.

- Steve Allen, comedian and former host of *The Tonight Show*
- William F. Buckley, writer
- Clint Eastwood, actor and director
- Jamie Foxx, actor, comedian, and singer
- Jeff Goldblum, actor
- Jack Lemmon, actor
- Denny McLain, former pitcher for the Detroit Tigers
- Dudley Moore, actor
- Richard M. Nixon, former U.S. President
- Paul Reiser, comedian and actor
- Condoleezza Rice, former U.S. Secretary of State
- Fred (Mister) Rogers, beloved children's TV personality
- John Tesh, recording artist and former host of *Entertainment Tonight*
- Harry S. Truman, former U.S. President

Chapter 20

Ten Questions to Ask Prospective Teachers

*A*fter you decide to hire a private piano teacher, your next step is to find one, a good one. Oh, sure, you think it's easy, but finding a good teacher takes time, commitment, and patience. Many pianists change teachers three or four times in the span of a career.

Before you take a single lesson, it's perfectly acceptable, and highly advisable, to interview each candidate and discover his or her history and strengths and weaknesses as a piano instructor. Don't be afraid to ask questions. Just remember, you're the boss — you're hiring the teacher, not the other way around.

Use this chapter as a checklist of the right questions to ask of your prospective teachers. Go ahead and take this book along with you on the interview.

Whom Else Have You Taught?

Possible answers:

- ✔ "I've had several students over the years and would be happy to give you some of their names and numbers so that you can contact them."

- ✔ "Just a few: Leonard Bernstein, Rudolf Serkin, and André Watts."

- ✔ "No one. You'll be my first."

Get a list of references from the teacher candidate and contact each person on the list, if possible. If a friend or relative referred you to the candidate, asking for another reference is still okay. A teacher's references should include current or former students, but it may also include other piano teachers or the teacher's former instructor(s) if the candidate is just starting out.

Assess your teacher's overall abilities by asking current and former students what they like and don't like about the teacher and how long they've taken lessons with the teacher. If you talk to other teachers or former instructors, ask them why they think the teacher is a good choice for a student at your level.

How Long Have You Been Teaching and Playing?

Possible answers:

- ✔ "Over 25 years, and I love it."
- ✔ "I retired from public performance three years ago and decided to start teaching."
- ✔ "Since lunch."

Whether it's years of playing, years of studying, or years of teaching, experience is a must for any good teacher. Without it, you'll both be learning as you go, but you won't be the one getting paid by the hour.

You may also want to know where the candidate received his education, what awards he won, or if he enjoyed a previous career as a performer.

How Much Do You Expect Me to Practice?

Possible answers:

- ✔ "An hour a day."
- ✔ "Fifteen minutes a day."
- ✔ "Until you can play 'Rhapsody In Blue' blindfolded."

This is an ideal question to ask a prospective teacher because it can open the door to an important part of your relationship: communication. Be honest about the time you have available for practicing. If you're comfortable with the response to your question, that's a good sign.

Let the teacher know your goals. Is there a special piece you want to play? A style of music? A teacher should be able to tell you whether your goals are realistic and whether he can accommodate them, and outline the steps you need to take to get there together.

How much you need to practice really depends on what you want to get out of piano lessons and how much time you're willing and able to dedicate to playing piano. Most piano teachers will be thrilled if you show genuine interest in improving, curiosity about playing the piano, and a passion for the music you want to play. If that's true for you, it will naturally translate into good practice time.

There's a difference between "good" practice time and "bad" practice time. When you do it for yourself, you're engaged and enthusiastic about improving. You can pretty much forget about improving if you only go through the motions of practicing your lesson material with one eye on the clock.

Would You Mind Playing Something for Me?

Possible answers:

- ✔ "Sure, what key would you like it in?"
- ✔ "Well, I'd be happy to play for you. How about a bit of Fats Waller?"
- ✔ "I don't really play. I'm just a good teacher."

How well does your candidate play? Ask her to play something for you — nothing too tricky but nothing too easy, perhaps Bach, Chopin, or even Scott Joplin. Your ears will tell you the answer. Are you impressed with the candidate's skill, or can your friends play just as well?

Don't head for the door if you get the third answer. Surprisingly, even someone who can't play very well can still be a good teacher. She may be very skilled in listening and correcting your technique without being able to make her own fingers play the music. If you like the answers the candidate gives you to the other questions in this chapter, she may be a good candidate despite not playing well for you.

What Repertoire Do You Teach?

Possible answers to the question of what repertoire an instructor teaches include the following:

- ✔ "I like all music. We'll start with the classics and work our way up to today's Top Ten."
- ✔ "The three B's: Bach, Beethoven, and Brahms."
- ✔ "Come again?"

Most likely, you have an idea of the pieces you want to play. It's important for every pianist to be able to play the classics — Bach, Mozart, Chopin — but, of course, they aren't the only composers. And classical isn't the only genre of music. (Chapter 17 introduces you to several styles of music.)

If you want to play rockabilly or jazz or R&B, find out whether your teacher is willing to teach you those styles. Granted, you have to work your way up to playing these other styles by starting with the basics. But as you improve, you want a teacher who lets you pick your own repertoire to some extent.

How Do You Feel about Wrong Notes, Mistakes, and Slow Learners?

Possible answers:

- ✔ "To err is human."
- ✔ "Mistakes are the path toward learning."
- ✔ *[Fist pounds the table]* "I abhor imperfection."

Patience is a virtue, and patience is an absolute must in teaching anyone anything. Learning to play piano is no exception. You want your teacher to teach you at your pace and be willing to adjust to your learning curve, as long as you put in the effort. Mistakes are a reason for taking lessons and should be approached with a positive, problem-solving attitude.

What Methods Do You Use to Teach Piano?

Possible answers:

- ✔ "I use the internationally respected blankety-blank method."
- ✔ "My method varies depending on the needs of each student. We can begin with. . . ."
- ✔ "Let's just see what happens."

Each teacher has his own method of teaching. It may be a tried-and-true approach, finely honed over the years. It may be a new method the teacher just read about in a book. (Read more about method books in Chapter 19.) Whatever the method, your teacher should teach piano in a way you're comfortable with.

Where Will the Lessons Take Place?

Possible answers:

- ✔ "Right here in my living room at my Steinway."
- ✔ "I am happy to teach at your home if you have a keyboard and feel more relaxed in a familiar environment."
- ✔ "In the alley behind the stadium after midnight."

As with real estate, location is everything. You don't want any excuses to skip piano lessons. On a hot summer day when a Hollywood blockbuster is opening at the theater down the street, you dream up a wealth of excuses. Don't let location be one of them.

Though having your lessons at your home may sound convenient, consider a few disadvantages. When your lesson time comes, you're responsible for minimizing interruptions (from pets, roommates, family members, phone calls, and cooking duties) and providing a reasonably clean area for the lesson. Interruptions and distractions can sabotage your lesson and may upset your teacher. A teacher's home or studio is often ideal because you can count on a comfortable, professional work environment and a good piano.

(Change teachers if the environment and piano aren't suitable.) When you go to your teacher's place, you're relieved of the responsibilities and distractions of home, and you dedicate a special place and time to your lesson. If you don't see the lesson location when you interview, or if you're concerned about the location for any reason, ask to take a trial lesson before making your decision.

How Much Do You Charge?

Possible answers to the question of how much a teacher charges include:

- ✔ "I require $45 per hour-long lesson. We'll meet once a week, and I ask that you give me plenty of notice if you must cancel."
- ✔ "We'll schedule four lessons per month, and you'll pay me $300 each month."
- ✔ "How can you put a price on art?"

On average, most teachers charge between $40 and $70 per hour. However, depending on a number of economic factors, including notoriety and demand, your teacher may command more than $100 per hour. But the good news is that you may be able to find less expensive rates. For instance, some undergraduate or graduate music students may offer inexpensive lessons on the side. If you live in a smaller town, rates are generally cheaper. Also, a church pianist, for instance, may offer a discounted rate to members of the congregation.

Do You Have Student Recitals?

Possible answers:

- ✔ "Yes. I rent the college concert hall and have a recital for all my students. You can invite as many guests as you like, and I serve soft drinks and cookies at intermission."
- ✔ "No, but that's an excellent idea for this year."
- ✔ "Sure, if Dad will let me use the barn."

Playing for an audience is fun, and for many, it's the main reason to play the piano. A teacher can help build your audience (and courage) through annual or semi-annual public performances called *recitals*. Your teacher should plan the recital, find the venue, advertise the show, and prepare you for the spotlight (whether or not there's an actual spotlight is another matter). Without a teacher, you're left to arrange and self-promote your public debut.

Appendix

About the Website: Audio Tracks and Video Clips

• •

*T*his appendix provides you with a handy list of what's on the accompanying website (www.dummies.com/go/piano). To access this information, use the username pianofordummies and the password wiley.

What You'll Find on the Accompanying Audio Tracks

The following is a list of audio tracks that appear at www.dummies.com/go/piano.

Track #	Chapter	Figure #	Description
1	2		Sound of an acoustic piano
2	2		Sound of a harpsichord
3	2		Sound of a pipe organ
4	2		Sounds from synthesizers
5	7	7-5	Mixing up all the notes
6	7		Same beat, different note values
7	7	7-14	Counting quarter and eighth rests
8	7		"A Hot Time in the Old Town Tonight"
9	7		"The Beautiful Blue Danube"
10	7		"Can Can"
11	7		"Lavender Blue"
12	8	8-3	Ties that bind: notes of the same pitch

(continued)

(continued)

Track #	Chapter	Figure #	Description
13	8	8-8	Practice with dotted notes
14	8	8-10	Counting triplets
15	8	8-11	Practice with triplets
16	8	8-12	Swing those eighths
17	8	8-15	"After You've Gone"
18	8		"When the Saints Go Marching In"
19	8		"Oh, Susannah"
20	8		"Scheherezade"
21	8		"Swanee River"
22	8		"By the Light of the Silvery Moon"
23	8		"I've Been Working on the Railroad"
24	8		"Limehouse Blues"
25	9	9-3	Melody of "Frere Jacques"
26	9	9-5	"Skip to My Lou"
27	9	9-7	"Chiapanecas"
28	9		"Ode to Joy"
29	9		"Autumn"
30	9		"Oranges and Lemons"
31	9		"Simple Melody"
32	10	10-5	A portion of "Joy to the World"
33	10	10-6	"The Farmer in the Dell"
34	10		"Danny Boy"
35	10		"House of the Rising Sun"
36	10		"Greensleeves"
37	11	11-4	"Swing Low, Sweet Chariot"
38	11	11-5	"Little Brown Jug"
39	11	11-15	"When Johnny Comes Marching Home"
40	11	11-16	"A Musical Joke"
41	11	11-17	"On Top of Old Smoky"
42	11		"The Sidewalks of New York"
43	11		"Stars and Stripes Forever"
44	12		"I'm Called Little Buttercup"

Track #	Chapter	Figure #	Description
45	12		"Marianne"
46	12		"Aura Lee"
47	12		"Shenandoah"
48	12		"Auld Lang Syne"
49	13	13-1	"Good Night, Ladies" in key of C (major)
50	13	13-2	"Good Night, Ladies" in key of F (major)
51	13	13-10	A portion of "After the Ball"
52	13		"Worried Man Blues"
53	13		"After the Ball"
54	14	14-10	A little suspension tension
55	14	14-12	"Bingo"
56	14		"Down by the Station"
57	14		"Sometimes I Feel Like a Motherless Child"
58	14		"Lullaby"
59	14		"Scarborough Fair"
60	14		"Red River Valley"
61	15	15-11	"Pop! Goes the Weasel"
62	15		"Polovtsian Dance"
63	15		"Camptown Races"
64	15		"Trumpet Voluntary"
65	15		"Also Sprach Zarathustra"
66	15		"Quiet Sunset"
67	16	16-1	Left-hand chords in varied rhythm patterns
68	16	16-2	Root-fifth-octave patterns
69	16	16-4	"Picking and Grinning"
70	16	16-5	"Octaves in the Left"
71	16	16-6	"Jumping Octaves"
72	16	16-7	"Rockin' Intervals"
73	16	16-8	"Berry-Style Blues"
74	16	16-9	"Bum-ba-di-da" bass pattern

(continued)

(continued)

Track #	Chapter	Figure #	Description
75	16	16-10	"Boogie-woogie" bass line
76	16	16-11	Intro #1
77	16	16-12	Intro #2
78	16	16-13	Intro #3
79	16	16-14	Intro #4
80	16	16-15	Intro #5
81	16	16-16	Finale #1
82	16	16-17	Finale #2
83	16	16-18	Finale #3
84	16	16-19	Finale #4
85	16		"Country Riffin'"
86	16		"Love Me Like You Used To"
87	17	17-4	12-bar blues progression
88	17	17-6	Rockin' bass line
89	17	17-9	Motown syncopation
90	17	17-11	"Yankee Doodle" swings
91	17		"Album Leaf"
92	17		"Playin' the Blues"
93	17		"Classic R&R"
94	17		"Motown Is My Town"
95	17		"Billy Boy Swings"

Viewing Videos on the Website

The following videos are available for viewing at www.dummies.com/go/piano.

Video #	Chapter	Description
1	2	Keys, hammers, and strings
2	5	White keys and black keys
3	5	Arching the hands and fingers
4	5	The pedals

Video #	Chapter	Description
5	9	Playing a melody in C position
6	9	Crossing over and under your fingers
7	10	The major scales
8	10	The minor scales
9	11	Left-hand melodies
10	11	Playing scales with your left hand
11	11	Basic left-hand accompaniment
12	11	Practicing melodies with both hands
13	11	Playing songs with both hands
14	14	Playing major chords
15	14	Playing minor chords
16	14	Exploring other chord types
17	14	Playing seventh chords
18	15	Incorporating dynamics
19	15	Articulating notes
20	15	Grace notes
21	15	Trills
22	15	Glissandos
23	15	Tremolos
24	16	Interesting left-hand accompaniment patterns
25	17	Piano styles: The blues
26	17	Piano styles: Rock 'n' roll
27	17	Piano styles: Country
28	17	Piano styles: Pop
29	17	Piano styles: Soul
30	17	Piano styles: jazz

Index

About the Reviser

Adam Perlmutter is a freelance music writer, transcriber, and engraver living in Los Angeles, California. He has authored a number of music books in the *For Dummies* series, including *Broadway Piano Songs For Dummies, Sing with the Choir For Dummies,* and *Classic Rock Guitar Songs For Dummies*, among others. Perlmutter's work can also be seen in music education magazines like *In Tune, Music Alive!,* and *Teaching Music.* His website is www.adamperlmutter.com.

Reviser's Acknowledgments

Special appreciation to David Lutton, Elizabeth Rea, Chad Sievers, Christy Pingleton, Andrea O'Neal, Sharon Stosur, Kathleen Jeffers, Shelley Lea, Eric Hurst, Kole Rushmore, Jennifer Midkiff, and all the other *For Dummies* staff who worked on this edition.

Publisher's Acknowledgments

Acquisitions Editor: David Lutton

(Previous Edition: Lindsay Lefevere)

Project Editors: Chad R. Sievers and Elizabeth Rea

(Previous Edition: Christina Guthrie)

Copy Editor: Christy Pingleton

(Previous Edition: Elizabeth Rea)

Technical Editor: Andrea O'Neal

Art Coordinator: Alicia B. South

Project Coordinator: Sheree Montgomery

Video Producers: Kathleen Jeffers, Shelley Lea, Eric Hurst, Kole Rushmore

Video Performer: Jennifer Midkiff

Cover Photos: ©iStock.com/alengo